Behind the Curtain

Behind
the Curtain

An Insider's View of Jay Leno's *Tonight Show*

Dave Berg

Foreword by Jay Leno

PELICAN PUBLISHING COMPANY
GRETNA 2014

Library of Congress Cataloging-in-Publication Data

Berg, Dave, 1948-
  Behind the curtain : an insider's view of Jay Leno's Tonight
show / by Dave Berg ; foreword by Jay Leno.
    pages cm
  Includes index.
  ISBN 978-1-4556-1996-2 (hardcover) — ISBN 978-
1-4556-1997-9 (e-book) 1. Tonight show (Television
program) 2. Celebrities—Anecdotes. I. Title.
  PN1992.77.T63B47 2014
  791.45'72—dc23
                                            2014007910

Printed in the United States of America
Published by Pelican Publishing Company, Inc.
1000 Burmaster Street, Gretna, Louisiana 70053

For Beverly Berg, my mom (1924-2012)

*Thank you for teaching me to appreciate
the wondrous art of storytelling.*

Contents

Foreword

I met Dave Berg the day we hired him as a segment producer for *The Tonight Show with Jay Leno,* which would soon be debuting. He was nervous that he wouldn't fit in because he had no experience in show business. He had been a journalist for NBC News.

I told him not to worry and that we were actually looking for someone who had worked in news. In general, we were seeking out people with diverse backgrounds. I'm not sure that made him feel better, but it was true.

We wanted to bring a little more variety to *The Tonight Show's* lineup of guests. The show was known for its popular entertainers, but we were hoping to add more journalists, commentators, politicos, and others to the mix. We assigned Dave to help us book and produce the segments that would feature some of those guests. As a veteran journalist, he had worked with them.

But it would take a while for Dave to feel comfortable in his new gig. The lead guest on our first show was Billy Crystal, who was very funny. The second guest was Dave's responsibility. He was an economics reporter who had anecdotes about Alan Greenspan, then chairman of the Federal Reserve Board. He didn't exactly kill after Billy's performance.

It was a rough start for Dave, but eventually he would get the idea. During his eighteen years with the show, he booked some of our most memorable guests, including Barack Obama, the first sitting president ever to do a late-night show.

Dave was passionate about politics, an interest that goes

back to his days as a news producer. As time went on, he encouraged us to get more and more politicians, both Democrats and Republicans. He was always professional while working with the guests. None of them had any idea about his political views—or mine, for that matter.

Among his colleagues at the show, though, he made it very clear where he stood politically. He was a conservative and was very vocal about his beliefs. I didn't always agree with him, and we had many spirited discussions, which I really enjoyed. Sometimes I shared his opinion but would play devil's advocate just to get him going. It was great fun.

Dave wasn't the only conservative at the show. He was joined by other Republican and Libertarian writers. We also had our share of liberal writers, including a former Democratic speechwriter. I wouldn't have had it any other way. I think our friendly disagreements helped us relate to our viewing audience, which held a wide spectrum of political views.

On the pages that follow, Dave has written about his experiences at the show as well as his thoughts about what it all meant. To be honest, I haven't read it. I'll read it when everyone else does. Who knows, I might even disagree with some of his points. It wouldn't be the first time.

But I trust Dave, and I'm certain he'll do right by the show. We both grew up watching Johnny Carson. Being part of *The Tonight Show*, one of television's few icons, meant something to me, and I know it did to Dave, as well.

Jay Leno
Burbank, Ca.

Behind
the Curtain

Chapter One

James Douglas Muir "Jay" Leno

In all my years at *The Tonight Show*, Jay Leno never raised his voice to me or anyone else. He was generous, fair and loyal. And, of course, he was always good for a joke—no matter what the circumstances. Did he have a big ego? Of course. So does every prominent person in show business, politics, sports, business, religion—you name it. But ego is not what drives Jay Leno.

What drives—and defines—Jay is an amazingly short attention span. It's about ten seconds long. Thirty seconds, tops. He's very intelligent and professionally successful but is simply incapable of paying attention for a long period of time; he gets fidgety and can't sit still. One knee is constantly bouncing up and down to a staccato rhythm. I believe this is because he has some form of ADHD. I don't claim to be an expert on the condition, but I'm very familiar with its symptoms. Many people in show business have it.

Jay's condition—whatever it is—affects almost everything he does. It may have even been a blessing in disguise for the show. Whenever I had to brief Jay or pitch an idea to him, I had to keep it short or risk the danger of losing his attention and not getting it back. This was good because I often tell long, meandering stories. With Jay I had no choice but to stay on topic and keep it simple.

His restlessness was perfect for the monologue. Each joke was short enough to keep his attention but long enough to keep him challenged to the point of obsession. He and his writers turned out hundreds of jokes daily, up to as many as 1,500, but only the twenty-five or so funniest ones made it into the twelve-minute monologue. The strategy was to keep throwing pasta on the wall until some of it stuck.

Consistently delivering relevant and funny jokes was a relentless, demanding, and tireless task, although Jay never looked at it that way. Whenever someone asked him how he was able to do it, he would say: "Write joke. Tell joke. Get paid." Of course, his answer was a joke in itself that always got a laugh because, obviously, there was more to it than that. But in a way, his glib answer was true. He did his job by making it into a routine.

Jay usually began crafting his monologue at his home in Beverly Hills the night before a show. While his approach appeared to be casual and relaxed, it was actually quite regimented. In fact, it was the same almost every night. He wanted it that way so nothing interfered with his job.

A typical day for Jay actually began in the evening. Driving himself, he would leave the NBC lot after the show, usually about 6 p.m., and head for his home in Beverly Hills, where he would heat up lasagna for dinner. Then he would begin the work of putting the next day's monologue together by reading through hundreds of jokes. When he had enough material for at least half the monologue, he would go to bed, usually about 2:00 a.m., and get up the next morning about 6:00.

After arriving at the studio around 8:15, often before anyone else, he would work out with a trainer—usually with little enthusiasm. Then he and his head writer would go over the jokes that came in from the writers overnight. Jay's search for material would continue off and on throughout the day until show time at 4 p.m. He would try out jokes on as many people as possible. Anyone caught near his office, where the door was usually open, was fair game.

Whenever he used me as a sounding board, Jay would often do a slightly off-color joke and see if I was offended; I was considered to be pretty straight-laced, at least by Hollywood standards. To Jay, I represented our conservative, middle-of-the-road viewers, which I appreciated. But sometimes I think he was just yanking my chain.

Jay used cue cards for his monologue, which I thought was odd at first. Teleprompters had already been around for years, even in the smallest stations. I had used one years earlier to give the farm news and commodity prices in Green Bay, Wisconsin; Sioux City, Iowa; and Omaha, Nebraska.

So why did Jay insist on using cue cards? I think it was because of another condition—dyslexia, a reading disability. He would often flub words and complicated phrases. It was hard enough for him to read static words, but moving words would have been even worse, resulting in a confusing jumble of letters.

Jay was open about his dyslexia and became very adept at making fun of himself when he made mistakes, which only reinforced his image as a likeable guy. I asked him one day if it was what prevented him from using a prompter. He quickly dismissed the idea, which didn't surprise me. He tended to instinctively reject any perceived attempt to pigeonhole him.

He struggled so much with dyslexia that I think he even memorized most of his monologue jokes, referring to the written words only for an occasional cue. That didn't mean he could get by on his memory alone, though. One night the cue card guy didn't show up on time for the monologue, and we had to stop the show until he arrived.

Many entertainers do not like the grind of a daily program, but Jay never saw it that way. Because of his short attention span, he was easily bored and liked moving on to a new show every day. Whether an episode was good, bad, or just okay, the next day he didn't think much about it other than the ratings.

He was already concentrating on that day's show, which was something new and different. Besides, he didn't like resting on his laurels. Just because the monologue "killed" today didn't mean it would tomorrow. Or as Jay put it, "You're only as good as your last joke."

Jay's attitude about doing a daily show reflected his very essence, his philosophy of life. A reporter for *GQ* magazine once asked him a telling question: if he could be any of the many engines he owned, which one would he be? On the surface this appeared to be a contrived question, which Jay would normally deflect with a joke. But he took it seriously, saying he would most likely be his 1866 steam engine: "Steam engines are probably my favorite, because they chug along at the same speed. They don't get too up. They don't get too down." That short answer revealed more about his character and personality than anything else I ever heard him say. I think it could be his epitaph.

Jay appeared in a number of films early in his career, and not just cameos. He had some decent parts in such films as *Silver Bears* (1978), *Collision Course* (1989), and *American Hot Wax* (1978). But he disliked film acting because of the endless retakes, which could take days. He just didn't have the patience for that kind of repetitive work, so he didn't stay with it.

Instead, he put all of his effort into his stand-up comedy and, eventually, *The Tonight Show*. Ironically, he would do a number of films during his time as the show's host. He mostly made cameo appearances, which he enjoyed, especially if they were shot in *The Tonight Show* studio, where he had to be every day anyway. (Such films include *Space Cowboys*, 2000; *Calendar Girls*, 2003; and *Mr. 3000*, 2004.)

Jay also liked doing voiceover parts in animated films and voiced characters in *The Flintstones* (1994), *Cars* (2006), and *Ice Age: The Meltdown* (2006). However, he didn't like watching these films. He was a very literal guy, and he could never get over the fact that cartoon characters literally weren't real people; they were just moving pictures. He even had a hard time with the idea of interviewing animated characters on the show and rarely did it.

Other than animated features, Jay loved watching films and talking about them—usually at the same time—during film screenings. Since many of the show's guests were actors who were promoting projects they starred in, Jay felt he should watch their films. Attending a screening with Jay, usually at NBC, was an experience I will never forget. Not only did you get to see a movie before it was released in theaters but you also often got Jay's thoughts about it while the film was playing. And there was always pizza, Jay's favorite food.

His running commentaries during the screenings could be annoying, but they were often more entertaining than the films themselves. He would say things like, "Would anyone do that in real life?" Or, "Who didn't see that coming a mile away?"

While Jay thought most films were flawed, he had no agenda. He was equally passionate about films he liked and those he didn't like. One time he was so upset by how badly a film was made that he just wouldn't stop ranting about it. So I told him, "Hey, it's free." He responded, "Yes, but I'll never get my two hours back."

After a screening, he would sometimes corner the first person he encountered and engage them in conversation about the film. If you were in a hurry to get home, it was best to avoid Jay. Sometimes he would go on for fifteen minutes. He even did this with my children, Melissa and David, who were teenagers at the time. They were thrilled that Jay was interested in talking with them, but at the same time they didn't quite know if they had permission to disagree with him.

They still remember Jay's thoughts about *Pirates of the Caribbean: The Curse of the Black Pearl* (2003), the first in the series. He told them he loved it partly because the director didn't put in too many CGI "ghost pirates." There were only about eighteen, which made the flesh-and-blood soldiers' battle scene against the "ghost pirates" more realistic than if there had been an endless swarm of them. That was a critique they could relate to as teenagers.

Jay genuinely enjoyed having film critics as guests, including the late Gene Siskel, the late Roger Ebert, and Richard Roeper. They weren't always the biggest ratings draw, but Jay so enjoyed bantering with them about films, both on and off the air, that they were frequent guests. And in many ways, his views were similar to those of the professional critics.

Like them, he tended to favor smaller, independent films that featured actors rather than action.

In 2006, Richard Roeper invited Jay to fill in for Roger Ebert while he was in the hospital and serve as a guest co-host on his show, *At the Movies with Ebert and Roeper*. I thought Jay's performance on the show was one of the best things he had done, but it wasn't as entertaining as sitting through a screening with him.

While critics tended to dismiss Jay as the middle-of-the-road guy, he is actually more complicated than he appeared and is very quirky. I don't mean phony, Hollywood, "I-must-have-Coke-in-a-bottle-and-only-green-M&Ms-in-my-dressing-room" quirky. I mean he is genuinely idiosyncratic. Much of it is probably related in some way to his dyslexia and short attention span.

But as odd as he seemed, Jay's behavior worked for him and the show. His quirks generally reflected his desire to be in total control of his life. He wanted to spend as much time as possible writing jokes and working on cars and as little time as possible doing things that prevented him from that.

Jay had no interest in owning the rights to *The Tonight Show* while he was the host, as Johnny Carson had done before him and as David Letterman has done with *The Late Show*. Instead, Jay just wanted to be an employee so he could spend most of his time actually working on the show.

He is a workaholic and genuinely liked his job more than anything else. Jay once asked me if I was familiar with the math seventh graders were doing, which he described as impossibly difficult. I had to agree, as I had seen my own kids' math when they were in junior high school and remembered being unable to help them with some of it. "Imagine if we had a real job where we had to know how to do actual work," he told me. "We're lucky to be in show business."

Jay almost never took a day off and detested even the thought of going on vacation, which he considered a "nightmare." Were it up to him, *Tonight* would have original episodes fifty-two weeks a year. At his first contract renewal he asked for less time off but was turned down for his staff's sake.

The show took six weeks of hiatus, while Letterman stops production for twelve weeks, which helped Jay's ratings since reruns drew fewer viewers. Letterman works four days a week, recording two shows in one day, while Jay insisted on doing a show every weekday so the monologue jokes and guest segments would be timely and topical.

Jay rarely seeks leisure time. While the show was in reruns, he usually made stand-up appearances. He told *Fortune* magazine that he once decided to spend a day on the beach in Hawaii while he was there on a gig. He said it felt like he was there for hours, so he checked his watch only to find he had been there just ten minutes!

His parents grew up during the Depression, and Jay said he had a fear of running out of money. As such, he never spent a penny of his *Tonight Show* income while he was host. Instead, he lived off his stand-up earnings. Jay didn't buy anything on credit; he purchased his house outright and to this day doesn't invest in stocks.

Surprisingly, he doesn't think of himself as a rich person. Once while in New York, he and I shared a limo to the airport. As we headed down 5th Avenue, we passed some very expensive department stores. We were both amazed at some of the fine clothes, furniture, and other items we were seeing in the store windows. Finally, Jay said, "Wow, if you had a lot of dough you could get some nice stuff here." "Jay," I responded, "you do have a lot of dough." "I guess I do," he said.

Despite his dough, he wore the same clothes—jeans and a denim shirt—all the time, except when he did the show or was making a scheduled stand-up appearance. Though he admits he's a little overweight, Jay hasn't actually weighed himself since 1973, saying he's already married and doesn't need to impress women. For such a hard-working guy, he doesn't sleep much: four to four-and-a-half hours a night is his maximum.

Jay's quirkiness is also reflected in his diet. He never drinks hot liquids, such as coffee or tea, and he doesn't eat soup. No alcohol or drugs, either. He hasn't had a raw vegetable since 1969 when his mom finally stopped trying to get him to eat them, and he proudly claims he has never had a salad.

He likes beef, chicken, potatoes, pasta, pizza, hamburgers, and hot dogs. He would eat the same thing for lunch every day for a year at a time. One year it was chicken legs and thighs. The next year it was turkey from the fast-food chain Koo Koo Roo. Jay did this so he could spend more time thinking about jokes and less time worrying about food.

He frequented the original Bob's Big Boy in Burbank, not far from the NBC lot. People occasionally see him with his wife, Mavis, at an Italian restaurant, but Jay generally avoids exotic or exclusive establishments. He once gave this impression of a European restaurant to *Fortune* magazine: *"Excuse me, I didn't order this! Excuse me!* Will you be having the eel's head in some kind of butter cream sauce?"

A creature of habit, Jay generally preferred to keep things the same, especially in his *Tonight Show* office or dressing room. This may have to do with superstitious tendencies, common to many celebrities. His first office, which he used from 1992 to 2009, had a pile of papers and other items approximately five feet tall and five feet wide, as did his dressing room.

He also had a corkboard in his office that was only anchored to the wall at the top left corner. The bottom right corner rested diagonally on the floor, where it had fallen on January 17, 1994, during the enormously destructive 6.7 magnitude Northridge Earthquake. After that, Jay continued to use the corkboard, but he never had it horizontally reattached to the wall.

When Jay began guest-hosting for Johnny Carson in 1987, Joe Drago, a props man, would stand backstage with a cup of ice water for him just before the show started. The first few times, Jay ignored Joe and the water. Finally, Joe asked if he should continue bringing the water, which surprised Jay.

"Was that for me?" he replied. Jay thought Joe was drinking the water himself. During the monologue that night Jay even mentioned Joe's kind gesture and how he had stupidly misunderstood Joe's intentions.

From then on, Jay drank from the cup prior to making his entrance for every single show. He did it methodically, waiting for the first note of the show's theme song before taking a sip and then bowing to Joe in appreciation. Jay continued the ritual when he took over as host on May 25, 1992, through the end of the first run on May 29, 2009, when he poured the water on Joe's head instead of drinking it. Jay and Joe continued the practice during *The Jay Leno Show* and the second run of *The Tonight Show*.

According to Joe, Jay also had a tendency to touch things while waiting to go on stage. He was particularly fond of little corners and certain pieces of the set, such as a railing that held camera cables back. He also liked to sweep his foot over electrical outlets.

Jay has an affinity for numbers, although I wouldn't say he's a numerologist. He married Mavis on November 30, 1980, the same day his parents were married. Jay once told Larry King: "They were married for fifty-seven years, and my wife and I got married on the same day because it seemed to work for them. They were the funniest people I ever knew."

Before he met Mavis, Jay lived at different times with five women. All six were born on September 5. Cathy Guisewite, creator of the comic strip *Cathy*, once appeared on the show as a guest. In her dressing room before the show Jay told her that he was happily married but was attracted to her in a non-sexual way. (He did this in front of me so she wouldn't think he was flirting.) Then he asked her if she was born September 5. Turns out, she was.

Jay rarely attends Hollywood parties or social events and has few show-business friends. He says he likes making showbiz money but doesn't like living the life, which he compares to marrying a hooker. He rolled his eyes whenever entertainers whined about how hard they worked and advised them never to do it in public because so many people were struggling just to make ends meet.

He would tell young actors who were overwhelmed by the long hours they had to spend on shoots: "The last thing people want to see is rich people complaining." And his definition of a rich person was "anyone making more money than you do."

Jay has close ties with police and firefighters and often does benefits for them. He once told me that everybody—not just kids in the ghetto—had to be in a gang, like it or not. The gang he preferred was made up of cops. Of course, he was kidding. Although, for some odd reason, he rarely gets speeding tickets. And he owns some of the fastest cars on the planet.

Early in his career, Jay had a few run-ins with the law. He was arrested for vagrancy two nights in a row at the same place, right in front of the Ripley's Believe It or Not! museum on Hollywood Boulevard. He was homeless at the time and had no place to sleep, so he walked all night.

In 2000, when he got a star on the Hollywood Walk of Fame, he requested that it be placed on the spot where he was arrested in front of the iconic Hollywood museum. At the ceremony, the late Johnny Grant, Hollywood's honorary mayor, granted Jay a pardon for his crimes. The police were also there—this time as Jay's invited guests.

Jay had come a long way since he told his first joke in fourth grade. His teacher was talking about how cruel the Sheriff of Nottingham was to Friar Tuck. And Jay said: "Do you know why they boiled him in oil? Because he was a fryer." He got laughs right from the get-go.

A number of show business greats influenced Jay, including Johnny Carson, Steve Allen, Jack Benny, and Rodney Dangerfield. But his favorite was Elvis Presley. He would often point out that every single one of Elvis's thirty-one films made money, despite the fact that critics couldn't stand them. When Jay was seven years old, he went to the movies and watched Elvis in *Loving You*. The girls swooned when he sang "Teddy Bear." That's when Jay decided to get into entertainment. At first he took guitar lessons, but when that didn't work he turned to jokes.

Jay impersonates Elvis all the time, saying, "Thank you, thank you very much." He used to do an Elvis bit, sneering and singing Shakespearean soliloquies as the King would have done. In fact, Dick Clark told him that Elvis only liked two impersonations of himself, and Jay's was one of them.

But no one shaped James Douglas Muir "Jay" Leno and his comedy more than his parents. You could see it in his stand-up routine, which was full of funny stories that illustrated the dichotomy of his father Angelo's Italian background and his mother Catherine's Scottish side.

Much of the humor was about food. On Sundays, dinner on the Italian side of the family consisted of more meatballs and spaghetti than anyone could eat. On the Scottish side, the family would go to his aunt's house; she kept Coca Cola in the cupboard rather than paying to refrigerate it.

Jay described it to Oprah this way: "We'd go from meatballs and lasagna to warm Coke and a stale scone. My poor aunt would pour half a glass of Coke, and it would overflow because it was so hot! When we'd go to the Italian side for dinner, my [Scottish] aunt would say, 'Look at the waste.' She'd be counting how many meatballs were left."

Jay's parents have both passed on, but they lived long enough to see their son become a successful comedian and eventually take over *Tonight*. However, they never quite understood it, which was also a rich source of comedy for Jay.

When Jay got the gig, he made the cover of *TIME*, and he called his mom to tell her to pick up a copy. "Now, which one is that?" she asked. "It's *TIME* magazine, Ma—one of the biggest. . . . Call Aunt Faye in New Jersey and everybody in New York, and tell them I'm on the cover." There was a long pause, and his mom said, "I don't think you'd be on the cover there, Jay. They just put you on the cover here in Andover [Massachusetts] because they know you're from the area."

Jay credited his mom as the inspiration for the title of his show, which was originally called *The Tonight Show Starring Jay Leno*. But his mom, who despised pretentiousness, recoiled at the idea that her son would be the star of anything. So Jay changed the name to *The Tonight Show with Jay Leno*.

He was a C-student, which probably stemmed from his dyslexia and his restlessness. His mom used to tell him he would have to work a little harder than the other kids. He took it to heart, and that's why he's a workaholic. No one— not even his harshest critics—would dispute the claim that he is the hardest-working man in show business.

Jay loves to tell the story about a meeting he and his mom had with his high-school guidance counselor, who told him, "Education isn't for everyone." He then suggested Jay might want to drop out of school and parlay a part-time job he had at McDonald's into a career.

The best part of this story is that after that meeting Jay continued to work at McDonald's, where he won a talent show and decided to go into comedy. He also went on to study at Emerson College in Boston, where he launched his career by writing and performing comedy sketches with his roommate.

But Jay doesn't resent his counselor for irreparably damaging his sense of self-worth. He thinks today's emphasis on self-esteem is overrated and often points out that Mafia hit men are more self-confident than anyone else. He really believes everyone else is better and smarter than he is. "Maybe there's nothing wrong with feeling like you're not the greatest," he once said. "Maybe you're not the best, so you should work a little harder."

In any competitive situation Jay portrays himself as— and is often perceived as—the underdog, even if he isn't. But how does he pull that off? He was the number-one guy in late night from 1995 to 2014. I think he subconsciously believed he was not as good as Letterman. But I also think he consciously portrayed himself that way because he knew everyone roots for the underdog. There's a reason he always insisted on being paid less than his *Late Show* counterpart.

One of my favorite *Tonight Show* features was "Jaywalking," Jay's version of "man-on-the-street" interviews. The concept was created by Steve Allen, the original host of *The Tonight Show*. But Jaywalking brought a unique twist to this well-known routine: The people being interviewed tended to be stupid—really stupid—about everything from world events to history to the identity of prominent political leaders. But it was funny simply because their blissful ignorance was so unbelievable:

Jay: Who was the first president?
Person: Benjamin Franklin.
Jay: In what country would you find the Panama Canal?
Person: I haven't a clue.
Jay: What year was Independence Day?
Person: July 4, 1864.

Sometimes the answers were amazingly clever, even though they weren't meant to be:

Jay: What was the Gettysburg Address?
Person: I don't know the exact address.
Jay: How many stars in the [American] flag?
Person: It's moving too fast to count them.
Jay: What president was named "Tricky Dick"?
Person: Bill Clinton.

Jay and the writers of Jaywalking were often asked how many people they had to talk to for each one that aired. The answer was: surprisingly few. At the same time, there was admittedly a little sleight of hand involved. A successful Jaywalking segment was all about location. The best spots were Melrose Avenue in Los Angeles and Universal CityWalk in Universal City. The key was to find the places where trendy people hung out. In the early days, Jaywalking was shot in Burbank, a typical family community where they found very few "stupid people."

I believe Jaywalking was really about Jay Leno himself. It

was his clever way of getting even with the world for all those Cs he got in school. He was thumbing his nose while winking at his fifth grade teacher, who wrote on his report card, "If James spent as much time on his studies as he does trying to be funny, he'd be an A student." But he was never malicious about it. He was having fun.

Chapter Two

Funny Is Funny

I used to watch *The Tonight Show* with my dad when I was a kid. I thought of it as a show for grown ups, so I felt privileged when he let me stay up late with him to see Johnny Carson tell jokes and his guests relate funny stories, which we laughed at together. I always made sure to laugh when my dad did, even though I didn't always get the joke. I sensed something special was happening; it was as if he was allowing me into the exclusive club of adults for the first time.

So when I was hired as a *Tonight Show* producer, I thought I had just been selected to join the elite ranks of such luminary humorists as Samuel Clements, Will Rogers, Bob Hope, Steve Allen, and Johnny Carson: all pillars in the great and unique American art form of topical humor. All right, maybe I got a little carried away.

Watching the show with my dad taught me that comedy resonates with us in a powerful, often enigmatic, way. A funny story can ease the tension in our lives like nothing else. It can help us tolerate someone with whom we disagree on just about everything. A good joke can even cause us to reconsider how we think about someone or something.

I believe we seriously need to laugh. It has to do with the old cliché "life is too short." We never think much about that phrase. We just say it and smile. But deep down in our bones we all know that, despite our best efforts, we're not going to get out of this life alive. It's the ultimate irony, and that's why irony is the essence of comedy.

When I got the job at *The Tonight Show* I had never thought much about what makes something funny. But it didn't take long for me to understand just how elusive comedy could be. We never really know if a joke will make people laugh. If we did, there would be no bad jokes.

I quickly gained a new respect for good comedians and began to understand that there is much wisdom in what they say. They've thought about life and have tried to figure it out. They've had to. You can't write funny jokes unless you have a consistent point of view, which makes you a philosopher— sometimes a good one. Jay Leno would've laughed me out of the room if I called him a philosopher to his face, though I've learned much about both comedy and life simply by being around him.

The heart of Jay's comedy was his monologue, which he considered the best part of his job. It was more than twice as long as Letterman's and more political than either Letterman's or Johnny Carson's. Among Washington's politicos, Jay's monologue was considered the one of record.

Jay's passion for topicality went back to his days as a club comic when he would incorporate the day's news into his standup routine. At that time his audience consisted of one hundred to two hundred people; at *Tonight,* he was reaching millions throughout the world with his timely humor.

The Center for Media and Public Affairs at George Mason University, which tracks late-night humor, studied 43,892 of Jay's monologue jokes about politicians, a figure that covered all but his last two weeks on the air. Jay told 4,607 jokes about Bill Clinton, earning the former president the dubious distinction of being Jay's biggest target. As center director Robert Lichter said, "Leno's monologues focused on power and scandal, and Bill Clinton was the top twofer."

George W. Bush came in second with 3,239 jokes. Al Gore got 1,026, President Obama garnered 1,011, and Hillary Clinton rounded out the top five with 939. The study said Jay told 10,885 jokes about Democrats, 15 percent more than the 9,465 jokes he did about Republicans, but a Democrat was president 13 of the 22 years Jay was on the air.

Lichter told the Washington Post in 2008 that Jay was

"responsible for making late night a source of political humor." He added, "Carson had political jokes, but they were mostly filler. For Leno, it was the main thing. Whenever a public figure was involved in some personal foible, you knew you'd hear about it on Leno."

But Jay's monologue wasn't all about biting political humor, because he knew his audience wanted more than that. "I'm doing this broad thing of a smart joke, a silly joke, and then a joke unrelated to politics. That's what *The Tonight Show* is—it's big-tent comedy," he told *Parade*.

His jokes were also observational, covering what was happening in people's everyday lives: eating habits, fast-food restaurants and the large portions they served, the differences between men and women, and the absurdities of government bureaucracy. Jay never tried to be preachy or push an agenda, as some late-night hosts do. Naturally, his humor reflected his personal opinions, but it also respected the views of his audience.

In recent years, Jay's monologue became more technically complex, relying more on video drop-ins, graphics, and special effects. However, the art of writing jokes hasn't changed much over the years. It's grueling, demanding, but uncomplicated work. Monologue jokes are made up of only two elements: a setup and a punch line. The setup provides the context for the punch line, the part of the joke that makes you laugh. A good setup should be brief. That allows you to get to the payoff, or punch line, quickly. There are variations to this format, but overall it's pretty basic, as you can see from this typical joke taken from Jay's monologue:

The economy is in bad shape. In fact, the economy is so bad, President Barack Obama's new slogan is "Spare Change You Can Believe In."

Setup: The economy's in bad shape.
Punch line: In fact, the economy is so bad, President Barack Obama's new slogan is "Spare change you can believe in."

Obviously, the purpose of a joke is to make people laugh. The setup and the punch line are just the means to an end. This topical joke works because it puts a surprise twist on President Obama's familiar campaign slogan by using the words "spare change" in place of "change."

Surprise, misdirection, and exaggeration are the three hallmarks of comedy, which is simply a form of deception. Good jokes are written by joining one idea to another in an unexpected way. Surprise and misdirection are often used together, though not exclusively. Here are two examples from Jay's monologues:

> In Austin, Texas, President Obama told an audience: If you want to go forward, put your car in "D". If you want to go backward, put your car in "R." But you know something, either way, the economy is still "F"'d.

> It's freezing across the United States. In fact, in DC, the weather is so bad, they actually hired convicted criminals to shovel snow at the US Capitol. Isn't that amazing? It's nice to see members of Congress doing something useful for a change.

Exaggeration is the true workhorse of comedy. Such jokes frequently use numbers:

> The number of Americans who are obese now outnumber[s] the number of Americans who are merely overweight. One-third of all Americans are obese. You know what that means? One out of every three people is three people.

I've just pontificated more about humor than I've ever heard Jay do in all the years I've known him. I think it's fun to figure out what makes something funny, even though it's a no-no in the business. You can analyze the laughs right out of a joke. Or, as E.B. White put it, "Humor can be dissected, as a frog can, but the thing dies in the process."

Jay has one basic rule: "Funny is funny." This means that if a joke or an anecdote makes you laugh, go with it, even if you don't understand why you just laughed. This idea was confusing to me at first. It implies there is no rhyme or reason to the process, and it sounds more like an absurdity than a rule. But then, comedy is absurdity.

Jay used to tell a joke about a cat that showed up on an airplane, causing the pilot to turn the plane around and land. He said the cat must have been a member of al kitty (as in al Qaeda). It was just a silly line, an absurdity. But it got lots of laughs. Funny is funny.

Jay would often turn down my comedy ideas for no apparent reason. I found this very discouraging until one day he told me a story, which I will paraphrase:

> Don't ever ask me to dress up in a gorilla suit and go out on stage. I won't do it. Just think about it. What if I'm out there in a gorilla suit, and nobody's laughing. Now I'm stuck out there in a gorilla suit, and nobody's laughing.

In other words: just because you think something looks or sounds funny doesn't mean it will be funny.

Jay's "Gorilla-Suit Rule" has surely saved him from thousands of really dumb ideas, including many of mine. There's nothing inherently funny about a guy coming out on the stage in a gorilla suit. He's essentially just a setup without a punch line.

The idea only works if it's part of a larger, cohesive concept. Let's say the guy in the gorilla suit is portraying a gorilla imitating a human who thinks he's funny just because he's wearing a gorilla suit. The "gorilla" thinks it's a pretty weak routine, and he tells this to the audience. With a look of incredulity he says, "I'm sorry, who evolved from whom?" Then he walks off stage.

The Tonight Show featured some very funny running comedy sketches, including Jaywalking, which consisted of interviews Jay did with average people. The point of this bit was that folks didn't know much about politics, history, or geography but were quite knowledgeable about pop culture.

And like many viewers, I loved the popular "Headlines" segment. In this bit Jay showed actual headlines, stories, and ads from newspapers and other sources, submitted by viewers. They were unintentionally funny because of double meanings, misspelled words, bad syntax, and factual or grammatical errors.

Jay himself brought this idea to the show after having written a number of "Headlines" books. Steve Allen, the show's original host in the '50s, would hold up and discuss offbeat newspaper stories. Jay perfected the concept and made it his own.

While some of the headlines were funny at first glance, many of them wouldn't have made you laugh if you had seen them in the paper. They were only amusing because Jay made them work with a punch line or a simple reaction. For example:

Headline: Menu from a restaurant featuring sandwiches with accompaniments such as lettuce, tomato, onion, penis, etc.
Jay: I'm just going to stick with tomato and onion.

Headline: Ad for a house at 1208 White Bitch Lane
Jay: My name is Susan. I live at White Bitch Lane. Why can't I find any men?

Headline: "Troutt Named to Salmon Board"
Jay: Seems like a conflict of interest to me.

I was privileged to be cast in bit parts in many of Jay's comedy sketches. Since I have the conservative look, I was usually featured as a guy wearing a suit. Following a string of Amtrak accidents, I played the president of the company wrapped head to toe in bandages and sitting in the audience as Jay told a joke about Amtrak's president insisting their trains were safe to ride.

As "Vice President Dick Cheney's Secret Service agent," I was shown running to keep up with Cheney as a stuntman portrayed him doing cartwheels after receiving heart surgery.

I was even cast as a hero on New Year's Day in 1997, bravely saving tourists at NBC from a "runaway champagne cork."

It was fun being included in the bits, but the comedy I most enjoyed consisted of the jokes Jay told the guests backstage before the show. These weren't necessarily his funniest, and most weren't even original. But they shed some light on how Jay carried out his job as the host of the show. Most of the time he saw his guests as just that—guests. And he liked to welcome them with a good joke.

It was an excellent strategy. Guests were often a bundle of nerves before they went on, and his jokes always helped cut the tension. What's more, he picked material they could relate to. For professional athletes, he had this story:

> A guy was working late one night with a female client. One thing led to another. They had a drink or two, ended up in bed and had sex. The guy immediately felt terrible about it and decided to come clean with his wife. When he got home, he told her everything and asked for her forgiveness. He said it was the first time he had ever been unfaithful and that he would never do it again. But his wife told him she didn't believe him: "You think I'm stupid enough to buy that? You were out golfing again, weren't you?"

For politicians and political commentators, both Democrats and Republicans:

> A guy was scheduled to speak at a political convention, but he was one of many speakers that day. And they had droned on well into the night. By the time he got to the podium there was only one man left in the audience. The speaker told the man he was flattered that the man had waited for this speech. The guy replied that he was only there because he was the next speaker.

For actresses whose priority was to look beautiful and sexy, Jay would tell naughty jokes. For child actors he would go through several knock-knock jokes and then listen to theirs.

For very young actors (six and under) he would do an impression of a bee.

The trick to doing "Write joke. Tell joke. Get paid." was that the next day you had to do it all over again with the same level of enthusiasm. And the day after that. And the one after that. Jay never seemed to get overwhelmed by the routine. He loved it. In fact, he craved it.

Chapter Three

The Dangerous Art of Booking Guests

The monologue was the show's cornerstone, the reason most people watched. While we never knew for sure which jokes would make people laugh, Jay had a very good idea—and was usually right. He had the monologue under control. The rest of the show was essentially a crap shoot, made up mostly of guest appearances. We couldn't select guests (mostly actors) the way Jay picked the jokes for his monologue, rejecting sixty for every one he used. Once we booked guests on the show, we weren't able to just cast them aside like rejected jokes. We had to work with them. So we learned to choose carefully. The art of booking required the skill of a diplomat, the fortitude of a high-stakes gambler, and the cunning of a spy.

Johnny Carson established the gold standard for guest segments. While our best guests were as good as Johnny's, his were consistently good almost every night at a level our guests didn't match. Part of the reason for this was Johnny's skill as an interviewer. He knew how to listen and ask follow-up questions better than any other late-night host, and he was the master of the zinger. No one would disagree with that, including Jay Leno. The truth is Johnny's show was essentially the only game in town. Entertainers had nowhere else to go to promote themselves and their projects. Oh, sure, there was Joey Bishop, Dick Cavett, and Arsenio Hall, but their late-night shows essentially drew niche audiences.

For comedians, the only road to success was through *The Tonight Show,* and it took years for most to get "discovered" by Johnny Carson. And if Johnny didn't like their set, they usually didn't come back. If they did get a second chance, it was usually not for a long time. One young comedian "killed" during his first set on Johnny. His second shot was good, but his third and fourth appearances were only fair. He didn't return for eight years. That comedian was Jay Leno.

Actors and other entertainers also had to meet Johnny's high expectations. As a result, his pool of guests became smaller and more exclusive. They were the best of the best. Toward the end of Johnny's reign on *The Tonight Show,* his cadre of regulars probably numbered no more than 150 people. Viewers were frequently treated to the likes of Frank Sinatra, Dean Martin, Sammy Davis Jr., Don Rickles, Bob Newhart, David Letterman, Jerry Seinfeld, Jonathan Winters, Robin Williams, Billy Crystal, Bette Midler, Dolly Parton, and Zsa Zsa Gabor.

Jay didn't have the luxury of being so choosy. During his run, there were many other talk shows out there. Getting big-name guests first was very competitive and dicey. If we passed on someone, he or she could—and often did—show up on Letterman and become his loyal guest. Some, like Tom Hanks, Bill Murray, and Bruce Willis, simply preferred appearing on Letterman. Some chose to do Leno and then changed their minds, often for very arbitrary reasons. Danny DeVito made his first and last visit with Jay on June 2, 1994, and for reasons that are very murky never accepted another offer. Helen Hunt was a guest in May 1994 while co-starring with Paul Reiser in NBC's *Mad About You.* When one of our producers gently critiqued her performance, making suggestions for improvements, Helen didn't come back for fourteen years.

In the early 90s, NBC Entertainment president Warren Littlefield came up with a plan to protect Jay from the fickleness of guests. He reduced their numbers from four to three per show, adding a comedy segment right after the monologue with regular bits such as Headlines and Jaywalking. With the new comedy segment, guests didn't appear until just before midnight (11 p.m. in the central time zone). In addition, music acts were almost always scheduled in the last segment because they usually had only a niche following. Singers who were big stars appeared as the first or second guest to talk with Jay and then returned as the third guest to perform their song. Some of these included Christina Aguilera, Lady Gaga, Garth Brooks, Blake Shelton, Tim McGraw and Dolly Parton.

Littlefield's new format featuring more comedy and fewer guests vastly improved the quality of *Tonight*. Even so, guests were still the single-biggest factor in an evening's ratings. We were rated for an entire hour, not just during the monologue and comedy segments at the beginning of the show. We knew viewers tended to tune out after the monologue. It was our job as producers to stop the hemorrhaging by booking and producing the best guest segments possible.

One of our best producers was Jay Leno himself. He was always willing to get on the phone to personally extend an invitation to a high-profile celebrity, and he was quite persuasive. Guests would often tell me the reason they chose our show over Letterman was Jay's personal call to them. He helped bring in almost every "big get," including President Barack Obama and former president George W. Bush. Eventually, we had to limit Jay's involvement in bookings to protect him from a barrage of mediocre comedians and other entertainers seeking a spot on the show. They would approach him in social settings or at comedy venues, taking advantage of the fact that he was, indeed, a very nice man. So Debbie Vickers, the executive producer, made a decision that Jay's job description no longer included booking guests, even though he continued helping us reel in the big names.

Despite the new policy, we often got calls from agents and publicists on the bottom rungs who insisted Jay promised their clients an appearance. He rarely did, but people heard what they wanted to hear. If Jay said, "I'll pass your name on to the producers," which he frequently did, that was interpreted as a booking. Many described their clients as Jay's "good friend," claiming Jay said he would "take care" of them, even though he didn't make an explicit offer. Most of the time, Jay barely knew their clients—or didn't know them at all. The ever-annoying agents were also predictable: the more aggressive they were, the less talented their clients were.

We tried as much as possible to bring in guests Jay preferred. If he disliked someone, we usually respected his views and didn't book that person. Jay felt strongly that O. J. Simpson was guilty of murdering his ex-wife Nicole Brown Simpson and her friend Ronald Goldman. When the jury found Simpson not guilty, most of his defense attorneys, including Johnnie Cochran, wanted to come on the show, but we declined because Jay dismissed them as opportunists. However, he liked the two main prosecuting attorneys, Marcia Clark and Christopher Darden, so we invited them to appear.

But we couldn't always book the show based solely on Jay's tastes. There were potential guests too famous, too topical, too attractive, or too good to pass over, no matter what Jay thought. He understood that and tried to cooperate with us, even though it didn't always work. In 2003, we booked Trista Rehn, the beautiful and popular reality star featured in the first season of *The Bachelorette* and in the first season of *The Bachelor*. Jay had never seen either show, and he had no interest in them other than writing monologue jokes about them. Shortly after the taping, Trista saw Jay in the parking lot and requested a picture with him in front of his car. He had no idea who she was and assumed she was someone from the studio audience, so he asked what her name was and where she lived. Oops!

While we occasionally made mistakes, we put much thought into our selection of guests. The first thing producers, including Jay, did every morning was look at the overnight Nielsen ratings to see how well the guests did the night before. The hourly numbers with quarterly breakouts trumped everything else, including our own preferences. As a result, we knew which guests—and comedy segments—held the audience and which ones didn't. This gave us a competitive edge over Letterman, whose producers weren't paying close attention to the ratings, according to our sources at CBS. We also studied Letterman's bookings, which confirmed what we had been told. His show repeatedly booked entertainers as lead guests who were ratings downers. We would never invite back guests whose numbers consistently tanked. Our booking decisions were based mostly on math, not instincts. Our knowledge of the Nielsen ratings helped us understand just how fickle viewers could be. Even one night of bad ratings could seriously change the show's momentum. We saw it happen to Letterman. His CBS show was number one from its premiere in 1993 until July 19, 1995, the day British actor Hugh Grant was booked as a guest on our show. That single, fortuitous appearance was literally responsible for launching Jay's nineteen-year reign as the King of Late Night.

Hugh, who had a long-time relationship with the beautiful British actress and model Elizabeth Hurley, had been arrested on Hollywood's Sunset Boulevard for engaging in lewd conduct in his car with a prostitute named Divine Brown. The story immediately got worldwide coverage, and Hugh's skyrocketing career as a bankable, likable comedic actor was on the verge of falling into the abyss. As luck—or perhaps fate—would have it, Hugh had already been booked on *The Tonight Show* before the scandal broke. He was coming on to promote his first major Hollywood film, *Nine Months,* which followed his hugely successful 1994 hit *Four Weddings and a Funeral.* But only days before his scheduled appearance, Hugh was having second thoughts and almost cancelled it. We encouraged him to reconsider, and Jay assured Hugh he would conduct the interview delicately, devoting only a few questions to the incident. Hugh thought about it and wisely promised to stay in, so he could own up to his transgression and publicly apologize for it. Less than two weeks after the arrest, he showed up for the interview.

"Let me start with question number one: What the hell were you thinking?" Jay enthusiastically asked Hugh as soon as he sat down at the panel. Jay had put much thought into that question and decided to add the word "hell," making it slightly tongue-in-cheek. The question resonated with viewers and the press and it soon became a household phrase. I have no doubt Hugh also thought long and hard about his answer, which was an unadulterated apology. He accepted full responsibility for his actions and didn't mince his words: "I think you know in life what's a good thing, and what's a bad thing, and I did a bad thing." He went on to explain that people had given him lots of advice about what to say: "I was under pressure, or I was over-tired, or I was lonely, or I fell down the stairs when I was a child. But that would be bollocks to hide behind."

The episode got huge press worldwide even though Hugh had reportedly asked that no journalists be present at the show. On the day of the interview, the NBC publicity department figured out a way to get around the restriction by setting up a conference call for reporters around the country and feeding them live audio of the show. Other reporters staked out the area outside the studio to get the audience's reaction, which was mostly supportive of the beleaguered actor.

That single appearance, combined with press accounts about it, saved Hugh's troubled career and set the bar for the modern-day celebrity *mea culpa*. Until then, celebrities who were caught up in a scandal would routinely cancel interviews, attack the media for distorting the story, and go into hiding. Many of them still do that today, but not the ones who are savvy about proper crisis management techniques, which call for dealing with an emergency head-on.

Hugh's public apology was even referenced in a popular thriller novel called *Gone Girl* by Gillian Flynn, published in 2012. One of the book's main characters, Nick Dunne, makes an appearance on a talk show to express contrition for being unfaithful to his missing wife, Amy, and to convince the interviewer that he did not kill her. In a classic case of art imitating life, Nick prepares for his interview by watching the Hugh Grant interview online. Nick is impressed with the

British actor's answers and decides to imitate him, both in substance and style: "I watched that clip so many times, I was in danger of borrowing a British accent. I was the ultimate hollow man: the husband Amy always claimed couldn't apologize finally did, using words and emotions borrowed from an actor."

As for Jay, his ratings, which had already started to turn around months earlier, were boffo that night, ending Letterman's late-night reign and launching Jay to the number-one spot. *The Tonight Show* maintained its ratings superiority from that day forward, except for the seven-month period in 2009-2010 when Conan O'Brien hosted the show. Hugh's appearance was a powerful reminder to the producers about the double-edged nature of ratings and the importance of guests, one that we never forgot. There's no question the Hugh Grant interview was a game changer in late-night television. But why? Here's my best guess: most guests are either celebrities or at the peak of their fifteen minutes of fame and are expected to be entertaining and funny. Some are booked simply because they're controversial. On any given night, no single guest had all those qualities. No one, that is, except Hugh Grant, who was famous, entertaining, funny, and controversial. And the timing was perfect for Jay. He needed something big to happen, something so different and unique that it would capture the attention of a worldwide audience in a way no other late-night show had ever done.

But there's more to this story. The episode that aired wasn't the one we had originally planned. That one would have had an even bigger impact. On the night Hugh was booked, Dee Dee Myers was originally scheduled as the second guest. The former press secretary to then president Clinton had been charged with a DUI in Washington, DC, after police stopped and later arrested her for driving on the wrong side of the road. Like Hugh, she had been booked before the incident. At first, she agreed to stay in. Later, however, she got cold feet and dropped out after her lawyer reminded her the judge would probably not take kindly to seeing her on a high-profile comedy show prior to her trial. I tried to convince her that Jay would not make fun of her DUI and that her appearance would give her the opportunity to express genuine contrition, just as Hugh Grant would be doing. She still thought it was too risky, as she was facing possible jail time of up to one year. I often wonder what would have happened if she had appeared with Hugh. The show would have featured two celebrities, one from the world of entertainment, the other from politics, both offering *mea culpas*. Would that have made for a better program? There's no way of knowing, but I'm certain we would have gotten even higher ratings.

As for the defendants, prosecutors dropped the drunk-driving charges against Dee Dee after she spent twelve hours in a special alcohol-education program. Hugh was charged with lewd conduct in a public place and fined $1,180. He got back together with Elizabeth Hurley, though they would announce an amicable split five years later. His encounter with Divine Brown, which cost him $50, seemed to have little effect on his successful film career. And Divine, whose real name is Stella Thompson, was fined $1,150 for parole violations and sentenced to 180 days in jail. She eventually left the life of prostitution, thanking Hugh for "changing" her life. But her story wasn't exactly Disney material. She parlayed the scandal into a financial bonanza, earning more than $1 million from media interviews by giving graphic details of the incident. For the record, we didn't book her.

After Hugh Grant, Jay became the go-to host for fallen celebrities who wanted to come clean. In 2009, singer Kanye West made an apology for upstaging country singer Taylor Swift at the MTV Video Music Awards. As she was accepting an award, Kanye grabbed the microphone from her and argued that Beyoncé was more deserving of the honor.

"It was rude, period," Kanye told Jay. Kanye was at a rare loss for words when Jay asked him what his late beloved mother Donda would have said about his behavior. Media critics questioned the appropriateness of Jay's question, but he had met Donda. And he routinely challenged guests about their parents' reactions to questionable behavior. Besides, Kanye had agreed to answer the question. Then, in July 2013, Kanye took back his apology to Taylor, telling the *New York Times:* "If anyone's reading this waiting for some type of full-on, flat apology for anything, they should just stop reading right now." When Kanye was reminded he had already expressed contrition, he implied he only did it because he had succumbed to peer pressure. Kanye's confused and pathetic attempt to take back his apology only served to bolster Hugh Grant's genuine *mea culpa.*

In July 2013, Jay asked Eliot Spitzer: "How could you be this stupid?" The question had a ring to it, much like "What the hell were you thinking?" And it resonated with the press much like the one directed at Hugh Grant. The dishonored former New York governor came on the show to express regret for having to resign from office five years earlier after spending thousands on a high-end prostitute. He was planning to make a political comeback by seeking the office of New York City comptroller and wanted New Yorkers to understand he had been humbled by his personal mistakes. Spitzer answered Jay's blunt inquiry this way: "People who fall prey to hubris end up falling themselves. And this is something that I think infected me. And the fall from grace is incredibly painful and is something through which you learn."

By sheer coincidence, Bill Hader, who did an impression of Spitzer in a 2010 comedy sketch on *Saturday Night Live,* was his fellow guest. Spitzer referred to the comedian as his "long-lost twin who got all the talent" and said: "I usually hit the remote when I see him."

While big celebrity *mea culpas* were a hallmark of the Leno years, they were very rare. On any given day, actors pitching their films and TV shows were our stock-in-trade. Naturally, our goal was to bring in the biggest stars, but sometimes the process could get complicated. In general, movie stars mattered more than TV stars. However, only about ten movie stars could be counted on to improve the ratings. Even they didn't always come with a guarantee. As the number of talk shows increased, big stars made the rounds to promote their films, decreasing their value to us. Naturally, we tried to book them before any other show, but that wasn't always possible.

Like monologue jokes, the best guest bookings were topical: actors in current, popular films and televisions shows and people with "buzz" created by critics. We learned not to get too far ahead of the curve. Frequently, viewers' awareness of the latest films and "hottest" actors lagged behind the critics by several weeks. So we often passed on rising but still relatively unknown stars, who would have done nothing for our ratings. Instead, we allowed, and even encouraged, them to do other, "smaller" shows first. Sometimes we took a risk on a young, relatively unknown but promising actor to establish a relationship with them before Letterman did, even though such a booking usually resulted in lower ratings. The idea was to reach out to younger viewers in the coveted eighteen to forty-nine demographic. We considered this the cost of doing business, an investment in the future, though it didn't always pay off. Young stars often suffered from a strange case of memory loss when it came to remembering who gave them their big break. But sometimes we were pleasantly surprised.

Shia LaBeouf was a sixteen-year-old comedic actor appearing in a Disney Channel sitcom called *Even Stevens* when my teenage daughter, Melissa, brought him to my attention. A year later he was starring in his first feature film, Disney's *Holes*, which I watched with Melissa. By then, she was insisting Shia would be a major star some day. I agreed with her and invited Shia on the show. He was as funny as any comedian and he did, indeed, become a Hollywood celebrity after appearing in such films as *Indiana Jones and the Kingdom of the Crystal Skull* and the *Transformers* trilogy, and we invited him back many times.

Anne Hathaway was an eighteen-year-old sophomore in college when we booked her for *The Princess Diaries*, her first feature film. She remained loyal to the show, making appearances to promote subsequent films, including *Les*

Misérables, for which she won an Academy Award in 2013.

Lindsay Lohan made her first and best appearance with Jay at age twelve while promoting her film debut in Disney's remake of *The Parent Trap*, which was shot in London. I remember how cute and innocent she looked as she told Jay how much she disliked British food and how thrilled she was to discover they had McDonald's in London. She was also feisty: when Jay mistakenly introduced her as Leslie Lohan, she said, "Hi, Jay Lemon!" She went on to become a loyal guest, though her return visits were often sad occasions. Stories about her troubling drunken behavior frequently turned up in the press. Like Hugh Grant, she apologized to Jay for her profligate lifestyle and promised to redeem herself. But unlike Hugh, she didn't. In 2007, she cancelled a booking the day she was scheduled to appear after being arrested the night before on suspicion of drunk driving. Someone suggested we replace Lindsay with comedic actor Rob Schneider dressed in drag, playing her. He came out wearing a blonde wig, a black dress, and an alcohol-monitoring bracelet like one Lindsay had worn strapped to his leg.

While I was partly responsible for booking Rob, I thought his performance was tasteless, mean, and unfunny, a trip down the low road. I remembered when Lindsay was a freckle-faced kid, and now she was a young adult, possibly headed for a tragedy. Like many young actors, she grew up on movie sets and never had a childhood. Ironically, Jay once asked her if she ever regretted not taking time off from her acting career to just be a kid. She told him that at age twenty-six, she still felt like one. It was an awkward moment.

As time went on, we were booking fewer actors and more newsmakers. Interviews with presidential candidates during primary and presidential elections not only boosted the ratings but also resulted in heavy news and social media coverage. Timely appearances by sports heroes brought energy and excitement to the show like no actor could. Journalists and commentators also became frequent guests, as Jay was a news junkie who watched cable news in his office all day.

But even newsmakers never came with a ratings guarantee. Only animals could be counted on to bring in consistently high ratings, usually beating the biggest movie stars and celebrities on the *Late Show with David Letterman.* Like the audience, Jay loved critters and furry creatures, particularly the big cats, and he was fearless around them. The humans who presented our animal guests, known as "animal ambassadors," were just as important as the animals. The best ones, who knew how to balance their dual role as educators and entertainers, made up a small, elite group that included Joan Embery, Dave Salmoni, Julie Scardina, Jarod Miller, and the late "Crocodile Hunter" Steve Irwin, who was a worldwide star in his own right. Irwin made *Tonight* his late-night home. He and his animals ranked among our all-time most popular guests, and their appearances were more crucial to Jay's success than any Hollywood celebrity.

Eventually, Steve pressed us for a sit-down chat with Jay without critters, which we rejected at first, believing the audience would resist the idea. We eventually gave in, booking Steve as a solo act. He didn't disappoint us or our viewers as he regaled Jay with a very funny story about his newborn son Robert. Steve and his wife, Terri, had been hoping to provide a brother for their daughter, Bindi. He told Jay that the key to having a boy is to keep your testicles cool, which he did by wearing plastic-mesh underwear. While telling the story, he held up a mesh bag containing two onions. Fellow guest Catherine Zeta-Jones could barely contain herself.

In 2006, Steve died in a tragic accident while swimming with stingrays. Jay gave his friend an on-air tribute and wrote an obituary in *TIME* magazine: "He called himself the Crocodile Hunter, but Crocodile Preserver was more like it. He taught kids—and all of us—that not just the cuddly animals are special. And he was the best ambassador Australia ever had."

On September 19, 2005, we turned to animals in an act of desperation to counteract a huge booking Letterman had just scored: Martha Stewart in her first late-night guest spot after serving a five-month prison sentence for insider stock trading. Our original lineup of guests that night was Benjamin Bratt, Nicollette Sheridan and B.B. King. Benjamin was a fine actor but not a huge star. With him as lead guest, we faced a ratings disaster against "M. Diddy" (Martha's nickname among fellow inmates). We rarely cancelled or postponed a guest as a matter of policy, but this time we knew we had to make a change. No one mentioned Hugh Grant by name that day, but we were all aware that if he could make us number one in one night, Martha could do the same for David. So we booked animals along with animal ambassador Jarod Miller. We offered the second spot to Benjamin, who declined to follow animals and was re-booked as lead guest on October 17, his last appearance on the show. Steve Carell, then a rising new star, agreed to go second, and we bumped Nicollette Sheridan.

The changes ruffled some feathers, but they worked. Facing near impossible odds, we led with animals and won the ratings battle against Letterman and Martha by .4 of a point, approximately a half-million viewers. I'm just grateful our original lineup didn't include a big-name Hollywood celebrity. We probably wouldn't have cancelled such a person, and Martha would have destroyed us.

Chapter Four

Guests

Next to Jay, his guests were the most important part of the show. They got paid about $500 per appearance, union scale, but most didn't come for the money. It was peanuts to them. They were selling something: a film, a television show, a book, or even a presidential run—which was a little scary when you think about it. They weren't employees who could be fired for doing a bad job. They had no skin in the game.

Our success depended on people we had absolutely no control of; we were essentially turning the show over to them during their appearances. That's why we vetted, as much as possible, what guests would be discussing during their interviews and why we invited the best ones back often. Most of the time our approach worked.

The best guests understood they couldn't just hawk their wares. They knew they had to put on a good performance by telling great stories. While they often appeared to be having a casual conversation with Jay, many spent hours developing material for their interviews. We were grateful for their efforts, which helped take the burden off Jay.

The quintessential guest was comedian Billy Crystal, who appeared on the first show, May 25, 1992. He and Jay had known each other for twenty years at the time, and they looked like two friends chatting and clowning around during the segment. At one point, Billy pulled out a lyric sheet and began singing a musical parody to the tune "You Made Me Love You":

You made me first guest.
I didn't want to do it.
My agent really blew it.

I like your set, but
That picture of the sea now,
It makes me want to pee now.

. . . I'm proud to be your first guest.

That same night, Jay asked Billy to do his last show. He promised he would, and twenty-two years later he made good on his promise. Billy showed up on February 6, 2014, to do another music parody as well as a tribute done to the tune of "So Long, Farewell," from *The Sound of Music.* He was joined by the "Shut Your Von Trapp Family Singers" as well as Sheryl Crow, Carol Burnett, Oprah Winfrey, Kim Kardashian, NBA star Chris Paul, and Jim Parsons.

Billy called Jay "America's night-light" and then invoked the name of his predecessor, Johnny Carson: "You were handed the baton by one of the all-time greats. But once it was in your grasp, you ran the race." Billy gave Jay a touching sendoff, just as he had given him a rousing kickoff. It was comforting to know we had a real pro on the first and last shows. But there were 4,608 shows in between, and not all guests could be as good as Billy. In fact, most of them weren't. That was the challenge.

Most guests were actors. And as odd as it may seem, many struggled with the idea of doing a talk show. These were people who read scripts for a living, pretending to be other people. They didn't seem to have life experiences of their own and often admitted their lives were uneventful and boring. My plumber actually had better stories than many of them. The guests I dreaded the most were the ones who said: "Let's just wing it. Jay can ask me anything." On the surface it sounded great, but they didn't mean it. What they were really saying was they couldn't think of anything to talk about and didn't want to try. My job as a producer was to help them get ready for their interview by doing a so-called pre-interview. I usually started by reminding them Jay was a workaholic who thoroughly prepared for his own interviews on other talk shows. Winging it was never an option for him.

With many actors, I had to go over the basics of storytelling. It's an art, but it's not complicated. And it hasn't changed much over the centuries. Johnny Carson had this advice for his guests: "Tell them what you're going to say. Say it. Then tell them what you said." Johnny didn't actually come up with that idea. Aristotle did. A good story has to be simple, clear, and consistent, and it should have a beginning, a middle, and an end. The world's greatest tales follow this ancient formula. I told my guests to imagine they were at a dinner party talking with friends. And I asked them to come up with three interesting, humorous topics and be prepared to talk about them at the party. The pre-interview usually worked well, but there was one notable exception.

In 2002, Christian Bale, an extraordinary actor, abruptly ended a pre-interview with me and cancelled his appearance on the show because my questions were too personal. I had asked him where he grew up (Wales), how big his family was (three sisters), and what his first gig was (a Pac-Man cereal commercial). I was amazed that a major star like Christian, who would win an Academy Award in 2011, didn't seem to have even a basic understanding of how *The Tonight Show* worked. I understand he's very protective of his privacy, but really; he's also a public figure. I just don't understand it. Still, I was glad he dropped out, thus averting an awkward on-air exchange with Jay.

Jim Caviezel, who turned in an Oscar-worthy performance as Jesus in *The Passion of the Christ* in 2004, had put a lot of thought into his upcoming interview with Jay but still needed a little guidance. He said he had recently visited the pontiff and had some great pope jokes. The trouble was, they weren't funny. I suggested he leave the jokes to Jay, but I could tell he was disappointed. Believe me, it wasn't easy saying no to the guy who had just portrayed Jesus better than anyone else I had ever seen. I knew he had much stronger material. He had literally been struck by lightning while filming the Sermon on the Mount scene. The skies were stormy, and he sensed an eerie vacuum as his hair stood on end. Then he was lit up like a Christmas tree. His eyes got very bright, and crew members saw flames coming out of the sides of his head. While this was happening, Jim saw what appeared to be a pink, static color and he heard a deafening sound like a jet engine. The strike left him stunned but—miraculously—unhurt. He joked that he looked up, as if to heaven, and all he could think to say was, "What, you didn't like this take?" I told Jim that his story would have been too good to be believed if his film crew hadn't witnessed it. But, then again, he was "Jesus." How could he be lying? I strongly advised him to go with it and lose the jokes about the Pope. Jim reluctantly agreed, and I'm glad he did. I heard thousands of anecdotes over the years, but I believe his lightning strike tale was the greatest story ever told on the show.

Jay usually didn't like to discuss the "craft of acting," which he thought was pretentious. He made exceptions for people like Jason Alexander, who could make anything funny. Jason, best known for playing George Costanza on *Seinfeld,* said he followed one basic practice as an actor. Whenever he had a difficult scene to play, he imagined he was passing gas. That facial expression covers the whole spectrum of human emotions, including sadness, pain, lust, compassion, sympathy, concern, and confusion.

Oscar-nominated British actor Ralph Fiennes was not a fan of the Harry Potter movies until he agreed to play the evil Lord Voldemort, starting in the fourth film. When Jay asked Ralph why he took the part, he said he only did it after his two nephews got excited when they learned their uncle might be in a Harry Potter film. It was Ralph's idea to shave his head for the role rather than wear a bald cap. A friend told him he looked tough as a bald guy, which he liked because no one had ever described him that way before.

Some actors were complicated, like Teri Hatcher. I called

her Teri One and Teri Two, though not to her face. Teri One was charming, smart, witty, and flirtatious. You couldn't make up a more perfect guest. Teri Two was moody. She would call me late the night before her scheduled appearance, scream at me for not having better ideas, and then hang up. The next day she would come to the show as Teri One, acting as if nothing had ever happened. Then she would put on an outstanding performance. I was intrigued by the behavioral patterns of the two Teris. They had an inverse relationship: the wackier Teri Two acted, the sweeter Teri One became. In spite of her eccentricities, I like Teri and can't help but smile when I think of her portrayal of Susan as a deeply conflicted character on *Desperate Housewives*. Teri played her perfectly.

As time went on, we added more diversity to our lineup with politicos, singers, authors, and even reality TV stars. Some of our best guests were sports people, many of whom were natural entertainers. Charles Barkley, NBA hall of famer and TNT commentator, was a total goofball. You couldn't help but laugh at anything he said, even if it wasn't funny. He especially loved making fun of his own golf game. He once talked about playing in a celebrity golf tournament in Lake Tahoe, California, where he finished 80th out of 81. As he was describing his struggles with his golf swing, Jay called for video of Charles muffing a fairway shot, which advanced the ball only a few yards. Ironically, his golf coach was one of the best in the world—his friend Tiger Woods, who compared his swing to a "speech impediment" he called "the yips." When Jay asked Charles what that meant, he answered, "That's what you get when you can't play golf anymore." The joke made no sense, but it got huge laughs because Charles said it as only he could.

Singers usually had great stories about the road, and Stevie Nicks of Fleetwood Mac fame had the best one of all, telling Jay about the time her tour bus broke down on the Grapevine section of the I-5 north of Los Angeles. The fan belt had broken, the driver didn't have a spare, and the band was late for a gig. What to do? Stevie suggested a pair of her pantyhose as a quick fix. It would be risky, as the Grapevine has many steep ascents and descents and has caused many overheated radiators. But desperate times call for desperate measures. The driver attached Stevie's makeshift fan belt to the pulley, started the engine, and the band got to its scheduled performance on time.

Country singers had the best tour buses. Decked out with every modern convenience, almost all included big screen TVs and Wi-Fi. Many didn't even use the show's dressing rooms. Instead, they just hung out in their buses. Willie Nelson's bus was the gold standard. Featuring beautiful, original Western murals and warm wood paneling, it was homier than most homes. Willie was the consummate host, always offering food and drinks. He once asked me to join him in smoking a joint, which I declined. But I think I actually got a little high.

The late Johnny Cash, known for his deep, resonant vocal timbre when singing such hits as "Ring of Fire," "I Walk the Line," "A Boy Named Sue," and "Orange Blossom Special" told Jay he had a high-pitched tenor voice as a teenager. Then at seventeen his voice changed after putting in a long, hard day on the farm. At the end of the day he returned home and started singing an old gospel song. All of a sudden, his voice dropped an octave. His mother said, "Who's that?" even though she knew who it was. When Johnny replied, "That's me," she simply said, "Keep it up." And from that day he did.

Stephen King, the great horror novelist, was an accomplished, witty storyteller. He admitted to Jay that he slept with a night-light on, even though he didn't believe anything was hiding under his bed. He also made sure his covers were always tucked in, which prevented non-existent monsters from getting in. He acknowledged his behavior appeared to be odd but insisted he was just taking reasonable precautions. Unfortunately for the show, Stephen never came back to our studio in Burbank because he was afraid of flying.

Cherie Blair, the wife of former British prime minister Tony Blair, told Jay how she became pregnant with her fourth child, Leo, while staying at Balmoral Castle during a visit with Queen Elizabeth II. She had left her contraception at home because she was afraid a royal maid would find it. She was forty-four at the time and assumed she would be safe, "and of course God was obviously laughing at me because nine months later along came Leo."

Sometimes a good story is as simple as a name. In 2013, reality TV star Kim Kardashian and singer Kanye West named their baby girl North West. As one would expect, Jay and other comedians made many jokes about it. But the story had an unexpected twist. Kris Jenner, North's grandmother, came on the show and said Jay was responsible for the name. Six weeks earlier, Jay was interviewing a very pregnant Kim about a rumor that Kanye favored the name North. She dismissed the rumor, saying she was partial to Easton (West). According to Kris, her daughter had second thoughts after talking with Jay: "This is a true story, and I am not messing with you," Kris said. "She called me and she goes . . . I never really took it seriously. I didn't think about it. And, mom, after Jay brought it up, I think I want to name the baby North."

"I think you're responsible," Kris said, pointing to Jay. "So, it's my fault?" he replied.

True moments of spontaneity were rare at *Tonight* and in all of television, inherently a crisis environment. The job of producers is to keep chaos contained by controlling as much as possible. Spontaneity was fraught with too many potential dangers. Even a few seconds of substandard programming could result in thousands of people reaching for their remotes. But sometimes things so bizarre and unexpected would happen on the show that they were compelling, albeit sometimes embarrassing. These moments often became show highlights, including the greatest train wreck in the history of *The Tonight Show*: In 1993, NBC executives decided to have Jay do an entire program live and on location in Boston with the cast of *Cheers,* following the beloved NBC sitcom's final episode after an amazing eleven-year run. The show would originate from the historic Bull and Finch Pub, the inspiration for both the sitcom and its set. It all sounded terrific. All of the cast members except one committed to be there, including Ted Danson, Woody Harrelson, Kelsey Grammer, George Wendt, John Ratzenberger, and Rhea Perlman. But after hanging out at the bar all day, most were intoxicated by show time. Besides, this was like a wrap party to them. And as Jay attempted to interview the cast, they were giggling and shooting spitballs at each other, which they frequently did on their own set. Jay repeatedly apologized for their drunken behavior, which seemed only to emphasize the fact that he had lost control. *Boston Herald* TV critic Monica Collins, who was at the bar, said all the cast members but Rhea Perlman behaved like "idiots" and "jerks." Obviously, this critic had never been to a wrap party.

The Tonight Show's Cheers episode wasn't all bad. Television train wrecks rarely are. Twenty-two million people were watching that night, making it the highest-rated show in Jay's twenty-two-year run. It did much better than the *Friends* finale episode in 2004 (12.6 million viewers), which featured Jay and the show's cast from their set in Burbank. So does that make the NBC executives geniuses? Yes, actually. If the ratings had tanked, the suits would have been blamed, so they deserve the credit for the stellar ratings. The experience also taught us an important lesson: all great shows start with great ideas, but not all great ideas lead to great shows.

We also learned a lesson from another humiliating disaster: never trust Howard Stern. In 1995, the radio shock jock was booked to promote a tawdry new book. Always the showman, he walked out to the strains of Miss America, flanked by two busty women dressed in tiny pink bikinis. Then he announced the women, who were actually porn stars, would stage "the first *Tonight Show* lesbian kiss," which they did. Later he performed "the first *Tonight Show* spanking" with one of the women, as some audience members, mostly Howard's fans, howled in support.

We were as surprised by this tasteless stunt as the audience.

Howard had hidden the women in his dressing-room bathroom prior to coming out on stage. Jay was absolutely furious and even walked off the set for the first and only time, although it was never seen on air. Backstage, he lit into Howard's executive producer Gary Dell'Abate for pulling off such a shameful and disrespectful act. *Tonight Show* executive producer Debbie Vickers warned Howard during the commercial break that his antics would not make air, and Jay repeated her warning on air. But Howard continued cavorting with the women, even as the next guests, Gene Siskel and Roger Ebert, vainly attempted to critique films with Jay. Debbie made good on her admonition, and the home audience didn't see much of Howard's sleazy antics, which were shot with a cameraman positioned in front of the women. Still, viewers were aware of what was happening. The next day, NBC put out a tepid press release, criticizing Howard for not staying "within acceptable boundaries" of taste and apologizing to "anyone (who) was offended." In fact, Howard had hijacked *The Tonight Show,* while holding Jay hostage, as he mocked the audience's middle-class sensibilities. As a result, the show's image was tarnished.

Chicago Tribune TV critic Steve Johnson called us (the producers) out for our role in the Stern travesty: "But Leno, his producers and his network, in allowing Stern's assorted offenses, airing them, then trying to distance themselves from them after the ratings had been notched, demonstrated an almost epic capacity for disingenuousness." Johnson was right. We weren't blameless. Howard was known for his obnoxious shtick, and we held our collective noses for the sake of higher ratings. We learned a valuable lesson from this incident: Jay pledged that no guest would ever be allowed free reign on the show again, and he stuck to that pledge.

Surprisingly, Jay even got support from an editorial in *Christianity Today* written by Billy Graham's publicist, Larry Ross. During the segment, Howard took out a Bible and announced that the Gideon Bible would be replaced in hotels with his new book. Jay quickly grabbed the Bible, held it up and said: "This book will strike you down as you go down the road. . . . I am sounding like an evangelist now, but I predict that's what will happen—suddenly all that is in this book is making perfect sense to me." Jay was speaking partly tongue-in-cheek, but even so, he was telling Howard to go to hell! *Christianity Today* lauded Jay by calling him "an unlikely man who took an unlikely stand in the unlikely forum of a late-night talk show." A more unlikely editorial supporting Jay from a more unlikely source has never been written.

As for Howard, he didn't return for five years, making a notably toned-down appearance in 2000, his last. I found his humor distasteful and embarrassing and was glad to see him go. I was always curious why he secretly staged such tawdriness. Until then, Howard had a good relationship with the show, one of only a few supporters in the early days when most critics were routinely pummeling Jay.

"Stuttering" John Melendez, Howard's sidekick at the time, later told me Howard was only trying to "outdo himself" with a stunt that would impress his own audience, not to make Jay look bad. According to John, Howard was genuinely taken aback when Jay walked off the set. I believe John's explanation, but I can't understand how Howard could be so unaware of *Tonight Show* standards.

In 2004, John was hired as our announcer and comedy correspondent, replacing Edd Hall. I thought John had shown a presence and a likability during a recent guest appearance on our show that would work well with Jay. Howard took this move as a personal affront, accusing Jay of "ripping off" his long-time sidekick. And his tasteless tirades against Jay never let up after that. In May 2012, NBC, then owned by Comcast, hired Howard as a judge on *America's Got Talent*. A few months later, he called Jay a "spineless maggot" after he took a 50 percent pay cut to save jobs when the network laid off twenty *Tonight Show* staffers. Howard's rant was laughably illogical, and he should have been fired for openly insulting NBC's biggest star. Instead, he received an obligatory letter from an NBC executive telling him to stop talking about Jay, which he openly mocked.

Some guests had an agenda only they understood. In 1994, Bobcat Goldthwait, a self-described comedian, lit his guest chair on fire using lighter fluid. Jay was visibly perturbed, as he and model Lauren Hutton quickly doused the flames with their drinking water. The studio audience laughed, thinking the stunt was part of a comedy bit, but it clearly was not. Bobcat insisted that he wasn't drunk or high. But he could never explain why he did it. Observers speculated he was protesting the recent cancellation of the *Arsenio Hall Show,* which he had strongly supported. Others say he was making a bizarre "artistic" statement. I usually discount professed artistic and altruistic motives. It's almost always about money and self-promotion. I think Bobcat was trying in his own confused and inarticulate way to draw attention to a film he had directed. He pleaded no contest in a Burbank courtroom to misdemeanor charges and was fined $3,880, including $698 for the chair, making him the only *Tonight Show* guest ever convicted of committing a crime on the show. He was never invited back.

In 1996, a woman came out of the audience and onto the stage, interrupting an interview Irish actor Colin Farrell was doing with Jay. She said something unintelligible to Colin, who quickly took matters into his own hands, as he grabbed her elbow, led her offstage and handed her over to security. "I'll see you in court," she shouted. "Darling, you're insane," he replied as he sat back down next to Jay, apologized to the audience, and said, "My first stalker." "Welcome to celebrity," Jay quipped. The show continued as if the incident had never happened, and the unscripted intrusion never made air.

Many moments of spontaneity became show highlights we could be proud of, such as the day Simon Cowell let down his guard. Simon, known for his cockiness and swagger, would talk to Jay about almost anything, including the many women in his life. He always seemed detached from and bemused by such stories. It was all an act, as Simon was actually shy.

And he covered it up well, except for one time in 2009.

The tabloids were reporting he had recently gotten engaged to his long-time makeup artist, Mezhgan Hussainy, giving her a six-carat diamond ring set in platinum worth about five hundred thousand dollars. On the day of the taping, he came with Mezhgan, a strikingly exotic brunette who had often accompanied him there as his makeup artist. This time he was proudly showing her off to the crew and even agreed to let her join him during his appearance. On stage, Simon was his usual cheeky, witty self. But when Jay brought up Mezhgan, Simon got a little flustered:

> Jay: The rumor is you are engaged. Is it true?
> Simon: Are they true, um, well I do have somebody in my life now, Jay, yes. I kind of made a decision this year to make somebody happy, so that's how I . . ."
> Jay: So you're doing this just to help someone?
> Simon: It's called giving back.
> Jay: For the first time on national television you are sweating.

Simon admitted he felt uncomfortable talking about himself but also admitted a wedding was in the plans.

> Jay: Within the next year?
> Simon: Within the next ten years.

The audience was eating it up. They had never seen the mighty, irascible Simon Cowell squirming. It got even better when Jay brought out Mezhgan. She sat on the couch right next to Simon, putting her hand on his leg. Then she kissed him, which was one of the show's most awkward moments. The *London Mail Online* wrote a scathing mock review of Simon's lackluster performance while kissing the love of his life: "The man whose withering judgments . . . turn contestants to jelly seemed remarkably ill-at-ease himself. . . . And in a hammer blow to romance, he kept his eyes wide open the entire time."

After Mezhgan left the panel, Simon regained his usual

composure, telling Jay he even wanted to have kids: "I'm kind of torn, because I'm a bit too old to have kids, but then again I think it would be important to have a lot of me's around."

Simon's engagement to his ravishing Afghan beauty would not last. They broke up two years later after a rocky relationship, which Simon called "a big mistake." He took full responsibility, telling British tabloid *The Sun*: "I'm attracted to crazy women. I encourage crazy behavior, and I make them crazy."

Four years later, Simon returned as an expectant father. Jay was incredulous: "I've known you what, twelve or fifteen years? I never thought I'd say this: Congratulations! You're going to be a dad." Simon admitted the news was "a bit of a shocker" for him, as well. He said he knew the sex of the child, but didn't reveal it: "If it's a boy, I kind of hope he turns out like me as I was older, not when I was a child—cause when I was a child I was obnoxious," he said, laughing. A few weeks later Simon announced the unborn child was a boy and that he was thinking of marrying the mother, his girlfriend Lauren Silverman, a New York socialite.

In one of the show's most romantic moments, New York Giants football star Jason Sehorn got down on one knee and asked actress Angie Harmon to marry him in March 2000. He walked out as a "surprise guest," which we had pre-arranged with him. Angie, a guest on the show, had no idea it was coming, which was obvious from the startled look on her face. She could barely contain her emotion as she answered: "Jason . . . oh, God . . . baby, yes," as fellow guest Elton John stood up and applauded.

Before Jason came out, Jay asked Angie questions about her love life, which annoyed her. She said she didn't talk about her personal life, but Jay persisted, suggesting Jason was backstage.

Jay: What if he wanted to come out?
Angie: He wouldn't.
Elton: He's not gay, is he?

A year later Jason returned to the show and said he had no regrets about the surprise proposal witnessed by millions. He then admitted he had been a little nervous when Angie hesitated about ten seconds before answering him. Then he told Jay how they met. It seems his mom, Nancy, was a big fan of Angie's. One Sunday after a Giants game, she spotted Angie outside the stadium and said: "You're that girl from *Law and Order*. I think you and that show are wonderful. Oh, and I'd like you to meet my son Jason." In June 2001, the couple married in Dallas before four hundred guests.

On Halloween day 1994, the show featured a wedding between the late singer Tiny Tim and "Miss Jan." It was actually a renewal of vows, as they were originally hitched in 1984. This was the falsetto singer's second matrimonial celebration on the show. His first was featured on *The Tonight Show Starring Johnny Carson* in 1969. A record forty-million viewers tuned in to watch "Miss Vicki" wed the man who had recorded the hit single "Tiptoe Through the Tulips." The second *Tonight Show* wedding resulted in only average ratings. No one seemed excited about it, including the couple, who got a divorce the following year.

The late Steve Irwin always turned in exciting, high-energy appearances with his animal friends. But the Australian Crocodile Hunter's best spot in November 2003 had more to do with his fellow guest and Aussie friend Russell Crowe than his animals. When Steve came out with his first critter, a beaver, he described it as his favorite American animal, prompting Russell to say, "I'm pretty fond of beaver myself," which set the tone for the whole segment. Later, Steve brought out two diamond snakes he described as very venomous. He handed one to Russell and the other to Jay. Russell went straight for the audience, holding his snake by the tail as its head swerved back and forth as if looking for someone to strike, causing a stir of nervous laughter. Diamond snakes are actually harmless, but Steve didn't bother to come clean with that until later. His boundless enthusiasm for animals combined with Russell's mischievous tendencies made for great fun.

Ironically, Russell never intended to be part of it, somberly telling me before the show that he absolutely had to leave right after his appearance as first guest even though his friend had asked him to stay. I implored Russell to reconsider, but he was adamant, so I dropped the matter, and told Steve to do the same. He bolted straight into Russell's dressing room, broadsiding him with information about all the cool animals he would be missing out on. Russell tried to resist, but Steve would not let up. Finally, Russell just held up his hands and said, "Okay, I'll do it." He was smiling, for the first time that evening.

We never really knew what would happen when Terry Bradshaw was a guest. He and Jay were constantly one-upping each other. Terry once sat through an entire segment with his fly down, which Jay was only too happy to point out since Terry would then have the embarrassing task of zipping it up in front of millions. On Terry's fiftieth appearance in 2012 Jay presented him with a big cake. Terry thanked Jay and then smeared frosting all over his face. It soon escalated into a major food fight, as Jay sacked the four-time Super Bowl-winning quarterback, sending the two of them to the floor covered head-to-toe with frosting.

In 1997, the lights went out in Studio 3 after a power outage as the show was being taped. As luck would have it, Robin Williams and Billy Crystal were the guests. Without missing a beat, Robin got up from his seat, saying, "It's the mothership, Jay," as the band played the theme from the television show *Star Trek*. Billy and Robin's antics that day would qualify as one of the best shows, except viewers at home never saw it. Without power, it wasn't recorded.

In 2003, German supermodel Heidi Klum had a wardrobe malfunction while wearing an eight million dollar, diamond-studded Victoria's Secret bra. She was planning to remove her blouse to reveal the multi-million-dollar undergarment. In the middle of her interview, she abruptly announced: "I think my bra is broken." Both Jay and Heidi's fellow guest Martin Short valiantly but unsuccessfully tried to help her reconnect the bra while holding up their jackets to cover the model. The faulty bra was finally fixed with sticky tape during the commercial break, allowing Heidi to do her striptease as planned.

In 1992, Mary Tyler Moore became the first guest to trip while making an entrance. It wasn't just a minor stumble. She almost fell down, and was very embarrassed, so Jay asked her to re-tape her entrance. The band struck up the music again, and Jay re-read the introduction as though nothing ever happened. For many years it looked like Mary would have the distinction of being the only guest to muff an entrance. Then in 2009 we launched *The Jay Leno Show* in Studio 11, which featured a set with a guest entrance requiring guests to walk down two steps. Not a good idea in the age of six-inch spike heels. Several made very awkward entrances. And one, teenage actress Joey King, actually fell. Luckily, she popped right back up.

The late Phyllis Diller was not only known for her rapier wit but also for her wacky hairstyles and huge collection of wigs. She once appeared on the show while it was taping in Las Vegas, wearing a wig. During rehearsal, a bird swooped down, lifting up her hairpiece. Phyllis was so surprised, she didn't even have a comeback.

Stage fright was a common occurrence, even for celebrities. Jesse Jackson had the worst case of it. I never would have guessed this prominent civil rights activist and one-time presidential candidate would be a nervous Nellie. One time he was shaking so hard backstage, he had to hold onto me for support.

In 2001, the show set up a mobile bar, primarily to help jittery guests loosen up a bit. The Jay Bar, as it came to be known (because it was Jay's idea), consisted of a cart on wheels stocked with wine and beer and operated by a bartender. If guests wanted a mixed drink, they just had to ask and it was provided to them. It was a throwback to the days of Johnny Carson. Even then, there was no actual bar or bartender. If a guest wanted a drink, he or she used to ask the guy in props. It was run like a speakeasy; you had to know somebody. But occasionally, the Jay Bar caused more problems than it solved. Some people just didn't know when to quit. In 2003, filmmaker Quentin Tarantino was slurring his words and was occasionally incoherent during his interview. Jay asked him, "Have you been drinking?" Quentin reminded Jay about the backstage bar, saying, "I'm bringing a little bit of old Johnny Carson onto the show when Oliver Reed was a little drunk." But that was a different time, when the guests got drunk responsibly!

Celebrities are known for being spoiled and demanding, but I think they often get a bad rap. Most made no demands beyond what the show routinely provided: hotel accommodations, car service, and sometimes airline flights. They were offered the services of the show's hair, makeup, and wardrobe departments. Their dressing rooms had showers and were supplied with an array of snacks and drinks.

Some guests had requests that seemed to be a little much, such as the time Eddie Murphy turned in an entire page of necessities for the forty-five minutes he spent in the dressing room prior to his appearance:

DRINKS (4 of everything)
    Snapple Fruit Punch
    Snapple Orange Aid
    Snapple Grape Aid
    Coke in glass bottles
    Dr. Brown's Crème Soda
    Dr. Brown's Root Beer
FRUIT
    Bananas
    Cherries
EVIAN BOTTLED WATER
JUICY FRUIT GUM
CANDY
    Snickers
    Milky Way
    Peppermints
    York Peppermint Patties
WRITING PAD/PENCILS/PENS
REGULAR-SIZED TOWELS
WASH CLOTHS/SMALL

This list has fascinated me for years, simply because it was so inexpensive and ordinary. Eddie could have asked for a full body massage with a salt scrub, a night at L'Ermitage Beverly Hills hotel, and a stretch limousine and he would have gotten them. By *Tonight Show* standards, Eddie was actually low-maintenance.

Ironically, the guests who most deserved special treatment rarely asked for it. Former president Jimmy Carter asked for very little, usually just dinner in his dressing room. We would have ordered him the most expensive meal from Wolfgang Puck's in Beverly Hills, but he was happy with chicken from the commissary. However, he expected to get what he requested promptly and efficiently. And if he didn't, I would get a disapproving scowl, which I tried to avoid at all costs.

He once came on to promote one of his favorite charities— Habitat for Humanity, a nonprofit Christian ministry that uses volunteers to build simple, affordable housing for needy families. He planned to work at a nearby Habitat site and then come directly to the studio with two volunteers. His dressing room request that day listed only a bottle of red wine and three glasses for his two guests and himself. He didn't even specify the type of red he wanted. As usual, I checked and double-checked to make sure everything was right. When I greeted Jimmy and his guests, I was shocked to see them holding half-full glasses of white wine. I immediately apologized for the mistake and promised a bottle of red right away. But Jimmy assured me with a toothy grin the white wine was fine. I was so upset that it took me a moment to notice that the two volunteers were beautiful, young women—and that Jimmy was sitting between them. They were laughing and exchanging worksite stories. It was all very innocent, but I couldn't help thinking: *Could there be a little lust in the heart going on here?*

Some guests were just plain quirky. A prominent political commentator insisted I brief him about the show with the door to his dressing-room bathroom open while he was urinating. I told him I could wait, but he was adamant.

A few female entertainers were not very modest backstage. One actress had a "wardrobe malfunction" when Jay and I walked into her dressing room after knocking. She was wrapped only in a towel, which just happened to fall off as we entered. Jay had a great comeback: "How could any towel withstand that kind of pressure?" Accidents do take place, but this one occurred again on her next visit. Even Jay was tongue-tied the second time.

Another actress wanted to prove to a producer her breasts were real, asking him to feel her up as evidence. He declined, but she persisted, so he checked out her claim and was able to confirm it. Trust, but verify, I always say. No, it wasn't me.

A female singer was found naked and wandering aimlessly in the corridor outside her dressing room. She was known to have drug problems, so I don't think she was trying to make a bizarre, artistic statement. She eventually returned to her room, closed the door and got dressed for the show.

Many actresses and female singers use and pay for their own hair and makeup people, spending several thousand dollars. In some cases the show picked up the cost, if it was reasonable. Once, Jessica Simpson said she would appear only if the show covered the $18,000 tab. We passed.

Some female performers were flirtatious with Jay, but most of the time it was just an act. After all, it was a late-night show. Many wore sexy and provocative dresses, and slightly cheeky behavior was actually appropriate under the circumstances. They all knew Jay was happily married to Mavis.

A few of our female guests had had relationships with Jay before he was married. He never discussed them, but we all knew who they were. Hollywood is a small town, and word gets around. The women continued to be friends with Jay, and nothing was ever amiss. For most of the show's twenty-two years, none of them ever publicly discussed their personal history with Jay. However in September 2013, Sharon Osbourne decided to go public. Why would the long-time wife of rocker Ozzy Osbourne spill the beans about a romantic fling with Jay Leno thirty-five years earlier? Ratings, of course. She just happened to "dish" about Jay and herself on the season debut of *The Talk,* a daytime television show she co-hosts. The theme of the show's premiere week was to have the hosts reveal secrets about themselves. Sharon said she had just moved from England to America when she met Jay at a comedy club. They were both single. Eventually he came to her house and they had a "flingy-wingy." It was short lived because it "was more fling for me and not fling enough for him . . . a couple of months into it, he brought around the real love of his life [Mavis, his future wife] for me to meet, and she was lovely and they took me to Fatburger and they showed me around town. . . ."

The Fatburger reference authenticated the story. Never a fan of fancy restaurants, Jay liked basic food. If he wanted to show Sharon and Mavis they could all get along, he definitely would have chosen the iconic hamburger restaurant over an elegant eatery in Beverly Hills. Sharon insisted the affair was not a "dirty little secret." She said she couldn't even remember if they had sex. (Wink! Wink!) But she was grateful it happened. She sent Jay a heart-shaped plant with a message: "Dear Jay, thanks for the memories and for driving me into the arms of the Prince of Darkness."

In earlier days she and Ozzy were regular guests on *Tonight* and were always entertaining, although it was often hard to understand Ozzy, as the drugs and alcohol had taken their toll. But in 2007, we had a falling out with the Osbournes and they never came back. It had to do with Ozzy's music. Sharon, who was also Ozzy's manager, demanded that he play two songs on the show, while our format limited guests to one.

Most guests came to the studio in a limousine, which we paid for, but a few preferred to drive themselves, including golfers Tiger Woods and Phil Mickelson (who came up from his home in San Diego). Teri Hatcher always drove her Lexus onto the lot, but one time the guard at the gate wouldn't let her in even though she identified herself as a guest on the show. The guard didn't recognize her and assumed she just wanted to come to the show. She didn't call me because she didn't have my number and was detained for more than a half hour. Finally, the guard called our office just before show time. We were worried sick and had been trying to reach her. Teri took it all in stride and joked about it with Jay on the air. Fortunately, she was Teri One that day.

Oscar winner Shirley MacLaine, who used to drive to the lot in her old, banged-up station wagon, wasn't as understanding as Teri when she was denied admittance. She just turned her car around and started to leave. Luckily for us—and the guard, who could have easily lost his job—he relented and let her in. Shirley also discussed the incident with Jay on the air, but unlike Teri, she was not amused. She said she was only a few seconds away from going home and had no intention of returning.

A man claiming to be Jack Nicholson once showed up backstage, as the show was being recorded, saying he wanted to make a surprise appearance. This guy was a dead ringer for Jack, and his impersonation was spot on. Still, how did he get past the guard while Shirley and Teri, who were both given clearance at the gate, didn't? I knew "Jack" was a fake, but for a split second he had me thinking: *Isn't this the kind of thing Nicholson would try to pull off?*

I had a good working relationship with most of the guests and became friends with many. But one really pushed my buttons. His witty, irascible, public persona made him seem like a lovable comedian, while his actual personality was darker than I care to go into. Even so, he taught me a valuable lesson. During our first phone pre-interview years ago, he sarcastically said he didn't hear me laughing at his jokes. I assured him they were funny, but I was preoccupied with taking notes to brief Jay. "Your job is to laugh at my jokes," he insisted. While I was in no mood to laugh after that, I realized he was right. I needed to show guests more positive feedback, despite my feelings. So I developed the ability to laugh on cue, even though I was usually faking it.

Hey, it worked for Ed McMahon, Johnny's sidekick! I'm sure he didn't think all of Johnny's jokes were funny.

Actually, when I really think something is laugh-out-loud funny, I emit a single, loud, staccato *HA!* Only my friends know this, which sometimes caused a problem for my guests who also happened to be friends, like Larry the Cable Guy. He once asked me during a pre-interview why I didn't like his material. I thought his stories were funny and didn't understand his reaction. Then it hit me: He sensed something was wrong because I hadn't let out even one *HA!* Instead I was mistakenly doing my genuine fake laugh for him.

I will forever be grateful to the nasty comedian for giving me the best career advice I've ever received. My genuine fake laugh served me well with just about everyone but him. His insults never let up, and one day he became abusive to both my assistant and myself. After that, I refused to work with him ever again. HA!

Chapter Five

The Real Reality Show

Reality shows are very popular, but most people know they're scripted. That's why they have writers. At *The Tonight Show,* we had a real reality show without the cameras. It was going on backstage, and it featured the same guests as the ones onstage. On a typical day guests arrived in limos, tended to their hair, makeup, and wardrobe. They hung out in their dressing rooms and chatted with Jay until show time. Then they left. Not much excitement. As a producer, I liked it that way. You try to anticipate every possible thing that can go wrong so you can deal with it. But sometimes stuff just happened. There were joyous moments, fun moments, silly, outrageous, uncomfortable, bizarre, and even touching moments. These are the stand-out episodes in our reality show.

Dr. Phil

As the world's most famous shrink, Dr. Phil McGraw could always be counted on to deliver the goods as a guest. The TV psychologist had little patience for whiny people who didn't accept responsibility for their own actions, and audiences never seemed to tire of his no-nonsense view of right and wrong. Like many of Jay's best guests, Dr. Phil was very competitive with Jay. This made for great discussions because neither wanted to be upstaged by the other.

They once had a spirited conversation about the nature of happiness. Jay called it a privilege: "I know a lot of people are depressed because they think they're supposed to be happy all the time. Happiness should be an occasional thing

. . . something you look forward to." Dr. Phil described happiness as neither a right nor a privilege but as a choice. He said people mistakenly confuse happiness with fun: "Happiness can be a feeling that comes from filling your days with what matters to you, living authentically, or working for what you want." Ironically, Dr. Phil chose to be unhappy with *The Tonight Show* and never returned after an October 2009 guest spot. Our publicity staff had promised him Jay's next appearance would be on *Dr. Phil,* but instead they booked him on *Oprah.* It was a tough call, but the right one, made under extenuating circumstances. Jay was on *Oprah* in January 2010 when his reputation was at an all-time low and his very future in television was at stake. *The Jay Leno Show* had been cancelled after a disastrous four-month run in prime time. Jay would be returning to host *The Tonight Show* in March amidst a barrage of horrendous press brought on by NBC's cancellation of Conan's stint as host of *Tonight.* Conan's run on *Tonight* was disastrous, hemorrhaging 50 percent of *Tonight's* viewers. He had failed to appeal to the show's mainstream audience, which didn't seem to matter to him, his angry "Team Coco" viewers, or much of the press. So Jay had a lot of "splainin'" to do. (See chapter fifteen.) Debbie Vickers and the publicity team decided *Oprah* was the best show to explain the crisis from Jay's point of view, which we believed the press was ignoring. Dr. Phil didn't see it that way. To him, a deal was a deal and Jay had broken his agreement. Of course, Dr. Phil was also aware an exclusive interview with Jay, then the most controversial man in America, would have been a ratings bonanza for him, as it was for *Oprah.*

Later, the matter came to a head when we offered to book Dr. Phil on our show again. His producers reacted sharply. Angry phone calls followed. My colleagues and I were called into the conference room to do damage control. Debbie got on the phone with Dr. Phil's people, taking full responsibility for the *Oprah* booking. She said our show was in a precarious position, and she thought the *Oprah* interview would best serve our needs under the circumstances. They weren't buying her argument, and the crisis escalated as Dr. Phil joined the phone conversation. We put him on speaker phone and listened as he angrily talked over Debbie's attempts to apologize and her pleas for understanding. His voice got louder and louder and then he hung up. Jay joined us and, ever the peacemaker, he wanted to talk directly to Dr. Phil. We warned him not to do it, but he made the call anyway. Dr. Phil would not be placated. He chose instead to continue not being happy with us and launched into a tirade, which seemed to go on for about an hour. There was no stopping the trained psychologist, who has counseled many on his show about anger management. Nevertheless, Jay continued to try to reason with Dr. Phil, calmly pointing out that he thought the TV psychologist was friends with Oprah, who had launched his television career. Jay's pleas fell upon deaf ears.

If this had been a reality show, it would have been great. But in real life there's no upside when a popular guest like Dr. Phil writes you off, no matter who's at fault. Not only did we lose a valuable, bankable guest, but Letterman gained one. As Dr. Phil is wont to say to his television patients when they make bad life choices: "How's that workin' out for ya?"

Judge Judy and John Elway

Judy Sheindlin was a regular on Jay's show from 1998 to 2000. The reality-show judge was always popular, even in the early days of her TV career. I understood her appeal. Like Dr. Phil, she didn't tolerate stupidity. In her courtroom she was the judge and the queen. I usually got along well with her, though we did cross swords in February 1999, when I told her I had to move her from the coveted first guest position to the second slot to make way for Denver Broncos quarterback John Elway and his coach Mike Shanahan. This was a huge, last-minute booking; the Broncos had just won their second straight Super Bowl and John was named MVP. The sports press was abuzz with speculation that John would soon be announcing his retirement, perhaps on our show. Of course, none of this meant anything to Judge Judy, who told me she wasn't happy to be playing second fiddle to a mere football player and coach she had never heard of. She didn't even know the Broncos had won the Super Bowl, or that they were in it, for that matter. I felt like a defendant on her show who had just been found guilty of some moronic crime. Nevertheless, she honored her commitment to do the show, and when she showed up, she was actually smiling. It seems her grandchildren knew quite well who John Elway was, and they were excited because Grandma had promised them all autographed footballs. She was carrying a huge plastic bag full of footballs when she arrived. I didn't have the heart to tell her that we did not allow excessive autograph requests. I don't think I could have stopped her anyway, and thankfully John was happy to oblige. Judge Judy was now John's biggest fan and was educating me about his career highlights.

Incidentally, John did not announce his retirement that night, but he did do so two months later. He would be inducted into the NFL Hall of Fame in 2004. Today he is the executive vice president of football operations for the Broncos. As for Judge Judy, her reality courtroom program became number-one on daytime TV, beating Oprah's numbers. She also became the highest paid star on TV, earning $47 million annually.

Garth Brooks

Garth Brooks was a friend of the show, and one of Jay's favorites. In fact, Jay extended Garth the honor of making the last guest appearance on the final episode, February 6, 2014. At Jay's request, the legendary country singer played his classic hit "The Dance." After that, Jay delivered a tearful goodbye to his audience and called on his old friend one last time. "Now that I've brought the room down, hey, Garth, you got anything to liven this party up?" Garth obliged with his iconic hit "Friends in Low Places."

Garth insisted on launching every one of his new albums

on Jay's show, saying it brought him good luck. That may be, but I think talent also had something to do with his phenomenal success. Only the Beatles and Elvis Presley have sold more albums.

Jay and Garth had an easygoing relationship backstage. One day while I was talking to the country music star, Jay joined us and just started singing an old country song called "Wolverton Mountain." The lyrics were silly, verging on absurd, but Jay had a penchant for corny, old songs and had memorized the lyrics to hundreds of them. Before Jay had finished the first verse, I joined in:

They say don't go on Wolverton Mountain
If you're looking for a wife
'Cause Clifton Cowers has a pretty young daughter
He's might handy with a gun and a knife

Jay signaled to Garth to join us as we started verse two, but Garth just stood there, staring in bemused bewilderment, saying he had never heard of the song. Jay and I were incredulous. How in the world could Garth—the world's most prominent country singer—not have heard of this classic song? It turns out the song was a big hit in 1962, the year Garth was born. Maybe we should have cut him a little slack.

Garth was a gentleman to all, backstage and onstage, but he was a little quirky. He would never travel anywhere without his wardrobe trunk number seven, which included buckeyes given to him by a fan in Ohio years ago. He was also obsessed with brushing his teeth, and I frequently encountered him in the bathroom, toothbrush in hand. When I asked him about it, he admitted he was addicted to clean teeth, brushing them fifteen to twenty times a day, once for as long as two and a half hours. His generosity was legendary. He would often buy luxury cars and other expensive items for members of his management team. One afternoon he and his band were rehearsing the song they would be playing on the show that night. Bob Whyley, our audio mixer, happened to comment to Garth that the Martin acoustic guitar he was playing was beautiful.

"You like it?" Garth asked. "Yes," Bob replied. "Then it's yours," Garth said as he handed Bob the $3,500 instrument. I had the same thought Bob did, but he said it first! After that, I had to literally force myself never to say anything to Garth about his guitar. Believe me, it wasn't easy.

Dolly Parton, Linda Ronstadt, and Emmylou Harris

A Dolly segment was like money in the bank. She was always cheerful and would talk about anything, including her chest size, her regular visits to the plastic surgeon, her vast collection of shoes and wigs, and her endless quarrels with her husband, Carl. Her singing voice was natural and pure even though she had no formal music training and had never learned how to harmonize. Even so, many singers loved to team up with her, including Linda Ronstadt and Emmylou Harris. They called themselves "Trio."

Trio sang beautiful songs, but while Dolly was always a pleasure to work with, Linda and Emmylou always seemed to be unhappy about something, especially Jay's monologue jokes about President Clinton. I tried to explain to them that Jay made fun of all politicians, but that just made them more agitated. I could never understand how Dolly was able to put up with those two. Of course, both Linda and Emmylou were solo singers, and without Dolly they could be very annoying. In a 1995 appearance, Linda told Jay she was barely able to get through her song because she was offended by something fellow guest Robin Quivers had said. Jay had asked Howard Stern's radio sidekick if she should stand up for blacks and women during his rants, which were often laced with racial and sexual overtones. Robin, who is black, replied: "People tell me I'm supposed to, but I don't find it necessary." The audience picked up on Linda's self-righteous attitude and booed her. Jay rescued her by saying she had a right to express her opinion and should be allowed to speak.

Rather than let it drop, Linda forged ahead: "I can tell you as a woman and a Mexican American I feel he [Howard] is very offensive and extremely irresponsible." Robin quickly defended her boss: "I think people who listen to the show understand what we're doing." To which Linda responded: "I don't listen to it. . . . I think you're shilling for him, and I think he's taking advantage of you." This little tiff went on for about five minutes and was painful to watch. The irony is that many people probably agree with Linda. I do. But an entertainer's primary job is to entertain, not preach.

The last time I worked with Emmylou, her publicist insisted she had plenty of fun stuff to talk with Jay about, such as her love of baseball and singing the National Anthem at baseball games. But when I asked her about those topics, she said I needed to come up with better questions. Twenty-five questions later she still had no stories. Searching for anything, I asked her how her dog was. I didn't even know if she had a dog. It turns out she did because she told me: "My dog just died two weeks ago. I hope you're happy." Of course, I had no way of knowing this and felt terrible. She didn't do an interview with Jay that night, and it was probably for the best.

George Jones

In my opinion, the late George Jones was the greatest country singer who ever lived, and he sang the greatest country song ever written: "He Stopped Loving Her Today." As a kid I used to go to his concerts. He had a great comeback for hecklers: "I thought I told you to wait out in the truck," he would say.

When he was booked to appear on Leno, I was thrilled at the thought of talking with him about his old concerts, but I soon realized he had no recollection of them, or much of anything else. I suspect his long battle with alcohol and cocaine addictions had taken a toll. It's sad when a country singer actually lives the life he sings about.

He was scheduled to do a duet with the legendary Loretta

Lynn. As they rehearsed their song, she suddenly took ill. So George decided he would sing his classic. I couldn't believe it. My favorite country singer was going to sing my favorite song. There was a great story to go along with the song; if only George had been capable of telling it to Jay. It seems George initially didn't like the poignant, ironic lyrics about a man's abiding devotion to a former love, which is so strong that it only ends when he dies. After recording the tune by Bobby Braddock and Curly Putnam, George told his producer, "Nobody will buy that morbid son of a bitch." Yet the song he so disliked won a Grammy, saved his sagging career, and launched his comeback.

And when it came time for the baritone singer to rehearse, I was shocked to see he requested cue cards. Singers often used cue cards, but not for their biggest hits. When George actually began singing the song, I changed my tune. His rendition was a tear jerker. It was perfect!

Ed McMahon and Johnny Carson

When *The Tonight Show with Jay Leno* debuted on May 25, 1992, Jay did not make any reference to Johnny Carson at the insistence of his then executive producer, Helen Kushnick. Jay knew it was a terrible mistake at the time and eventually did right by Johnny during the farewell broadcast, February 6, 2014, almost twenty-two years later. Calling his iconic predecessor "the greatest guy ever to do this job," Jay signed off the way Johnny used to: "I bid you all a heartfelt goodnight."

Jay also devoted an entire show to Johnny after he died on January 23, 2005. He dropped the monologue to spend more time honoring Johnny's memory. We invited the late Ed McMahon, who had been Johnny's sidekick and announcer for thirty years, to join Jay in the tribute broadcast. Ed said Johnny was like a "brother" and shared stories about recent phone conversations he had with his old boss. His presence helped draw fourteen million viewers.

We owed Ed a favor for that appearance, and he called it

in later that year, asking to come on to promote a new book he had written about Johnny appropriately called *Here's Johnny!* The book was filled with positive anecdotes, but the Carson family was reportedly not happy about it, as the legendary host valued his privacy and deliberately avoided the limelight during his retirement years.

This put us in a difficult position because we didn't want to offend either Johnny's family or Ed. We ended up booking Ed, but Jay played down the book, giving it only an obligatory mention. No one complained, and *Here's Johnny!* became a bestseller.

Nevertheless, Ed died broke four years later at the age of eighty-six. He had amassed debts of nearly $1.5 million even though he had made millions over the years as Johnny's sidekick.

Paula Abdul

Simon Cowell is one of the most entertaining people on American television, but his public persona as a grumpy, cantankerous guy is mostly an act. He's actually polite and easygoing. His fellow judge and sparring partner on *American Idol* and *The X Factor* Paula Abdul wasn't playing a character. She was, indeed, as ditsy as she appeared. She was also complicated. For twelve years she was secretly struggling with an addiction to painkillers she had originally taken to ease the pain caused by arduous dance routines. Her behavior was consistently erratic. She would cancel appearances for strange reasons, and when she did show up, her speech was often so slurred we could barely understand her. But we always gave her a pass because she seemed normal on air. Well, normal enough.

Greeting her before a show was awkward. I was really there to make sure she was coherent enough to appear. I dreaded the thought of telling her we would have to cancel her segment; and, as it turned out, I never did. But there were times when I wasn't sure what to do. It was a tough call. Many guests would get tipsy with just one glass of wine. Where do you draw the line? I reasoned that she was a professional who had always come through in the past, not only on *The Tonight Show* but also on *American Idol* and *The X Factor*. So why did we keep booking Paula? Ratings! She was very popular. Part of her appeal, ironically, was that you never knew what she might say, particularly about Simon. I think she was attracted to him, and in her heightened state of awareness she often dealt with it like a giddy school girl. People loved it.

In 2007, Jay asked Paula about a story that reported she thought of Simon as either a big brother or a lover. She denied the latter, saying she would rather have a "surprise colonic." But she did own up to the former. Then she talked about her experience as a guest judge on the British version of *The X Factor*. She said Simon caressed her back to comfort her after one of her favorite contestants was voted off, but he warned her not to expect that kind of treatment in the States. Her face lit up, as it always did, when she gossiped about Simon. That was for real. There was nothing phony about Paula.

Jerry Mathers

In February 2001, Jerry Mathers of *Leave It to Beaver* fame was part of a parody our writers came up with of CBS's *Survivor*. It was called *Hollywood's Ultimate Survivor*. He was joined by Charlene Tilton (*Dallas*), Gary Coleman (*Diff'rent Strokes*), Danny Bonaduce (*The Partridge Family*), Dawn Wells (*Gilligan's Island*), Florence Henderson (*The Brady Bunch*), Adam Rich (Eight Is Enough), and Alison Arngrim (*Little House on the Prairie*). The group competed against each other for the title "Hollywood's Ultimate Survivor." In the four-week competition, patterned after *Survivor,* these eight stars were "marooned" in a separate studio, divided into two teams and pitted against each other in a series of silly games. After each game, the losing tribe had to vote a member off the set. The celebrities were put through the rigors of such challenges as searching through mud to find a match that would light an aromatherapy candle and participating in a "repulsive food" relay race, which involved eating whole brussels sprouts, Spam, poached fish eyes, and giant grub worms.

Finally, it got down to two survivors, Jerry Mathers and Florence Henderson. They competed against each other, and the six losers, who were then named as members of a tribal council, helped determine the winner. Jerry and Florence were given fifteen seconds to explain why they should be named "Hollywood's Ultimate Survivor." Florence said she enjoyed being with everybody on the "island;" "the Beav" said he had no hard feelings and working with the other stars was great. The tribal council voted for the Beav, who walked away with the trophy but almost didn't survive the experience. A month later, Jerry went to the doctor after experiencing stomach pains and having lost fifteen pounds. Tests revealed the grub worm, known as a Suri, had chewed through his intestinal lining, causing rectal bleeding, intestinal cramps, and diarrhea. Suris, common in the Amazon, grow to be about four inches long and have "sharp, biting pincers." The creatures are, indeed, edible live, but the natives always bite the heads off first.

"This was a race and I didn't have time to study what they were giving me to eat. It was just bam! And I swallowed it," Jerry told the *Daily Telegraph* in Sydney, Australia. His manager, Brian McInerney, said the Beav nearly died as a result. "I was dazed and confused," Jerry said. "They put intravenous tubes into me. It took three or four days before my body could even tolerate food."

All turned out well. According to Richmond.com, Jay called Jerry several times to apologize and to check on his condition. He eventually recovered. And just as one would expect from the good-natured Beav, he never sued *The Tonight Show* or NBC over the incident.

Robin Williams

No one was ever funnier or had more energy than Robin Williams. He worked very hard on his material and then would often set it aside and improvise. And he was always on, even when the camera wasn't. In 1992, he played Peter Pan in the film *Hook*. My two kids loved it and jumped at the chance when I offered to take them to the show to meet Robin the night he came on to promote the film. When Robin saw the little ones, he bent down to their level and asked them if they had any questions. My four-year-old son, David, wanted to know how he could fly. Without missing a beat, Robin replied: "A little magic and very tight pants." Both the kids and the adults laughed, but for different reasons!

During another guest spot some years later, Robin "killed" as usual with a variety of antics. After the taping, Robin and the other guests joined Jay to shoot a quick promotion that would be aired that night on local NBC stations. Such promos were routine, but what happened next wasn't. Robin tripped over an audio speaker and fell onto the hard studio floor, injuring his arm. The audience laughed, thinking he was just doing another pratfall. Ever the performer, he made the accident look like a stunt, as he clutched his arm and let out exaggerated howls of agony. In fact, though, he was feeling severe pain and was immediately taken to a hospital in Burbank where doctors determined he had dislocated his shoulder.

Lucy Lawless

Lucy Lawless, star of the hit television series *Xena: Warrior Princess*, performed most of the stunts on her show without any major injuries. But the plucky New Zealand native wasn't so lucky at *Tonight,* where she was seriously injured while doing a routine stunt for a taped comedy sketch in October 1996. She was riding a horse that slipped on the studio parking lot tarmac and fell on her, fracturing her pelvis. I was in my office at the time, but a colleague who witnessed the mishap said it happened in the blink of an eye. All of a sudden, Lucy was on the ground, crying out in excruciating pain. Someone called 911 and Jay immediately ran out of the studio, got down on the ground next to her, and took her hand in an effort to comfort her. He assured her she didn't have to worry because the show would take care of everything. And he told her a joke, saying "We'll even re-book you." That got a smile out of her. Ever the gracious guest, Lucy blamed herself for the accident and said she hoped it didn't ruin the show that night.

Paramedics quickly arrived and transported her to the hospital, where she was listed in stable condition. Everyone was grateful her injury wasn't worse. Still, it was the most severe injury sustained by a guest at the show. Jay said on the air that night how sorry he was and that he wanted Lucy back as soon as possible. In the days that followed, he sent bouquets of flowers to her hospital room, visited her, and called her. Miraculously, Lucy was able to return to the show in only twenty-two days, only this time she wasn't riding a horse. She was carried on stage by two very muscular men dressed in loincloths, an entrance befitting a warrior princess. She assured everyone she was all right, although she had not fully recovered. Then she related an anecdote about a mysterious visit she had recently made to a fortune teller while vacationing in Turkey. The clairvoyant had warned her: "You are going to get very, very hurt, and a man will fall into your eyes, and he has got a very big chin." The fortune teller described the man's hair as long and grey. Lucy said she was lying in a fetal position after the accident and remembered seeing Jay come into her vision just as the fortune teller had predicted. Was she telling the truth or just a tall tale? I worked with Lucy for almost a decade, and she was always a straight shooter. But you never know!

Shirley MacLaine

The 1994 Northridge earthquake in Southern California was one of the worst disasters ever to hit North America. While seismologists attributed the cause to a previously unknown fault nine miles beneath the earth, actress Shirley MacLaine had a different take. She told an audience in Kansas City the quake happened because Mother Nature was sending a message that "she" wasn't happy with the way we humans were treating the earth.

Shortly after that, I booked Shirley to appear on the show. A writer told me he had an idea for her segment and handed me a sketch of a fake printout from a seismograph. The squiggly lines spelled out the word REPENT in large, bold letters. I thought it would be fun if Jay brought the sketch out during the interview. She was famous for her off-the-wall ideas and usually had a sense of humor about them.

When Shirley showed up for her appearance, I was excited to show her the printout. I thought it would get a big laugh out of her, but I was wrong. She looked at it, gave me an icy stare, and asked: "What part of this do you think is funny?" Needless to say, the "seismograph printout" was removed from her segment, and Shirley performed splendidly without it.

I could never bring myself to throw out the modern-day prophetic warning, so I placed it on the wall over my office door. It stayed there for fifteen years, enduring several more earthquakes.

Abigail and Spencer Breslin

There's an old adage in show business: Never follow kids or animals. Cute kids and furry creatures are a draw, but there's a downside with kids. Hollywood is full of very messed-up adults who were once child actors. I witnessed the ruin of many young lives over the years. It was so common that whenever a child actor debuted on the show my colleagues would speculate how long it would take him or her to go over to "the dark side." Six months? One year? Two? It was dark humor, but often when the child returned for a second appearance they were already showing noticeable signs of disrespect for their parents and handlers. In subsequent visits, it got even worse. It was sad to watch cute, smart kids turn into spoiled brats—and then monsters—in only a few years. Not all cases were this extreme, but suffice it to say that Hollywood was not a family-friendly place.

There were some notable exceptions, especially Abigail and Spencer Breslin, who were entertaining guests and wonderful kids. Best known for his roles in Disney's *The Kid, The Santa*

Clause film sequels, and *The Cat in the Hat*, Spencer first came on the show at age four. Abigail made her debut appearance at age eight and had often accompanied her brother in the dressing room during his guest spots. She was in *Signs, Little Miss Sunshine* (for which she received an Oscar nomination), and Broadway's *The Miracle Worker*. Thanks to their mom and manager, Kim, Abigail and Spencer lived relatively normal childhoods, attending public schools, going to church, and doing chores like taking care of pets for small weekly allowances. Kim was involved in making decisions about every aspect of their young careers, including the films and television shows they were in. As a result, the Breslin family stayed strong, and the dark side of Hollywood was held at bay.

Most child actors have no childhoods, instead growing up on movie and television sets. They have few friends their own age and are educated by studio-hired teachers. So when they were on the show, they were essentially acting the way they thought children should act. On the other hand, Abigail and Spencer, who experienced all the joys and frustrations of being kids, were for real, and they told Jay all about it. Abigail loved to chide Spencer for his unromantic treatment of his long-time girlfriend Skye, suggesting that he do such things as give her flowers. In turn, Spencer called out his sister for having a secret boyfriend, which she adamantly denied.

Jay had watched the Breslins grow up over the years, and there were many heart-warming, genuine moments with them. During the Christmas season, Abi often brought him homemade gifts, such as cookies and gingerbread houses. And when she was nominated for her amazing performance in *Little Miss Sunshine,* she told Jay it wouldn't have happened without him. The director gave her the part after he saw her on *The Tonight Show*.

Shia LaBeouf

We began booking Shia LaBeouf at age seventeen after his first starring role in the Disney film *Holes*. The Emmy-winning actor went on to star in *Indiana Jones and the Kingdom of the Crystal Skull* and the *Transformers* franchise. I believe his best work is still ahead of him, if he decides to continue making films. He has done well as a young actor despite growing up poor in Los Angeles with "hippie parents." Shia once brought his divorced parents to the show to introduce them to Jay and me.

His dad, Jeffrey, had long, unkempt hair and looked like a homeless guy. He had once worked in the lower rungs of show business as a rodeo clown and as the opening act for the Doobie Brothers. During Shia's childhood, Jeffrey didn't work much and wasn't often around. When Jay and I met Jeffrey, he was living in a car.

Shia told me he was very close with his mom, Shayna, who he affectionately called a "gypsy." When we met her, she was wearing a tie-dyed dress and lots of beads. She had essentially raised her son alone, selling fabrics and brooches to earn money. As one would imagine, Shia had a colorful childhood and often talked about it with Jay at the panel. He never spoke about his background in a negative way, though. Shia found humor in every experience. He said that he was the only white kid at his school, making him the minority, and that he did whatever he could to stay out of fights. He even shaved his head, figuring that would help him be accepted. It actually had the opposite effect as his schoolmates then thought he was a skinhead.

Shia sought to become an actor as a way to escape poverty. He began searching for an agent at the age of twelve by looking through the phone book. The first name he decided to call was John Crosby. Disguising his voice to sound older, Shia told John he was the manager of a great European actor named Shia LaBeouf. John knew right away Shia was lying but was impressed with the young man's resourcefulness and took him on as a client. John continues to represent Shia to this day.

The Civet

Animals were the perfect guests. Unlike actors, they never showed up saying "I have nothing to talk about with

Jay today." They didn't have demanding publicists. They didn't ask for anything. They and their handlers, or animal ambassadors, were usually a pleasure to work with. And their appearances usually resulted in higher ratings. We worked with many potentially dangerous and unpredictable wild animals over the years and experienced only one minor incident: A civet once ran away and hid under the set during an appearance by zoologist Jarod Miller. After the show, Jarod and his crew were unable to coax the two-foot-long, cat-like mammal out. So Greg Elliott, the prop master, drove home and got his "varmint trap," which Jarod baited with the civet's favorite food. Later that night, they heard the trap snap, and the civet was captured unharmed.

The Bigfoot Playmate

I once booked a Playboy Playmate who claimed she had seen Bigfoot—and had video to show for it. When I pitched the idea for Thanksgiving Day 1995 I fully expected to get shot down, but my colleagues were intrigued, and wanted to know more. Besides, we were having a hard time booking the holiday, and the Playmate sounded as good as any of our other choices.

The Playmate, Anna-Marie Goddard, was a beautiful Dutch model who had made a successful appearance with Jay two years earlier, telling funny stories about working as a milkmaid in her childhood. My colleagues were understandably concerned about the legitimacy of the five seconds of night footage Anna-Marie had sent me, which was grainy, dark, and shaky, but definitely showed a large, eight-foot tall, hairy creature walking on its hind legs. She had made a very convincing argument to me that she actually believed she had seen Sasquatch, even though at the time she had never heard of the hominid and thought it was a bear. She, her husband, Colin, and a crew had been in the California Redwoods near the Oregon border filming a pilot for a show she was hosting. They had wrapped the shoot and were returning home in their recreational vehicle late at night when they got lost deep in the woods. That's when "Bigfoot" made his cameo, crossing the road in front of their vehicle.

While my colleagues liked the idea, they thought the video—shot by the crew's videographer—could have easily been faked, even though I had statements from Bigfoot experts that the footage appeared to be genuine. I thought they were missing the big picture. To me, the story was that an attractive model had seen a big, hairy monster and had video to back it up. Maybe it was a true story. Maybe it was a publicity stunt. Maybe it was both. But she sounded like she believed it. My colleagues remained skeptical, but as Thanksgiving Day approached and we still couldn't find a big-name guest, they warmed up to Anna-Marie, and I booked her.

Jay didn't buy the story at all but was concerned that if he made fun of Anna-Marie on the air it would look like he was picking on her. So he decided he would be a neutral observer. Besides, the story had an angle that was perfect for late-night humor, which appealed to Jay. It seems one of the so-called scientists who had examined the video was able to discern a prominent appendage, convincing him the creature was an excited male. Jay mined that comedy vein for all it was worth, and the segment was very entertaining.

While my colleagues never let me forget about the Bigfoot Playmate, Sasquatch experts took her footage and story seriously, initially naming it the "Playmate video." Dr. Jeff Meldrum, an anthropologist and Sasquatch researcher, found the footage compelling and renamed it the "Redwoods video" to give it credibility. Loren Coleman, a respected Bigfoot chronicler, wrote a book in 2003 called *Bigfoot!: The True Story of Apes in America* and devoted almost an entire chapter to Anna-Marie and her account of the incident on *The Tonight Show*. Coleman wrote a blog in 2010 commending Anna-Marie for "her bravery in coming forward as an eyewitness" on *Tonight*.

Greg Kinnear and the Donkey

Oscar-nominated actor Greg Kinnear once hosted an NBC

late-night talk show called *Later,* which debuted in 1994. It was taped in a studio adjoining *The Tonight Show.* One time, Greg was shooting a comedy sketch for his show that involved putting a surprise donkey in the dressing room of one of his guests. The segment didn't quite turn out as planned. With the camera rolling, Greg went in to check on the animal. As if on cue, the donkey lifted its tail and let loose a projectile of diarrhea like water from a fire hose. Greg was horrified as he bolted from the dressing room, slamming the door behind him. When you're working with animals, it's always a crap shoot.

Chapter Six

Gets I Didn't Get

People are always surprised to learn that not every celebrity wants to appear on *The Tonight Show*. Most come on only if they have something to promote. A few prefer other shows. Some of the country's biggest stars, such as Al Pacino, Robert DeNiro, and Woody Allen, just don't like the process and rarely show up on any programs.

Some of the biggest "gets" never did Leno because they didn't like his monologue jokes—about them. The late Michael Jackson, even in death one of the world's biggest stars, would have been ratings gold. But Michael also made great monologue fodder, and there's no way he would have ever done an interview with Jay while he was regularly reeling off jokes like these:

> It looks like the Democratic field is really starting to get narrowed down. For Democrats it's going to be Barack Obama versus Hillary. So it's a black man or a white woman. You know, this is the same decision Michael Jackson has to make every morning of his life.

> Good news for Michael Jackson, not guilty on ten counts! The bad news—he's going to Disneyland.

> Early today Michael met with his priest—not for spiritual advice. They went on a double date.

During Michael's 2005 trial on child-molestation charges, Jay was listed as a possible witness, and the judge put him under a gag order not to discuss the trial publicly. That

91

technically meant Jay couldn't tell monologue jokes about Michael, so instead Jay brought in comedians Roseanne Barr, Dennis Miller, and Brad Garrett to do the job. The judge allowed it.

When Jay was finally called to take the stand, ironically as a defense witness, he talked about it on the show: "Apparently, they've never seen the program."

He was asked to discuss "suspicious" calls he got from a boy who was Michael's accuser. Jay testified he got several phone messages from a twelve-year-old male cancer patient who called the late-night host his hero. Jay often makes calls to children who are ill, but he had reservations about this boy. "I'm not Batman," he said. "It seemed a little unusual."

Michael's attorney, Thomas Mesereau Jr., said Jay told Santa Barbara police he thought the boy's family was "looking for a mark," although the boy didn't ask Jay for money. Michael was eventually cleared of all charges, and Mesereau, an extraordinary attorney who fervently believed in his client's innocence, agreed to come on the show to discuss the case with Jay. The lawyer was a great guest. Still, he was no Michael Jackson.

Bill Clinton would have been compelling, but he never appeared. I made him offers for ten years that he neither declined nor accepted. In the political world people rarely say no. Instead, they just never give you an answer.

This put me in a perpetual state of limbo, because to Jay and executive producer Debbie Vickers, only "no" meant "no." So I had to keep trying. What is it with Bill Clinton and two-letter words? He famously told a grand jury his answer would depend "on what the meaning of the word *is* is."

I made countless offers to the forty-second president. Each was pegged to dates I knew he would be in Los Angeles and to events he would want to promote. I called him when he

1. left the presidency and was establishing himself as a speaker;
2. published his 2004 memoir, *My Life*;

3. published his 2007 book, *Giving: How Each of Us Can Change the World*;
4. built his presidential library in 2004;
5. set up his foundation;
6. campaigned for Hillary in senate and presidential races;
7. campaigned for Barack Obama for president;
8. raised funds in 2005 with former president George H. W. Bush for Asian tsunami and Hurricane Katrina relief.

The list goes on for pages, but you get the idea. All the while, Mr. Clinton was making himself available to many other shows, including Letterman, so he probably wouldn't have made a big difference in the ratings. It's just that you always want what you can't have.

We tried to reach out to him by sending elaborate flower arrangements with notes, having Jay call his people directly, and going through political confidants like James Carville and Paul Begala. In the fall of 2004, the former president had quadruple bypass surgery and was sent to his home in Chappaqua, New York, to recover. We decided to give him a practical gift that would help him regain his strength, so we bought him a twelve thousand dollar, custom-made tandem bicycle. I cleared the idea with Oscar Flores, the operations director at his home. Gifts to politicians can be sticky because of federal restrictions, so you always have to check. I got approval to ship the bike because Mr. Clinton was no longer in office. However, our present was soon returned to us. It seems his legal adviser was concerned that a bike with two seats was really meant for both the former president and his wife, then Senator Hillary Clinton, who legally could not accept a gift exceeding fifty dollars. So we built Mr. Clinton another bicycle with one seat, which he accepted. Still, he never did our show.

Jay always believed Mr. Clinton rejected our offers because we once turned him down. In his first presidential bid against President George H. W. Bush in 1992, Mr. Clinton approached *The Tonight Show* requesting an appearance, which would feature him playing the saxophone. But the late

Helen Kushnick, then the executive producer, said no. She reasoned that if we were to book him, at that time a long-shot in the campaign, then we would have to do the same for the other candidate, President Bush, which she thought was a bad idea. She assumed no one would be interested in watching either candidate.

We had only been on the air a few weeks at the time, but Helen's decision would stand as the worst one in the show's twenty-two-year history. A successful Bill Clinton guest spot would have established Jay early as a late-night force to be reckoned with, a host worthy of following Johnny Carson.

In June, Mr. Clinton took his tenor saxophone to *The Arsenio Hall Show*, where he played Elvis Presley's "Heartbreak Hotel" while wearing dark sunglasses. He then did a remarkably frank interview with Arsenio, discussing his infamous statement that he had smoked—but never inhaled—pot. He said his explanation was so absurd that no person in their right mind would have dared to use it, unless it was true. His answer was pretty convincing and very funny.

Arsenio's ratings that night were spectacular, resonating with young and minority viewers. Shortly after that, Mr. Clinton moved ahead of President Bush in the polls for the first time. Many analysts believe the appearance galvanized his campaign and led to his eventual victory, making it the most important guest spot in late-night television history.

I don't agree with Jay that Bill Clinton snubbed us over the years because we refused to book him in 1992. He simply didn't like Jay's never-ending Monica Lewinsky jokes. I confirmed this with several former Clinton aides, but it took me years to get them to admit it, and they would only do it anonymously.

Another former president, George H. W. Bush, also declined my long-standing offers. I understood Mr. Clinton's reluctance but not Mr. Bush's. He invited Jay to visit the White House during his presidency and later to perform at the 2009 commissioning of the USS *George H. W. Bush* nuclear aircraft carrier in Norfolk, Virginia.

Mr. Bush said he was interested but only available by

satellite from Houston. Since our guests always appeared before a live audience in the Burbank studio, it wasn't really an option, which was a shame. Any former president who at age eighty-five parachuted out of a plane, as Mr. Bush did, was worthy of an interview.

Multi-billionaire Warren Buffett, once ranked at the top of the *Forbes 400* list of America's 400 richest people, was always right up there with Bill Clinton on my guest wish list. What I admired most about the Sage of Omaha was that even though he was the world's greatest financial wizard, he was a regular guy. He lived in the same Omaha house he bought for $31,500 in 1958 and took home a modest one hundred thousand dollar yearly salary from his company, Berkshire Hathaway. In 2006, he announced he would give away his entire fortune.

I had many conversations with his secretary, Debbie Bosanek, inviting her boss on the show—all to no avail. I liked the idea that I didn't have to go through a high-powered, self-important publicist to reach him. I could just call Debbie, who was always pleasant when she said Warren just didn't do shows like ours. She never failed to invite me to call back in a few months, which I did for about ten years.

Jay would sometimes phone Debbie himself. One time he even got through to Warren, who wanted Jay's opinion of a comedy routine he had shot for an upcoming shareholder meeting. The 2009 bit featured Warren as a mattress salesman at his subsidiary, the Nebraska Furniture Mart. After failing to sell a woman a couple of mattresses, he offers her the Nervous Nellie model, saying: "This has been the best seller ever since the Dow fell below 10,000." It was a reference to the country's Great Recession that began in September 2008, precipitated by the stock market implosion. The woman is not convinced at first, but then he shows her a hidden compartment—called the "Night Depository"—built into the foundation of the mattress. She notices it's full of cash, presumably Warren's, and then announces she wants the mattress. Warren calls the warehouse to order a mattress for the woman pronto, but she insists on the floor model. She then temporarily leaves the scene, at which time Warren clears out his money as well as his stock certificates and a couple of *Playboy* magazines, which he quickly pages through.

Turns out Warren himself wrote the bit, and the mattress would become a best-seller after the ad hit YouTube. What did Jay think of Warren's performance? "We're talking Emmy here," he told the budding, billionaire thespian on the phone, as he smiled at me.

As for Debbie Bosanek, she would become a celebrity in her own right after Warren wrote a well-circulated op-ed in *The New York Times,* pointing out she unfairly paid a higher tax rate than he did (34 percent *v.* 17.4 percent). President Obama saw this as a great example of how rich people weren't paying their "fair share" of the taxes and invited Debbie to be his guest at his 2012 State of the Union address. As he spoke about her plight, the camera showed her sitting next to First Lady Michelle Obama.

One thing the president and Warren neglected to mention was that Debbie wasn't exactly poor. According to the *Wall Street Journal,* she was earning an estimated $400,000 in adjusted gross income, which made her a so-called one-percenter. Not bad for a secretary. She would have made a great guest, as well.

Many of the world's greatest athletes stopped by to chat with Jay, including Michael Jordan, Dennis Rodman, Shaquille O'Neal, Charles Barkley, Kobe Bryant, Tiger Woods, Phil Mickelson, Terry Bradshaw, Troy Aikman, Brett Favre, Joe Montana, John Elway, Steve Young, Kurt Warner, Drew Brees, Tim Tebow, Lance Armstrong, Andre Agassi, Pete Sampras, the Williams sisters, John McEnroe, Wayne Gretsky, the Chicago Blackhawks, the Chicago Cubs, Cal Ripken Jr., Dale Earnhardt, and David Beckham, to name a few.

Some of them were regulars, like Dennis Rodman and Terry Bradshaw. Still, I wanted the sports greats who consistently

ay and I doing a faux interview at the desk in Studio 11 right after the show had been
ecorded. (Courtesy NBCUniversal Media, LLC)

lere I am in The Tonight Show audience playing the president of Amtrak as Jay (not
ictured) tells a monologue joke about the railroad company's uneven safety record.
Courtesy NBCUniversal Media, LLC)

Hugh Grant making his famous mea culpa *to Jay Leno in 1995.* (Photo by Margaret Norton/NBC/NBCU Photo Bank via Getty Images)

John Elway, former Denver Broncos quarterback, with me backstage during his only visit to the show in 1999, after leading the Broncos to their second consecutive Super Bowl victory and being named Most Valuable Player. (Courtesy NBCUniversal Media, LLC)

Garth Brooks was one of Jay's favorites and the last guest ever to appear on The Tonight Show with Jay Leno. *Here he is performing as Barbera Libis, music co-producer, and I watch.* (Photo by Margaret Norton/NBC/NBCU Photo Bank via Getty Images)

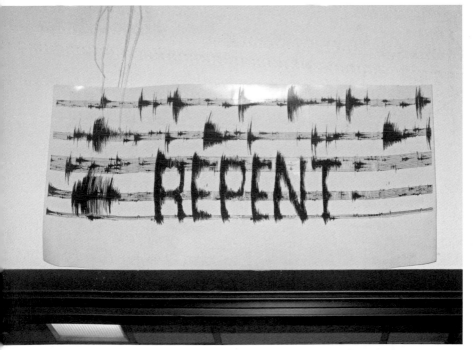

The fake seismograph printout, mounted over my office door, that Shirley MacLaine didn't think was funny.

Dennis Rodman with me backstage. This is actually a conservative look for him. Dennis wa. *always a ratings draw and a favorite of the staff.* (Courtesy NBCUniversal Media, LLC)

Jerry Seinfeld, John F. Kennedy Jr., and Jay Leno during John's only appearance (1998, (Photo by NBC/NBCU Photo Bank via Getty Images)

Mr. Obama arriving at The Tonight Show with Jay Leno *on March 19, 2009, for his appearance as the first sitting president on a late-night show. (l-r) Walter Lewis, President Obama, me, Jay Leno. (Official White House photo by Pete Souza)*

...ay and President Obama in the dressing room. Mr. Obama made six appearances. ...Official White House photo by Pete Souza)

Former president Jimmy Carter and me during one of his eleven appearances. Mr. Carter was our first major political "get." (Courtesy NBCUniversal Media, LLC)

Former senator Bob Dole with me in 1996 during his presidential run. Mr. Dole was the first presidential candidate to come on the show (Courtesy NBCUniversal Media, LLC)

Then Texas governor George W. Bush in the hair and makeup room during his 200 presidential bid. (l-r) Mark McKinnon, Logan Walters, aides; Mr. Bush; Meta Hahn, ha design artist; me. (Courtesy NBCUniversal Media, LLC)

George W. Bush wearing an Al Gore mask and Jay Leno wearing a Bush mask on October 30, 2000, during Mr. Bush's run for president against Mr. Gore. Mr. Gore came on the show the following night, Halloween. (Photo by Paul Drinkwater/NBC/NBCU Photo Bank via Getty Images)

Jay Leno with former senator John Kerry after Mr. Kerry made a dramatic entrance, riding a Harley-Davidson motorcycle up a ramp onto the stage during his presidential bid in 2003. (Photo by Paul Drinkwater/ NBC/NBCU Photo Bank via Getty Images)

Then senator Hillary Clinton and me backstage in 2003 during her first of two appearances with Jay. (Courtesy NBCUniversal Media, LLC)

Jay Leno and former House Speaker Newt Gingrich with piglets during Mr. Gingrich's first appearance in 1996. (Photo by Margaret Norton, NBC/NBCU Photo Bank via Getty Images)

turned down my invitations. Like Super Bowl-winning quarterbacks Payton Manning, Eli Manning, and, especially, Tom Brady, a California guy who grew up watching his idol, 49ers quarterback Joe Montana. I'll bet Tom even saw Joe on our show, which he always chose to do over Letterman. Tom's agent, Steve Dubin, frequently asked me for VIP seats to the show for his friends. I obliged him, hoping he would eventually reciprocate by offering us Tom. But it never happened.

I was big on world leaders, but I was never able to book any of them. For many years we assumed Americans didn't care about foreigners, so we didn't make offers to them. But thanks to the Internet and the global economy, the world got smaller in the two decades we were on the air. Suddenly international politicos didn't seem so remote, and I got the green light to go after some of them.

I extended an invitation to former Soviet leader Mikhail Gorbachev, and was surprised—no, shocked—to learn he was interested. I was curious if the guy who tore down the Berlin Wall and won the Nobel Peace Prize genuinely wanted to make an appearance with Jay, or if he just thought it would help him sell more copies of his latest book. At first, there were months of discussions as to where we would do the interview. He insisted that it be in San Francisco. It seemed strange to be negotiating with the man who hammered out the Intermediate-Range Nuclear Forces Treaty with President Reagan.

Obviously, I was out of my league, but I held fast to my position that we could only do the show before a live audience at Studio 3 in Burbank, so Gorbachev would have to come to our location. He eventually agreed. Then he insisted on speaking Russian during the interview. I knew he could speak English fairly fluently, but he denied it. I tried to explain that having a translator would be cumbersome on a late-night entertainment show, but I think my explanation got lost in translation. He never did the show.

Other international luminaries who passed on my offers

included the Dalai Lama, Bishop Desmond Tutu, and British Prime Minister Tony Blair. But two Israeli leaders interested in appearing with Jay actually contacted me: the former prime minister Benjamin Netanyahu and the then prime minister Ehud Olmert. My colleagues thought Mr. Olmert was boring and Mr. Netanyahu was polarizing, rejecting them both. I wish I had pushed harder. Netanyahu was educated at MIT and was a former anti-terrorist commando who took part in a dangerous rescue mission of a Sabena airliner that had been hijacked by Palestinian terrorists at Ben-Gurion Airport in 1972. He was an important voice in his country and would be re-elected prime minister in 2009, becoming a powerful, high-profile world leader. Mr. Olmert, on the other hand, would not have been a good get. After leaving office, he went on to face seemingly endless charges of corruption.

In 2007, I almost fell out of my chair while reading a *Condé Nast Traveler* interview with Jordan's King Abdullah II. The king, who was primarily promoting tourism in his country, said: "I watch Jay Leno at night [on satellite TV], and when he asks Americans questions in the street about history or culture, their responses are still pretty shocking."

King Abdullah watches Jay Leno?!, I thought. By making a specific reference to Jaywalking, he was saying he actually was a fan. *What a great guest he would make!* Here was a young, forward-thinking king from the Middle East who liked skydiving, riding motorcycles and science fiction, especially *Star Trek*. And his wife, Queen Rania, was incredibly beautiful. *I'd certainly stay up to watch him!* I had a strong feeling King Abdullah would be interested, if I could just figure out how to get to him. I didn't have many contacts in the Middle East, and government bureaucracies could be impossible to deal with under the best of circumstances. But the king was easier to reach than I thought.

Peter Greenberg, a travel reporter I knew who had done a special on the king, contacted His Majesty on my behalf and confirmed that he was interested in making an appearance. But I was never able to make it happen. My colleagues and our executive producer were intrigued, though they didn't think he was a big enough draw. These decisions were never easy. Maybe they were right. But if we had booked King Abdullah, one thing is certain: we would have owned the ratings in Amman that night!

Chapter Seven

Spying on Dennis Rodman in Nashville

Dennis Rodman is a child of God. A lost child at times, as evidenced by his recent trips to North Korea. Still, he taught my colleagues and me to focus on the book, not the cover. In his most recent book, *I Should Be Dead by Now*, Dennis listed me in the acknowledgments. I have no idea why, but I'll take it.

He was a gifted and graceful basketball superstar known for his incredible rebounding abilities and was inducted into the NBA Hall of Fame in 2011. But he was also self-destructive. I'm not talking out of school here; Dennis was aware of his limitations and said as much.

He made twenty-eight appearances on *The Tonight Show with Jay Leno*, each uniquely bizarre yet oddly predictable in its own way. He was one of Jay's most popular guests, even after his halcyon days on the basketball court ended. People liked Dennis because he was an NBA titan with a lot of bluster. Underneath it all he was a sweet person who was flawed and vulnerable.

We had few rules for our studio guests. The most important one was to show up on time. But Dennis was almost always late, which was potentially disastrous even though the show was pre-recorded a few hours before it aired. After all, we had the audience in place and other celebrities standing by who were often on tight schedules as well as a deadline to make the satellite feed to the eastern time zone. Besides, being late was just plain rude to Jay.

This was one battle I rarely won as tardiness was part of Dennis's persona. He even said in his book, *Bad as I Wanna*

Be, that he didn't believe in punctuality. Nevertheless, I went through the motions and over time realized I was essentially just a player in Dennis's chaotic game. Every guest worth getting was a challenge, but Dennis added a new dimension. After much trial and error and its consequential pain, I became an expert on Dennis's antics, which always began during the booking process.

Here's how it worked: I would call his agent, Dwight Manley, to see if and when Dennis was available. This could take weeks because of his demanding NBA schedule, his proclivity to selectively answer Dwight's calls, and the mysterious "Dennis factor." In other words, Dennis would only agree to do the show if and when he felt like it.

There was also the "Dwight factor." I didn't trust him at first: he looked a bit too slick and projected a little too much self-confidence. So I looked him up and discovered he had no background as a sports agent or manager before he met Dennis at a Las Vegas casino. Until then, he was best known as a coin expert who had a legendary collection known as the King of Siam.

I eventually realized that Dwight was a perfect match for the eccentric NBA star, and in many ways I changed my mind about him. My opinion didn't alter entirely, though. I never quite got over my first impression of Dwight as a flimflam man trying to pull a fast one, but I did come to like and even respect him. Working with Dennis was not an easy job. Dwight was essentially on call 24/7, and I believe he did his best to help Dennis earn and keep as much money as possible, despite Dennis's efforts to spend it all.

Whenever Dwight would call me to say Dennis agreed to an appearance, I usually had mixed feelings. I knew Dennis was good for the ratings, but I also dreaded the inevitable headaches that would result from our phone conversations. "Promise me he'll be on time this time," I would say. Dwight would never concede any wrongdoing. He just denied the truth and claimed Dennis always got to the show on time.

True, but just barely, and that was only because of the extreme measures I had to take.

Debbie Vickers also had lingering concerns about Dennis and Dwight, and she never let me forget it. She had an acerbic wit that was both funny and cautionary. Her mantra was simple: "a little paranoia never hurt anyone." She lived by it, especially when it came to Dennis.

Dennis lived in Newport Beach, California, an hour's drive from our Burbank studio in good traffic, and we taped during rush hour in the late afternoon. We would send a limousine to his house to pick him up. We did this for almost all of our guests not to pamper them but to make sure they would arrive at least forty-five minutes before the taping. This worked well for most, but not for Dennis. He would never get into the limo on time, even though we called the handlers at his house numerous times. It was obvious Dennis wasn't running late; he was creating chaos and reveling in it. This was his protocol, and I soon learned how to abide by it.

After one too many close calls, I added a helicopter to the routine. So now whenever Dennis decided he felt like sauntering into the limo, he would be rushed to nearby John Wayne Airport, where the chopper was standing by to fly him to the NBC lot. He usually arrived in twenty minutes with no time to spare.

I will never forget the time Dennis pushed his protocol beyond the pale. I was suspicious from the beginning when I offered him a spot on September 25, 1997, and he quickly agreed to it. There were no apparent conflicts with either his NBA or personal schedules. *This was too easy*, I thought. *Way too easy*. And I was right. Soon after, Dwight called to inform me that Dennis was going to be on the Country Music Awards program in Nashville the night before his appearance on our show. That was a huge no-no. One of our few rules stipulated that a guest couldn't appear on any other show prior to ours unless we had agreed to it at the time of the booking. And Dwight knew that.

I usually didn't raise my voice, but this time I did. "You can't do that," I yelled. "Cancel the CMAs." But Dwight insisted Dennis would just be making a cameo appearance during a Deana Carter performance of her hit song called "Did I Shave my Legs for This?" Dennis would be seen wearing a dress in silhouette and then be revealed at the end of the song. It would just be a quick visual. All right, it was short and funny. Still, Dennis would be in Nashville, two thousand miles away from *The Tonight Show*. When I told Debbie about it, she went ballistic. To her, any change in the routine was a potential disaster. She let out a scream that was probably heard throughout the Hollywood Hills: "They absolutely can't do that. Tell them no."

This was merely her way of expressing frustration. She knew about Dennis's antics and was aware that it didn't matter how loudly she yelled. Dennis would be going to Nashville, and we wouldn't be canceling his booking on our show. She, too, was fond of Dennis and in a strange way viewed him as our prodigal son. Still, she was angry, and she wanted Dwight to know it. So I went through the motions, telling Dwight to pull Dennis from the CMAs. But Dwight insisted Dennis couldn't break his commitment. I expected that answer and went straight to my biggest concern: how would he get Dennis from Nashville to Burbank in time for our show all in the same day? Dwight assured me he would be with Dennis at all times and told me not to worry. Yeah, right!

When I told Debbie this, she came up with a new plan on the spot: "Looks like you're going to Nashville to shadow Dennis. Make sure he gets back here in time. But don't let him see you."

"I'm sorry, what?" I said. I thought she was kidding, but she wasn't.

"You heard me."

Okay, Debbie was going off script here, and I was incredulous: "How exactly do you expect me to do that?"

Without missing a beat or looking up she said, "You make

the big bucks. You figure it out." It was her sardonic way of closing conversations.

I was stunned and didn't have the slightest idea what to do next. There was no template for this. But I had to do something and time was running out, so I drew upon a lesson I had learned during my earlier years at the show: when backed into a corner and you don't know what to do, do something you know how to do. I booked a round-trip flight to Nashville and a hotel. I also figured it would be a good idea to attend the Country Music Awards where Dennis would be performing, so I got myself invited to the show, which had no available audience seats. But I had friends in low places: Garth Brooks and his people, who got me a ticket.

I called a friend of mine who was the publicist for Word, a Nashville record company. I asked her where to hang out in Nashville the night before the CMAs. "Sunset Grill," she said without hesitation. "It's where the songwriters will be." I never considered myself a Hollywood guy, but Nashville was different. I loved everything about this center of country and worship music. I had written a number of country songs, and when my friend said the words "songwriters" and "Sunset Grill," I knew one place where I definitely wanted to go.

Then reality hit again. Here I was doing what I knew how to do without giving much thought to carrying out Debbie's cloak-and-dagger assignment. I did know one thing: The plan didn't feel right. I would be going to Nashville in four days and didn't have a clue about Dennis's travel plans, including his flights to and from Nashville, his hotel, or his rehearsal time at the CMAs. Some spy I was. And that's when I realized there was a pit in my stomach, reminding me of another lesson I had to learn, un-learn, and re-learn almost every week: your gut is very real . . . never ignore him. Everyone has gut instincts. Mine are very real, especially when I'm desperate. I actually experience a persona. His name is Mr. Gut. I've had a life-long, love-hate relationship with Mr. Gut, who through his still, small voice is always giving me advice that I mostly ignore. The funny thing is that when I have listened to him, I've rarely regretted it, although I hate letting him know that.

When I was trying to figure out what to do about Nashville, Mr. Gut became unusually aggressive. He wouldn't leave my conscious mind, and he wouldn't take no for an answer. He made it very clear that stealth was not my style, and that I needed to stop trying to come up with a way to carry out the boss's plan and start coming up with my own.

I commiserated with my real-life colleagues, who thought my dilemma was the funniest thing they had ever heard. While I didn't share their amusement, I was struck by the absurdity of the situation. They assured me Debbie would change her mind about shadowing Dennis if I came up with a better idea. So I headed home for the weekend to formulate a new strategy by Monday morning. But what?

I told my wife, Mary, I felt a little like Peter Graves playing Jim Phelps on *Mission: Impossible*. *Your mission, Mr. Berg, and you* will *accept it, is: First, become invisible. Second, get Dennis Rodman to show up on time at* The Tonight Show. *I realize the second part is harder, but you'll figure it out.*

Then Mr. Gut had some advice: *Tell Dwight you're going to Nashville, but don't tell him the real reason. Spying on Dennis would be much easier than shadowing him.*

Me: *How would that work?*

Mr. Gut: *Tell him you just got invited to the CMAs yourself, and wouldn't it be fun to hang out together in Nashville?* Sometimes you can tell a little while lie.

Me: *Where are you going with this?*

Mr. Gut: *Just say Garth Brooks invited you and you couldn't say no.*

Me: *That would be a lie. Garth didn't exactly invite me. I invited myself with his help.*

Mr. Gut: *It's a white lie. Close enough.*

I never liked lying because, well, it's just plain wrong. And it's bad business. People never trust you once they find out you've deliberately misled them. Besides, I'm a bad liar because I can't keep my stories straight. Mr. Gut admitted it was a grey area, but not over the line, and the white lie was so simple that even I could handle it. I had to agree. Besides, it might work.

On Monday morning I said a prayer as I walked into NBC. I had to call Dwight as soon as possible before self-doubt took control. When I got to my office I took a deep breath and dialed. I had two diametrically-opposed thoughts: 1. Please don't be there. I don't know if I can do this, and 2. Please be there. I have to do this, now!

Turned out Dwight was in, and when I told him I had just been invited to the CMAs, he was predictably incredulous: "Why would they invite you?" I told him country music was one of my specialties at the show, and many artists had offered me seats to the CMAs over the years, which was true. This year it was Garth Brooks. How could I say no?

Long pause.

"You like country music?"

"Yeah."

Another long pause.

"You don't seem the type."

He was suspicious, but I was standing on solid ground. "Didn't you ever hear of Dave & Pete, my bluegrass band in college? Or Bobby Williams and the Loco-Motives? I was a Loco-Motive," I said.

He never questioned the Garth Brooks' invitation but was instead skeptical about my country music credentials. I felt confident because on this point I was actually telling the truth. Besides, how could I have made up a name like Bobby Williams and the Loco-Motives? So I moved in to close the deal. "Maybe we can hang out in Nashville," I said. I was hoping against hope he would ask me to join Dennis and him for something—dinner, lunch, breakfast, the CMA rehearsal, the CMA show itself—anything.

Yet another long pause.

"Dennis and I are flying to Nashville on a charter jet. It's an eight-seater. Plenty of room. You should come with us." I couldn't believe what I was hearing. I had to force myself not to overreact by accepting too quickly: "You're too generous. Are you sure?" I asked.

"I'm not being generous. The CMAs are paying for the jet. Besides, Dennis likes you. It'll make our trip more fun."

"Well, if you insist. . . ." He told me to show up at noon the next day at the AMR-Combs Terminal at John Wayne Airport in Orange County. I was familiar with that airport, as I had booked many helicopter flights there for Dennis.

Then I hung up the phone and sat there in a stupor. I wasn't really sure what had just happened. I couldn't have made up a better scenario. And just to be safe, I didn't cancel my flight to Nashville.

Now it was time to deal with Debbie. I wasn't sure she would like my new plan, but Mr. Gut was. He reminded me she was usually cheerful on Monday mornings before the crises of the week started piling up.

Debbie had a larger-than-life personality, even though I don't think she was taller than five foot four. She was a sharp dresser. Uniquely classy, never flashy. A little country, actually: cowboy boots, high-end jeans, and western shirts. We had a lot in common. She was from Kansas, born and raised in Wichita and a graduate of the University of Kansas. I attended graduate school at Kansas State University and once was a television farm reporter in Wichita.

My relationship with Debbie was complex. She was both a friend and a boss. Great as a friend: caring, protective, lovable. Intimidating as a boss: tough, demanding, smart. She yelled at people as loudly as she laughed with them, sometimes all in the same conversation. A perfectionist, she was hard on people but harder on herself than anyone else. Everyone, including Jay, knew she was just as responsible for the show's success as Jay.

The Hollywood trade magazines have annual articles on the hundred most powerful women in Hollywood. There are many similar lists (most powerful men, directors, agents, producers, etc.), but everyone in town understands that you don't get on a top-100 list unless your people have lobbied for it. In other words, you only get on the list if you put yourself out there. As the executive producer of the number-one late night program since 1995, Debbie never made that list because she never sought the limelight. There's no question she merited a spot not only *on* the list but at the top.

When I got to her office, she was in a Monday-morning mood and immediately embraced my new game plan. She thought it was funny. I was the token conservative among the producers, and I think she was amused that I was spinning a web that had the potential to get really tangled. She told everyone about my Nashville scheme. Mr. Gut was gloating and reminding me that I should listen to him more often. But I had a different take because I knew no matter how much scheming I had done, I couldn't possibly cover every base. Something was bound to go wrong.

The next day I showed up at the hangar on time. Dennis and Dwight were late. I expected that, but half an hour later I started to get concerned even though the charter company assured me I was in the right place. Okay fine, but after an hour I was feeling queasy. Did they charter another flight? Did they decide to call it off and not tell me? Would I be waiting for Godot all day? They finally arrived an hour and a half late with no apologies.

I had been on charter flights before, but this one seemed strange. Three guys on a Learjet with eight seats, yet still I felt cramped. Dennis was six foot eight inches tall. He looked like a giant, and I felt like a Lilliputian. Dennis and I were friends, but he's not much of a talker, so a five-hour flight with him had me feeling a bit out of my element. This was the extent of our conversation:

"Hey Dennis, you doing okay? Are you cramped?"

"No."

"Thanks for letting me come with you. This should be fun."

"Yeah."

Okay, now what? About an hour later I noticed Dennis was reading about the NBA in the sports section of the *Los Angeles Times*.

"Hey Dennis, what's going on with the Bulls?"

"Not much."

"You guys should have a great season this year. How are the negotiations going?"

"Okay."

Dennis had not yet nailed down a contract with the Bulls for the 1997-98 season. In fact, it would be his best year ever. He was part of a basketball dynasty coached by the Zen master Phil Jackson. Dennis was the biggest name in basketball behind Michael Jordan and was recognized worldwide. He was a great player to be sure, but his fame had as much to do with his bad-boy image and all its accoutrements, such as tattoos, nose rings, changing hair colors, and numerous outrageous outfits, including a wedding dress.

The Bulls would win their third consecutive NBA Championship that season. Not bad for Dennis since it was his third straight year with the team. At the end of the season, he would have five rings and seven consecutive rebounding titles.

As an NBA superstar, he seemed to have everything the world had to offer. Yet there was a sadness and vulnerability about him, as well. In his book, *Bad as I Wanna Be,* released in June 1997, he admitted, "From the outside I had everything I could want. From the inside I had nothing but an empty soul and a gun in my lap." I worried about Dennis, but at the moment I was more concerned about myself. We were about to land, and I didn't know what to expect next. I was . . . ah . . . flying by the seat of my pants.

"Where are you staying?" I asked Dwight.

"The Renaissance Hotel. The CMAs are picking up four rooms, and we're only using two. You can have one."

Not bad for my first time as a spy, I thought. Plus the Renaissance wasn't too shabby. After we checked in, Dwight invited me to join them for dinner: "You amuse Dennis. He really wants you to come with us." Dennis smiled.

"Okay," I said instinctively and with Mr. Gut's tacit approval.

Then Dennis spoke up: "After dinner we're going to a titty bar (strip club) and you're coming."

"That's not really my style, but thanks for the invitation."

"Oh no, Bro, you're coming with us."

"No, I don't do that,"

"You do now," Dennis insisted.

"You heard what he said," Dwight said.

I have to admit, for a moment I was tempted. Mr. Gut loved the idea of going to a strip club with Dennis Rodman. *You'll never get this chance again,* he insisted. *Besides, Mary would have to understand the demands of the job. Wouldn't she?* But I was a guy who at least tried to do the right thing in my own flawed way. Dennis and Dwight knew that. If I had followed them to a strip club, they would never let me forget it.

"Let's talk about it at dinner," I said. I didn't want to risk getting myself uninvited.

"All right," Dwight said. "Come to our room in fifteen minutes."

When I got to my room, the first thing I did was call Mary to tell her what happened, and well, to bask in her expected adoration of my noble sacrifice as a husband. But she actually suggested in a teasing way that I accept Dennis' invitation.

Mr. Gut: *You idiot! She's okay with the idea. I told you so.*

Me: *No, she's not. She was just joking.*

That's where I put a stop to Mr. Gut's rants. That day, September 24, also happened to be our wedding anniversary. Not a good day to go to a strip club.

I called to update Debbie and my fellow producers, who urged me to go even though they knew I wouldn't. They thought this whole adventure was pretty funny. I, however, wasn't amused at all. Dennis could still pull any number of stunts, which I tried to impress upon Debbie. She just laughed and told me she expected a full report on the strip club in the morning.

The story took a new twist when I knocked on Dennis's door and he didn't answer it. Then I tried Dwight's door. Still no answer. So I called Dwight. No response. "You have to be kidding me," I said out loud. I knocked again, and called again. Nothing! I had lost control of the situation in fifteen minutes and felt completely helpless. Mr. Gut told me not to worry. Dennis had a very short attention span and probably didn't feel like waiting around for me, so they went to dinner. Sure, but Dwight could have let me know. Red flag!

I updated Debbie, who couldn't believe I let them get away. She advised me to check every nice restaurant in town and, if that didn't work, the strip clubs. I called my Nashville friend for help. "Impossible," she said. Nashville had way too many nice places to eat, and even more strip joints. She recommended that I go to the Sunset Grill and at least try to enjoy myself. So I did.

It turned out to be a very homey place teeming with Nashville luminaries. I recognized many faces, and people were calling me over to their tables. I loved it. I finally settled in with a group of songwriters who had all heard Dennis was in town and wanted to know why. I figured the more people who knew my "secret mission," the more eyes and ears I would have to help me find Dennis. Some of them even volunteered to go to the strip clubs with me, including the women.

Their curiosity seemed inexhaustible: *Was spying part of my job?* No. *Who else had I spied on?* No one. *What was Jay like?* Great. *Who was the best guest I ever worked with?* JFK Jr. *Who was the worst?* Lots of competition. Then someone asked me if I wanted to meet the people from Sony Records who were there in a private dining room. Duh!

I felt like I was being escorted into the holy of holies. There were about thirty people, all seated at a long table. I was introduced to everyone from the president of Sony to several of the company's biggest artists. But one person captured my attention: the late Harlan Howard, perhaps the greatest country songwriter who ever lived. At age seventy he looked fragile. With a shock of pure white hair and a big nose full of veins, he was sitting slightly stooped over. His years of hard drinking had taken a toll. I could tell the "Irving Berlin of country music" was a larger than life guy, and I wanted to meet him.

Most people outside of Nashville have never heard of Harlan, but they knew his amazing songs, which totaled about four thousand. His hits included Patsy Cline's classic "I Fall to Pieces," Ray Price's "Heartaches by the Number," the Judds' "Why Not Me," and Ray Charles' "Busted."

When I was finally introduced to him, I froze. My mind was racing: What could I say to impress him? Should I bring up Dennis Rodman? If he didn't know the background, the story would be too complicated to explain. Should I say I was a big fan of his ever since I was a kid in Chicago listening to the Grand Ole Opry on WSM in Nashville? Or that I wrote and played country music? That would seem like I was kissing up. Then a story came to mind that I thought would really impress him, so I forged ahead: "I heard something about you that I have always wanted to know."

"Shoot!" he said.

"A while back I was listening to Don Imus on the radio. He's a big country music fan, as I'm sure you know." Harlan seemed interested, so I continued. "Imus was talking about divorce and how messy it can be. He's been divorced twice. He said you had been divorced four times and claimed it wasn't all bad. That you had also gotten four hits as a result," I said, laughing.

But I soon stopped because Harlan wasn't laughing. Nor was anyone else. There was an uneasy silence that lasted an eternity. Where was Mr. Gut when I needed him? Drinking beer with the songwriters? That's when I noticed the beautiful young woman sitting next to him. "Son, I would like you to meet my fifth wife, Melanie," he said with a slight, wry smile.

"Nice to meet you, Melanie," I said, uneasily. She smiled politely, but that didn't make me feel any better. I had just made the biggest *faux pas* of my life, and there was nothing I could do about it. An apology would have been insulting. I wished I could just disappear.

"Son, I only write happy songs these days, always from the girl's point of view. She's much more emotionally invested than the guy."

"What an insight," I said.

He didn't respond, which was my cue to leave. Too embarrassed to give my card to all the big-wigs at the table, I made a quick exit and took a cab back to the hotel. I checked to see if Dennis and Dwight had returned to their rooms, but they hadn't. It was midnight, so their evening was probably just getting started.

I had a restless night and woke up at 6 a.m. central time, 4 a.m. Pacific, which I was still on. It was way too early to check on my wayward friends, and I couldn't get back to sleep. So I just lay there and worried about things I couldn't control: Where did they go the night before? Why did they ditch me? Would they return to the hotel? Where else could they possibly be? Should I have tried to find them instead of going out on the town? Will I ever find them on this trip? Will I still have a job when I go home?

By 10 a.m. I couldn't wait any longer. Even though it was still too early to disturb the party animals, I called Dwight, but there no answer. I tried knocking on his door—several times. Still no answer. I was beginning to feel desperate. Time to call anyone and everyone who could give me any information that would lead me to Dennis. I started with the woman at the front desk, who told me Dennis and Dwight had checked out. I called Shannon Heim, the publicist for the CMAs, asking what time Dennis's rehearsal was scheduled. She told me the bit had been scratched.

"*Are you kidding me?*" I yelled.

"Excuse me, sir?"

"Why was Dennis cut?"

"I'm not sure. You'll have to check with him."

"Where is he?"

"You'll have to check with him."

Circular conversation. I hung up, haunted by the possibility that my worst case scenario was fast becoming a reality.

Next, I called the hangar at the airport, and they confirmed what I most feared. Dennis and Dwight had taken off. I asked for their ETA in Los Angeles but was told the itinerary had changed. They were headed for Las Vegas! I immediately called Dwight's assistant in Los Angeles to try to find out where they would be staying, but Dwight hadn't told her about their new destination, so I asked her to have him call me the moment he checked in.

I reported the bad news to Debbie, who wasn't sure how to react, which was a first. She knew I had done everything I could. "I can't believe those guys," she said. Then she started teasing me about not going to the strip club. "You wouldn't be in this mess if you had just done it. Besides, Mary would have been okay with it, right?"

"Ah yeah, sure."

"Well, I think what you need to do now is catch the first plane to Vegas," she said.

"Huh?"

"You need to find Dennis."

"He could be anywhere. I don't even know for sure if they're actually there."

"You said they were flying to Vegas."

"Who knows with those guys? They could've changed their minds mid-flight."

"Oh come on, there's no way Dennis would change his mind about Vegas."

She was right. Dennis once appeared on our show when it originated from Las Vegas. We had seen him around show girls and gambling. That was his comfort zone. Actually, more like his obsession.

"Look, Deb, let me talk to Dwight first. Maybe he'll tell me the name of the hotel. I left him a message. I'm sure he'll get back to me."

"Oh, you want to rely on Dwight now?"

"I just feel funny about flying off to Vegas because I'll be in the air for several hours and out of pocket."

"Well, do what you have to do."

That went well, except I didn't really know if I would ever hear from Dwight. So what next? Sit around and worry all day like a high school girl waiting by the phone for that special guy to invite her to the prom? I decided to stay in Nashville and do something I knew how to do: eat!

It was late morning, and I headed for the iconic Pancake Pantry, where a friend had invited me to meet up. When I arrived, there was a long line outside the restaurant, but that was okay. I was about to experience the best pancakes in the world, concocted from secret family recipes. Except I don't remember tasting them. Just as the pancakes arrived, my cell phone rang. It was Dwight.

"What's your problem?" he asked, clearly taking the offensive.

"What's my problem? First of all, you're in Vegas, and I'm in Nashville!"

"So what?" Confirmation they were in Vegas.

"What hotel are you at?"

"What's it to you?"

"What's it to me? Let's start with you guys standing me up for dinner."

"You said you didn't want to go to the strip club."

"I said I didn't want to go to the strip club, not that I didn't want to go to dinner."

"Dennis was getting impatient."

"Well, thanks for letting me know. And thanks for letting me know you were checking out the next day, and that Dennis was scratched from the CMAs. And that you were going to Vegas. What am I supposed to do now?"

"You're supposed to go to the CMAs. That is why you're there, isn't it?" *Busted!* Dwight was on to me.

"Okay, okay, but what happened to Dennis's bit?"

"It's not a very nice story." He was clearly angry.

Then Dwight hit me with an odd question: "Are you telling me you don't want Dennis to do your show now? Because that wouldn't be good."

"No, I'm telling you I'm worried he won't be on time for

our show. He's in Las Vegas. You'll never get him out of there."

"Trust me, Dennis is where he should be. He likes it here. And we'll be at the studio on time tomorrow, so stop worrying."

"You're right, I am worried. Can you just fly him home tonight?" I pleaded.

"No, this is better than home for him. He'll be occupied and distracted here. He wouldn't know what to do with himself at home."

"Look, why don't I just join you there? I'll feel better knowing where he is."

"No, you're better off there. I promise. Dennis will be on time tomorrow. I won't even let him go home. We'll check into a hotel in Los Angeles. That way we'll be even closer to the studio."

"Yeah, but I can't send a helicopter to downtown Los Angeles to pick him up."

"Relax, Dave. We don't need a helicopter. We'll show up tomorrow."

I called Debbie, who was as curious as I was about what happened to Dennis at the CMAs. She didn't like the idea that Dennis would be spending the night in Vegas and still thought I should fly there. I told her I believed Dwight. Something happened at the CMAs that really hurt Dennis, and now he wanted to do our show to boost his morale and maybe take a swipe at the CMAs. She encouraged me once again to go to Las Vegas to find Dennis and Dwight but told me to do what I thought was best. But no matter what I did, I better make sure Dennis showed up.

By then I had lost all enthusiasm for the CMAs. I had to force myself to attend, but I ended up having a wonderful time. When Deana Carter performed "Did I Shave My Legs for This?" the audience loved it, but I thought it would have been much better with Dennis in a dress as the kicker. It would have been a great topic for Jay and Dennis to discuss on our show, too. Now we had a new topic: Why was Dennis mysteriously dropped?

The highlight of the evening for me came when it was announced Harlan Howard was inducted into the Country Music Hall of Fame. I was glad to be there to see it, but figured it was best not to seek out and congratulate him after the show. Ironically, I was grateful to Dennis for the chance to go to the CMAs. It was the only time I attended the program.

The next day at *The Tonight Show* I briefed Jay and Debbie about possible topics for Dennis's segment. The producers met with Jay every day at noon to discuss the guests scheduled to appear on that day's show. Jay had the final say about the questions he would ask, but it was the producer's job to do the research and come up with a list.

He was very amused by the Nashville story, particularly the part about the strip club. No surprise there. He was a comedian, always trying to find humor in a situation. I know what he was thinking: What could be funnier than to get the "Christian guy" to admit going to a "titty bar" with his buddy Dennis Rodman? No matter that it didn't happen. Why let the truth stand in the way of a good joke?

Debbie saw what was happening and asked Jay not to bring up the strip club because it would embarrass me. While I appreciated her sweet gesture, I was actually glad Jay had diverted her attention from Dennis's arrival time.

I had done a lot of worrying for nothing. Dennis showed up on time, thus breaking his own protocol. Halleluiah! Maybe he figured I had suffered enough in Nashville. Yeah, right! I was just glad something turned out as planned. Now my job would be pretty routine: Encourage Dennis to have a good time and speak up. The real Dennis was really a shy guy who had been picked on as a kid, and he often spoke too softly to be heard.

His outfits were always loud, outrageous and expensive, costing several thousand dollars. It was his trademark, and his look bolstered his confidence. That night he was wearing a pink-leather jacket, a leopard-print open-collar shirt, black-leather pants, and black high-top tennis shoes. He was sporting a stylized black-fur Derby hat, which had a band of rhinestones and bright, pink feathers on the side of the brim. He also had a huge chain necklace, but his facial jewelry was very minimal: two small hoops in the left ear and a small nose ring in the left nostril.

Dennis's wardrobe always made me smile because I knew it was just his way of saying: *This is my world and my protocol, such as it is. Now you're all part of it.* And we were, even Jay. He always had the same reaction to Dennis's outfits: "You remind me of Huggy Bear."

It was a reference to a character on the 70s television show *Starsky & Hutch*. Huggy Bear was a jive-talking guy who wore absurdly ostentatious outfits. Few people probably even remembered Huggy Bear, but that didn't matter. Jay always cracked himself up when he said it, and so he began each interview with Dennis on a happy note.

That night, Dennis put on one of his best performances. He even got in a light-hearted dig at Deana Carter by suggesting she dropped him from her act because she didn't want to be upstaged by the "great Dennis Rodman." He said it tongue in cheek, but I think he meant it. For the record, I was never able to find out why Dennis was cut. When I asked Deana and her people about it, they said the CMAs told them to do it.

As for my secret Nashville assignment that Debbie had asked Jay not to mention, he did it anyway, telling our millions of viewers, including my family, church, and friends, that he had sent his most conservative guy—Dave Berg—to Nashville to keep an eye on Dennis in a strip club.

Jay to Dennis: "You leave him there. You take off for Vegas on a jet, and he's stuck in a topless bar." Dennis immediately agreed. Then he glanced over where I was sitting off-camera and winked.

Hey, I was working for a comedian at a late-night show. Being the butt of jokes came with the territory. And to this day, Mary says a little part of her is not quite sure about that strip club story.

The Nashville caper was always a mystery to me. Why

did we spend so much time and money just to make sure Dennis Rodman showed up on time when we had never gone to such lengths for any other guest? I had convinced myself the real reason Debbie did it was to help me jump-start my songwriting career. Years later I was at a dinner party with her and my colleagues, and I asked her why she did it.

"I sent you to Nashville because I didn't trust Dennis," she said. "That's it."

"That's funny . . . because I thought you were trying to help me get connected in Nashville."

"What are you talking about?"

Okay then. Mystery solved.

Chapter Eight

John F. Kennedy Jr., the Favorite Guest

Jay was twelve years old when President Kennedy was assassinated in 1963. He was sitting with his mother in their living room watching the funeral procession on television as three-year-old "John John," dressed in a shorts outfit, saluted his father's casket passing by.

Jay's mother was crying hysterically as she asked: "What's going to happen to that little boy?" Jay wanted to help her stop crying but felt helpless. After all, he was only a kid and she was an adult. What could he do? It was a terribly sad moment, but it eventually faded from Jay's memory.

Thirty-five years later, on May 14, 1998, the late John F. Kennedy Jr. was booked as a guest on *The Tonight Show*. He was a great "get" and everyone, including Jay, was excited. When he went into the dressing room to meet with John before the show, he had no recollection of the moment with his mother. That wouldn't happen until John actually made his entrance onto the stage. Jay reached out to shake his hand, and as he did so, he happened to glance into the monitor where he witnessed the handshake as it was happening. That's when it hit Jay, and tears suddenly came to his eyes. He wanted to say to his mom, "Look, he's right here. He's fine. It's okay."

Like Jay, I had vivid memories of "John John" at his father's funeral. The assassination and funeral were landmark events for the baby boomer generation Jay and I belong to. The three major networks (ABC, CBS, and NBC) provided round-the-clock coverage for four days. There had never been anything like it on television.

While JFK Jr. came from the world's most prominent political family, he transcended politics. He was American royalty. I booked and worked with his sister, Caroline, and had already experienced the magic of the Kennedy name. I saw how reverential the studio audience was of her. John rarely did television interviews and had never done one on a late-night show, so I knew he wouldn't be easy to bring in.

I figured my best—and maybe only—chance would be to go through a new magazine he co-founded called *George*. Magazines were always a risky venture, and this one was really headed for uncharted water. Aptly subtitled "Not Just Politics as Usual," *George* was a slick, hip, monthly fusion of politics and celebrity in a way that had never been done before. The debut issue featured a sexy cover picture of Cindy Crawford as George Washington, dressed in a white wig and a revolutionary soldier uniform. Other cover pictures portrayed George Clooney as Thomas Jefferson, Harrison Ford as Abraham Lincoln, Barbra Streisand as Betsy Ross, Julia Roberts as Susan B. Anthony, and Charles Barkley as George Washington. Contributors included Ann Coulter, Paul Begala, Al Franken, Norman Mailer, and Madonna, who wrote a piece called "If I Were President."

I called *George's* publicity director, Nancy Haberman, offering John a spot on the show. I was fairly confident they would take my invitation seriously. They had too much at stake to dismiss *The Tonight Show* outright. Still, John was media shy, so I didn't expect to get an answer in a week, or even a month. But I never thought it would take six years.

Nancy stopped taking my calls after a year, though I kept calling her. I wasn't a pushy guy, but I was paid to book A-level celebrities, so I never stopped making offers until I was asked. Then I would start again in about three months.

I realize this sounds counterintuitive. The normal response would be to dismiss Nancy for being rude and move on. But a good producer can never let ego stand in the way of a booking. I had dealt with many people like Nancy, and I tried to look at the world from their point of view. Most people don't like to deliver bad news, and I had a feeling John was probably losing interest in our show. I figured she didn't want to tell me that and was hoping I would figure it out on my own.

One day I called Nancy and was transferred to John's executive assistant, RoseMarie Terenzio. She confirmed my assumptions about John but made it a point to tell me she was a fan of *The Tonight Show* and wanted to stay in touch. So that's what I did for the next four years. I would call her whenever I read news about John or *George* to get her take on it. In turn, I would bring her up to date on *The Tonight Show* and Hollywood gossip. We were both keeping the lines of communication open, and in so doing we became friends.

RoseMarie was very aware about what was going on in John's life. It was obvious to me she was more than John's assistant. She had become his confidante. So the day she finally told me he wanted to do our show, I was pretty jazzed; but I wasn't surprised because I knew she played a big part in the decision. Nevertheless, I was skeptical. It wouldn't be a sure thing until he actually showed up at Studio 3.

She said John would do the show only if we agreed not to promote it beforehand. That threw us for a loop. Only one guest had ever made such a demand: author Salman Rushdie, and he was the target of a fatwa calling for his death. When the show scored a name as big as John Kennedy Jr., we wanted to shout it from the highest mountaintops to bring in as many viewers as possible.

Obviously, promotions help both the show and the guest, so why did John make such a strange demand? RoseMarie said at the time her boss was concerned that news of his booking would upset David Letterman's people, and he didn't want to deal with their inevitable relentless phone calls. I didn't tell RoseMarie that I didn't buy it. JFK Jr. wasn't born yesterday. If she was telling me the full story, he didn't owe Letterman anything. Despite my concerns, we agreed to John's terms and decided to make the best of it by calling him our "mystery guest," which turned out to be a pretty effective promotion.

I routinely worried about everything. As a producer, it came with the territory. In Debbie-Vickers-style, my colleagues and I used to say, "You're only as good as your paranoia." It comes off as negative, but you have to think that way in a world where even small mistakes can lead to major consequences. In this case my instincts turned out to be right, but I'll get to that later.

John had another stipulation: He was only available one day—May 14, 1998. This one put my stomach in knots because we had already booked Jerry Seinfeld that night as the lead guest, and he couldn't be bumped. His appearance was scheduled on the same night as the very last episode of *Seinfeld*. I dreaded the thought of telling JFK Jr. he would have to follow Jerry. To most Hollywood elites, being offered the second guest spot was considered an insult. I had never talked with John, so I suggested to RoseMarie that she should probably be the one to discuss this with her boss. She said it would be better coming from me, and she didn't seem that concerned. I was surprised, but I took it as a good sign.

When John called me for our pre-interview, he seemed excited about his upcoming guest spot. Then I took a deep breath and told him Jerry would be first out. There was a long pause—maybe the longest in my life. All I could think was: *Oh no, I've lost him. I've lost John Kennedy Jr.* Then he broke the silence: "Do you think I'm good enough to follow Jerry Seinfeld?" I wasn't sure if he was serious. His voice sounded sincere. So I asked, "Are you kidding me?" He assured me he meant it. He didn't understand why anyone would want to watch him after seeing Jerry reminisce about one of the most beloved shows in the history of television. RoseMarie had warned me he was a humble guy, but I never expected this.

I told him I was certain he would have at least three good stories that would hold the audience's interest, such as his family background, his views on politics, and some of the great articles in *George*. He wasn't convinced, but at least he did agree to do the show. Then he promised he would come up with some decent material so he wouldn't embarrass himself. As if!

RoseMarie insisted John was not feigning modesty. Then she revealed something new: John had already agreed to appear on Letterman's upcoming one thousandth episode as the featured guest with Pearl Jam in the second spot. But he was having second thoughts about being promoted as such a high-profile guest. Obviously, I didn't know about the Letterman deal when I explained to John that he would be following Jerry. As I said earlier, I suspected something was amiss when RoseMarie insisted on no publicity.

Turns out she had just cancelled John's booking on *Letterman*, and his producers were predictably upset, as I would have been. They would have been merciless with her and John, had they known JFK Jr.—the most celebrated resident in New York—was turning down their show to do Jay in Los Angeles.

The two shows were bitter rivals from the very beginning. Most of the hard feelings were coming from Letterman and his people, who never got over their resentment that David didn't get the hosting job at *Tonight*. It didn't matter to them that Jay was the number-one show in late night. They had constructed their own parallel universe in which David was a true comedic genius and Jay was lowbrow.

RoseMarie was wise to protect both John and herself from Letterman's wrath at being upstaged by Jay. Letterman routinely badgered prospective guests on the air for not doing his show.

John called me three more times to discuss his interview, and each conversation was fairly lengthy. I spent more time on the phone with him than any other guest. I knocked off most pre-interviews in one phone call, lasting no more than a half hour, which I could have easily done with him. Yet he never thought his material was strong enough and felt he needed to keep working on it. Actually, his jokes and anecdotes were some of the best I had ever heard. I told him he was overthinking the segment and actually had too much material. The big challenge would be deciding what to cut out.

RoseMarie told me years later that shortly before his scheduled appearance John informed her he didn't want to go through with it. He asked her to "fall on [her] sword" and alert *The Tonight Show*. Her immediate reaction was, *Oh my God!* But she didn't say it. She calmly suggested to him that he give it little more thought before making a decision. He took her advice and never brought it up again.

On the day of the show I felt confident John would "kill," as they say in the business. He had prepared extensively for the segment, but he was still worried. He made the Sign of the Cross as he left the dressing room and headed for the studio.

When Jay finally introduced the "mystery guest" and John walked out on stage, the studio audience immediately shot to its feet and let out a thunderous applause. He was incredibly handsome, even by Hollywood standards, and women were screaming, including my wife and five of her friends, who were aware he would be coming out.

John was visibly surprised by the raucous reception. I could see him mouth the word *Wow!* When he sat down between Jay and Jerry, he admitted he was feeling overwhelmed: "I gotta tell you . . . my judgment in following Mr. Seinfeld on the biggest night in television . . . they always tell you in politics you gotta watch who you follow, so I don't know what I was thinking."

John had reminded me in our pre-interview that he was portrayed, but didn't appear in, a hugely popular Emmy-winning Seinfeld episode in which Elaine (Julia Louis-Dreyfus) was smitten with him. He thought it might be a good topic with Jerry out there. He was right, but I think what he was really trying to do was take the spotlight off of himself and put it on Jerry. It didn't work. Jerry was as interested in what John had to say as everyone else. When John said he had a tip for Jerry, he played along:

John: There's this great soup place. I don't know if you've heard about it.

Jerry: No, I haven't heard. How's the service?
John: He's kind of an ill-tempered guy.
Jerry: I'll check it out.

John's ode to the Soup Nazi got a huge laugh. Jay followed it with a question about the *Seinfeld* episode with "JFK Jr." in it. Jerry excitedly pointed out how popular it was. John said he hadn't seen the show when it aired. The next day as he was heading for his office, where he worked as a district attorney, he was causing a huge commotion, as people were yelling and honking their horns at him. He had no idea what was going on, but when he got to work, colleagues filled him in on the *Seinfeld* episode, which prepared him for what was about to happen:

> John: I had a trial and I walked into court. The defendant is sitting over there, and he goes: "You were on *Seinfeld*." And I said, "No, no, I wasn't on *Seinfeld*." And he leans over to his lawyer, and he says, "The guy's an actor, too. No wonder he failed the bar exam."

The studio audience loved it. Then Jay asked the question that was on everyone's mind:

> Jay: You've been around politics your whole life. Would you ever run for office?
> John: Other than people asking me, "Were you ever on *Seinfeld*," that was the second most-frequently asked question. Being an editor of a political magazine, you're able to be in politics without really being in politics. It's like being the vice president, I guess. [Huge audience response.] I have a great time doing that, and we all know politics is a tough profession these days, but I think a very rewarding one.

In fact, John had thought about getting into politics. He was approached about running for Senate against Hillary Clinton, but he declined. There was also some discussion about a possible gubernatorial run in New York, but

RoseMarie told me what really intrigued John was the office of mayor of New York City.

Jay then asked John about a poem he published in *George*. It had been written by Monica Lewinsky when she was nine years old. It was his best story, even though he had strong misgivings about doing it, which he expressed to Jay:

> John: I know I'm going to eternally rot in Hell for this. The poem is a poignant rumination on how "I Can Be a Delicious Lunch, Dinner or Breakfast—If You're Weird." She goes on to describe herself as a "round and flat piece of dough with lots of topping. I am a mouth's best friend. I make you say, *yum, yum.*"
>
> Jay: It's amazing how kids know at such a young age what they're gonna do with their lives.

The show was enormously successful, drawing fifteen million viewers, the third-largest audience in its history. I believe John put on the best guest performance I've ever seen on *The Tonight Show*. He was my favorite guest, and Jay's, too. Not bad for a guy who was so afraid he would bomb that he almost cancelled his appearance. Without question, the *Seinfeld* finale and Jerry's outstanding appearance helped drive the numbers, but it was John who made the show truly memorable.

A little more than a year later, we heard the news that John had died when the plane he was piloting crashed into the Atlantic Ocean. His wife, Carolyn Bessette-Kennedy, and sister-in-law, Lauren Bessette, were also killed. All of us, including Jay, were deeply saddened. We talked fondly about the day our "mystery guest" showed up. I felt like I had lost a friend.

Chapter Nine

Mr. Sitting President

March 19, 2009, 4 p.m.

I was standing in a short line outside our studio waiting to greet President Barack Obama and his staff as they arrived for Mr. Obama's guest appearance. Jay and his wife, Mavis, were in front of me.

The president's motorcade was running a little late because of heavy traffic on Highway 101, but I knew it was getting closer because of the increasing Secret Service chatter. I had worked with the agency many times for political guests, including Mr. Obama, but this day was different.

It would be the first time a sitting president had ever made an appearance on a late-night entertainment show, and the Secret Service was there with a full contingent: twelve agents from Washington, DC, and eighteen more from different government security agencies in Los Angeles, as well as four snipers, two on rooftops and two in disguise at undisclosed locations. In the past, they had sent only a few agents to cover politicos.

Normally, the dignitary would be driven into the building through large "elephant" doors, traveling about twenty-five yards down the corridor to Studio 3, where the show was produced. But the president's new Cadillac limousine, known as "the Beast," had so much armor that it weighed upwards of fifteen thousand pounds. It was too heavy to bring inside for fear it would crash through the floor to the basement.

I heard from the radio chatter that the motorcade had arrived at the entrance to NBC, and I instinctively glanced at the elephant doors, which were wide open. The sun was unbelievably bright as it reflected off a shiny, white tent where the president would be getting out of his limousine.

Finally, the president's limo pulled up. My eyes darted toward the elephant doors again, though they now seemed to be shrouded in billows of fog coming off the light. I wasn't sure why I was seeing fog. Maybe it was the excitement of the moment and a week's worth of sleep deprivation. Then a person stepped through the fog, a staffer. Followed by another, and another. They just kept coming, and they all seemed to be moving in slow motion. It reminded me of an old Keystone Cops movie where the cops just keep streaming out of the paddy wagon.

After about ten people came through, I started recognizing them: David Axelrod, the president's political adviser; Hilda Solis, the labor secretary; and Robert Gibbs, the press secretary. Finally, I heard the president's voice: "Hey, Jay." His waving hand was reaching through the white veil of fog. Then he emerged, smiling and looking unbelievably presidential.

All of a sudden, he was there, shaking hands with Jay and Mavis. Then he was shaking hands and exchanging pleasantries with me. This was Mr. Obama's third visit, but somehow he wasn't the same person. And it wasn't just about the Secret Service, the presidential limo, and the coterie of aides. He was now the most powerful person on earth.

The president, a few of his aides, Jay, and I were then escorted to his dressing room. Actually, it was two adjoining rooms, a Secret Service requirement as would-be assassins can shoot through walls. I asked Mr. Obama if he had any questions about the show or the interview, and he said with a smile that he thought he could handle it, which ended the formalities. He had a story about the Secret Service, and he was anxious to tell Jay about it.

The day before, he had made an appearance at the Orange County Fairgrounds. After arriving there by Marine One, the presidential helicopter, he decided to take a short walk to the site where he would be speaking. But a Secret Service agent quickly nixed the idea because the distance—seven hundred fifty yards—was too far.

When the president said it would only be a five-minute walk, the agent replied, "Yes, sir. Sorry." They did let him walk on the way back since the doctor was there with a defibrillator. Jay loved the anecdote and told the president to bring it up on the show.

Although Mr. Obama's closest aides, Robert Gibbs and David Axelrod, were in the dressing room, the guy he really related to was his personal assistant and so-called "body man," Reggie Love. Reggie had been with the president since his days in the US Senate, starting in 2005. When he was hired, he was given no formal job description. He was simply told to "take care of stuff." And from all appearances he did that quite well. At six foot five, he played on Duke University's 2001 NCAA Championship basketball team and was the president's teammate in the many pickup basketball games he played. While Reggie was a better player than Mr. Obama, the president was quick to point out to Jay that his friend didn't always understand the politics of the game. During the presidential election they had traveled to a small Northeastern town where they played a pickup game against some of the townsfolk. Reggie was running up the score with some hot-dog moves. Mr. Obama had to pull him aside and remind them they were trying to get votes, not win the game. He took great pleasure in busting his friend with this story.

After our visit, I returned to my office to wait for the show to begin. I had about ten minutes, and I couldn't help but think back on the fascinating series of events that led to that moment, beginning five years earlier. I had never heard of Illinois State Senator Barack Obama before he delivered the keynote address to the Democratic National Convention in Boston on July 27, 2004, which I thought was amazing. I had not seen such a powerful speaker since President Reagan, and I was convinced I was watching the future of the Democratic Party by the time his speech climaxed with these rousing words: "Tonight, there's not a liberal America and a conservative America; there's the United States of America. There's not a black America and white America and Latino America and Asian America; there's the United States of America."

"*Who is that guy?*" I said out loud to the television over and over as I was watching the seventeen-minute speech. But I wasn't the only one impressed by the forty-four-year-old, no-name politician from Hyde Park in Chicago. The entire nation was electrified.

And the very next day I made an offer to Mr. Obama that would eventually lead to today's historic presidential appearance. Of course, I had no way of knowing that when I called his staff for the first time. They were overwhelmed by the reaction to his game-changing speech and suggested I stay in touch. I was just happy they took my call, which I'm sure was one of hundreds. Their guy was thrust into the national limelight overnight, and I suspected they weren't quite sure how to deal with it, so they opted to keep the lines of communication open.

Two and a half years and several hundred phone calls later we got our first booking with Mr. Obama, then a national senator and a likely presidential candidate in the upcoming primary election. But he made no major announcement in that appearance, nor did he have anything to say about his famous speech. Instead he had a self-deprecating story about the first Democratic National Convention he attended four years before "The Speech," where he was not the keynote speaker. He wasn't even a delegate. He was a gate crasher.

He told Jay he was broke after losing a Democratic primary bid for a House seat and wasn't planning to go to the convention. Then at the last minute friends and supporters talked him into catching a cheap flight to Los Angeles. When he got to the Hertz counter at LAX, his American Express card was rejected after several tries. Then he couldn't get a pass to the convention floor, so he had to watch most of the speeches on television screens around Staples Center. He was so discouraged he caught the first flight back to Chicago.

Mr. Obama related his woeful tale to Jay with great flair and political savvy: "It's not as if I was that much smarter in 2004 than I was in 2000. I'm the same guy. I've gotten some good breaks."

Jay asked Mr. Obama if he was running for president, but he deflected the big question with a joke: "I'm already committed to the Food Network." Two months later he made a dramatic entry into the presidential race in Springfield, Illinois, home of Abraham Lincoln, the nation's sixteenth president. Thousands filled the town square to hear him say: "It was here in Springfield, where North, South, East, and West come together that I was reminded of the essential decency of the American people—where I came to believe that through this decency, we can build a more hopeful America."

From that point on we put a full-court press on him to make another appearance. I believed our chances were good because he had told me he preferred Jay's "regular guy" persona over Letterman. My optimism panned out, but not until October, eight months later. It was well worth the wait.

He was still trailing Senator Clinton in the polls, campaign funds, and support of Democratic heavyweights. But at the show he was a textbook case of grace under pressure. On stage he came across as the leading candidate, as he turned his negatives into some pretty funny material: "When your name is Barack Obama, you are always the underdog."

When Jay pressed Senator Obama on it, he pushed back:

Jay: Hillary appears to be a shoo-in. How discouraging is that?
Obama: It's not discouraging.
Jay: A little bit?
Obama: Hillary is not the first politician in Washington to declare mission accomplished a little too soon. [Much laughter and applause.]

Of course, Senator Obama would eventually defeat Senator Clinton in a close and exciting primary election. He would go on to win the presidency over Senator John McCain and then appoint Mrs. Clinton his secretary of state.

Had the stock market not taken a freefall in September 2008, Senator McCain had a real chance of becoming the commander-in-chief. He was ahead in the polls at the time, but when the economy definitively went south, voters decided to go with the new guy who was offering "hope and change." And when Mr. Obama was declared the winner, he delivered a momentous speech in Chicago's Grant Park that had commentators buzzing well into the next day. My thoughts drifted to the Illinois state senator who had given "The Speech" only four years after crashing the Democratic Convention four years before that. I got carried away in the moment because I felt as if I had been watching from a front-row seat as history was unfolding.

I told my assistant I wanted to do something that had never been done in almost sixty years of late-night television: book the president. I knew the chances would be slim, but it was worth a try. An interview with the popular new president would define Jay's watch as the host of *The Tonight Show,* which I thought would be ending in June 2009 when Conan O'Brien was to take over.

I had a good relationship with the new president and his staff and wanted to take advantage of it by calling regularly, though I didn't want to wear out my welcome. So I decided to be aggressive but clever about it. I would make many calls, sometimes contacting the president's staff two and three times a week, often under the guise of making offers to presidential staffers, such as Robert Gibbs or Chief of Staff Rahm Emanuel. These gentlemen would have made terrific guests, but I knew they would never agree to appearances that could potentially upstage their boss. I was just keeping the lines of communication open.

One day Jay called Gibbs, who—to everyone's surprise—put President Obama on the line. He told Jay he wanted to do the show when the time was right. It was an exciting moment, to be sure. Still, we didn't have a date. Every sales person knows you don't really have a deal until it's closed, and I wasn't going to relax until that happened. Jay wouldn't let me. Every day it was the same: He would see me getting coffee in the staff kitchen and ask me if the president was booked yet. I would tell him we were still working on it. Then he would want to know why it was taking so long, and I would say I didn't know, followed by an awkward pause. I felt a little like Phil, Bill Murray's character in *Groundhog Day,* who woke up every morning to find it was the same day all over again. I understood Jay's impatience. It's just that he didn't concern himself with the details, such as the fact that the president couldn't just jump on Air Force One any old time just to do our show. He was now the new guy in charge of running the free world. We would just have to wait until he scheduled a trip to Los Angeles.

Finally, we got the word: the president was booked on March 19, the following week. It would be his fifty-ninth day in office, not even two months since his inauguration and not quite five years since "The Speech." Our dream booking had come true! My first order of business was to let Jay know the news as soon as possible. He was as happy as I've ever seen him, and I was glad that I would be able to get my morning coffee in peace again—at least for the time being.

Five minutes later—after the euphoria wore off—I realized I had some loose ends to deal with: Teri Hatcher, star of *Desperate Housewives,* was already booked as the lead guest that night and would have to be bumped to another night. Since she was an Obama supporter, I didn't think it would be a problem. He was the president, after all, but I didn't know how she would react. We rarely moved guests, and when we did it was usually messy.

I sent Teri an e-mail with the news but didn't hear back from her. Instead, I got a call from someone on her staff, who said Teri understood my dilemma and would be happy to make way for the president. Still, I was told, "a girl likes to be appreciated." I told her not to worry because I was planning to send Teri some flowers. There was a long pause.

"You know," she said, "girls like Louis Vuitton . . . maybe a handbag?"

I had no idea such a purse could cost up to $2,000. I figured it would run about one hundred dollars, no more than a nice bouquet of flowers. Just as I was about to ask what style of handbag would suit Teri, I was interrupted by my assistant, who had been listening to my conversation. She came rushing into my office, waving her hands, shaking her head from side to side and mouthing the word "no." I quickly revised my answer and said I would have to check our budget, which was a little tight. We ended up sending Teri the flowers, and we worked out another date. She was very gracious about it, but I'm not sure how she would have reacted had I promised a designer handbag and then reneged on my word.

Now that Teri was re-booked, I returned to the most pressing matter: what should we ask the president of the United States? Working with political guests was always tricky for an entertainment show like ours. We couldn't look like we were shilling for the White House. The Washington press corps would have a field day. We also couldn't pretend we were *Meet the Press*. The challenge was to come up with some topical and newsworthy questions—maybe even make some news—but to have a little fun along the way. I didn't get much sleep for the next week.

Jay had lots of questions about his favorite subject, automotive technology—enough to fill the entire show several times over. He was especially interested in a local research facility the president would be visiting where they were working on batteries for electric cars. He was also incensed about the millions of dollars in bonuses bankers and others who had been bailed out by the government were getting and wanted to know if somebody should go to jail.

I also added a question about plans to set up a basketball court on the south lawn of the White House, hoping we'd make some news with this small but fun scoop.

I ended up making more revisions to President Obama's notes than I had for any other guest—at least ten rewrites, adding and deleting questions and changing the order, right up until just before the president walked out on stage. I even reworked his introduction numerous times before settling on the simplest one, which reflected Jay's true feelings: "I'm excited and honored to introduce my first guest . . . the forty-fourth president of the United States. Please welcome . . . President Barack Obama.

When it came time for Jay to read those words on the show, I watched from the wings in disbelief as the president entered the stage and took his seat next to Jay. The audience sprang to its feet, cheering wildly. And I noticed that everyone on the crew was dressed up in suits and ties. Something they had never done before.

The Secret Service agents were spread throughout the studio, all doing their jobs in the shadows. Nothing escaped their attention. One of them even had the task of filling and refilling the president's water cup to make sure he was not poisoned.

The president opened the interview with a joke: "I do think in Washington it's a little bit like *American Idol*, except everyone is Simon Cowell." Then he brought up the story about the Secret Service he had told Jay in the dressing room. The audience loved it.

Most of the interview covered the faltering economy, as planned. Mr. Obama said he was "stunned" by the bonus payouts. When Jay asked him if someone should go to jail, he replied that "the dirty little secret" of the mortgage crisis was that "most of the stuff that got us into trouble is perfectly legal." He said laws needed to be changed.

The interview ran about twenty-five minutes with commercials, although it seemed like only a couple of moments to me. I thought it was excellent, but I was a little concerned about a question Jay threw in at the end. He wanted to know if the bowling alley in the basement of the White House—installed during the Nixon administration—had been taken out. It was a dated reference to the presidential campaign when Mr. Obama bowled a dismal 37 (out of 300), worse than most kids. I couldn't hear all of the president's answer in the studio because Jay was talking over it. What he said was that the bowling alley was still there, and he had scored a 129. "That's very good, Mr. President," Jay said, mockingly. "It's like the Special Olympics or something," Mr. Obama shot back. The president was just going for a joke, but it was a potentially offensive remark.

I learned about the president's gaffe right after the segment but didn't worry too much about it. The audience didn't seem to be bothered, and neither the president nor his staff brought it up. So I decided to go to dinner with my wife and some friends. I was ordering my second margarita about an hour later when I got a call on my cell phone from the executive producer, Debbie Vickers. She told me Keith Olbermann had just reported the president's Special Olympics remarks on his MSNBC show. *The Tonight Show* had not yet aired, but Olbermann had seen the internal NBC feed.

Debbie said some of our colleagues were suggesting we edit the president's "politically incorrect" words out of the interview before airing it. We occasionally did this for guests who made gaffes. In this case I thought it was a very bad idea. Olbermann had already broken the story, and the traveling White House press corps had watched the feed, as well, from an adjoining studio. Debbie agreed with me and asked me to check with Robert Gibbs.

When I reached Gibbs, he was already aboard Air Force One with the president en route to Washington, DC. He emphatically asked that the show not make any edits and said the president and his staff would deal with the problem, which they summarily did. While still en route home, the president called and apologized to the chairman of the Special Olympics, Tim Shriver. And the next day Gibbs put out a statement that President Obama believed the Special Olympics were "a triumph of the human spirit" and that he understood they deserved better "than the thoughtless joke that he made last night."

The president's Special Olympics joke became a big story.

While we were hoping to make news with his appearance, this is not what we had in mind. However, the story had no legs, and it was gone within a day because of some very efficient damage control.

The interview with President Obama on that day will always be remembered as Jay's crown-jewel show and my crown-jewel booking. It resulted in our highest ratings in four years. President Obama eventually showed up on other late-night programs and would make three more visits with Jay, for a total of six. During the president's final appearance in August 2013, he gave Jay a special parting gift. Referring to Jay's legendary car collection, Mr. Obama said: "Well, there's one piece that's missing." He then handed Jay a Matchbox replica of his limo, "the Beast," describing it as "the one I drive in." "I assume the real car will be at my garage after the show," Jay said, as the president autographed the roof of the miniature limo.

The mini-Beast, a ⅟₄₃ scale model of the 2009 Cadillac DTX, was actually only worth $29.99, as listed on the website of the manufacturer Luxury Collectibles. But since it was a gift from President Obama and features his autograph, it is one of the most valuable possessions in Jay's extensive, rare collection of expensive vehicles.

Chapter Ten

Political Moments

In 1979, Johnny Carson agreed to a rare interview with *60 Minutes* correspondent Mike Wallace, who asked him why he didn't deal with controversies on *The Tonight Show.* "That's not what I'm here for," the King of Late Night said.

Johnny referred to comedians Jack Benny and Red Skelton, neither of whom ever dealt with issues on their television shows, and cited the danger of an entertainer becoming self-important and using his or her show as a forum. Johnny's concise, thoughtful answer revealed the essence of his late-night format.

While he did monologue jokes about politicians, including seven presidents, he never pushed a political agenda and generally avoided political issues. In his thirty-year reign as *The Tonight Show's* host, Johnny interviewed only four political guests: John F. Kennedy, Robert F. Kennedy, Hubert Humphrey, and Ronald Reagan. In the beginning, we—like Johnny—didn't feature politicians. But that would change—out of necessity.

In its first two years, Letterman's show was consistently drawing larger audiences than Jay's. Our strategy to overcome the CBS late-night show was to book the biggest stars we could. But they were never a ratings guarantee, even if we booked them first. They invariably showed up on Letterman and other shows shortly afterward to promote their multi-million-dollar films, thus diminishing their value to us.

So we turned to politicos to boost our viewership and to attract attention in the press. Jay enthusiastically supported the idea from the beginning. Next to cars, politics was his favorite subject. He was already doing far more political jokes in his monologue than Johnny or David, and he loved the idea of interviewing the leaders of our nation and the free world.

In the beginning, we didn't know if adding politicians to the guest mix would pay off. It seemed risky because, after all, Johnny didn't do it. But as time went on, it would be the political guests, combined with Jay's heavy reliance on political jokes in the monologue, that would be the biggest factor in establishing Jay Leno's *Tonight Show* as truly unique.

Our foray into political bookings started with former president Jimmy Carter in February 1993. Working with him the first time was a bit nerve-wracking. While he comes across as an affable grandfather, privately he's all business. In our first phone conversation, he tersely instructed me to be direct and get to the point, which was unnerving, to say the least. On the day of his appearance, I was there at the studio entrance to greet him and his retinue of Secret Service agents. As we walked down the long NBC corridors, we were silent; I was afraid to make small talk with him for fear of being lectured.

When we reached his dressing room, Jimmy walked in and the Secret Service agents motioned for me to follow him while they waited outside. This surprised me. Stars were often joined in their dressing rooms by large contingents of agents, managers, publicists, executives, makeup artists, hair stylists, friends, family, boyfriends, girlfriends, and self-important people whose title or role was never clear.

When the door closed, it was just Jimmy and me. I nervously asked him if he had any questions. And he said, "Yes, where is the little boy's room?" I pointed out that it was right behind him and started to leave, but he told me to stay as he entered the bathroom and closed the door. *There's something wrong about this,* I thought. *Should I be listening to presidential tinkle?* But I had no choice. Besides, it didn't sound presidential, and for some odd reason I felt more relaxed after that.

Still, I was concerned. We never had a former president on the show before, and he was quiet and business-like. I couldn't help but wonder if he understood that our show was different from CNN. *What if he started talking to Jay about something dull like foreign policy?* I thought. Then Jay stopped by to visit with the thirty-ninth president. When he left the dressing room, he motioned for me to follow him to a place out of earshot of the Secret Service agents. He asked me what I thought of Jimmy, which was code for "Are you sure this is gonna work?" "Terrific," I said, but I had no idea.

As it turned out, Jimmy came alive onstage, proving to be a talented raconteur with some great stories, including an "embarrassing moment" at a recent book signing. A "very nice young lady" approached him, saying: "Mr. President, if you still have lust in your heart, I'm available." No one saw that coming, and it brought the house down.

Jimmy seemed to have a magnetic effect on women. In 1996, he was on with actress Jamie Luner, who was noticeably smitten and gave him an awkwardly long hug after her entrance. During her interview, she couldn't keep her hands off of him and kept touching his arm and grabbing his hand. After that appearance, we advised all political guests to leave the stage after their interviews.

Jimmy's candor as a guest was a refreshing change. While many actors shied away from personal questions, Jimmy didn't hesitate to tell Jay he and his wife Rosalynn almost got divorced over a dual electric blanket that wasn't working properly. And he was serious! On cold winter nights, he was too hot and she was too cold. The dual controls were mistakenly reversed, and when he turned down the heat, her side of the blanket got cooler and his side got hotter.

Rosalynn made her own visit with Jay to talk about another sticking point between her and Jimmy. She thought her husband should never have told *Playboy* magazine that he, a Christian, had lust in his heart in the middle of his 1976 presidential campaign against President Gerald Ford. When the magazine came out just two weeks before the election, his support in the polls dropped precipitously, and he almost lost.

It was fascinating to work with Jimmy as a person and not as a public figure. He had grown up during the Depression, and like many from his generation he did not believe in wasting anything. We had several thousand guests on our show over the years, but he was the only one who left with the complimentary dressing room gift basket and refreshments, including water, soda, and snacks.

He also didn't believe in wasting time, and did everything as efficiently as possible. At book stores he was billed as the "fastest book signer alive," autographing twelve hundred books an hour (which he considered to be a record). When Jay told him Colin Powell could beat that, Jimmy quickly replied that his autographs were more legible.

After Jimmy's success, we put a priority on political bookings. Republican senator Bob Dole came on in 1996 as our first presidential candidate, enduring Jay's jokes about his age (seventy-three). His wife, Elizabeth, appeared in the first comedy sketch ever done by a politico, riding onto the stage on the back of a motorcycle driven by Jay. Before mounting the bike, she said, "Yeah, rev it, baby. Let's get out of here."

By 2000, the major presidential candidates were making regular stops on Leno and, to a lesser extent, David Letterman, who had followed our lead into the political arena. They saw late-night shows as an opportunity to come across to viewers as a regular guy in a way that news and political shows did not afford them. Commentator Christopher Buckley wrote in *TV Guide* that talk shows (especially Leno and Letterman) had become "essential milestones on the road to the White House."

In the presidential contest of 2000, both major candidates, Vice President Al Gore and Texas Governor George W. Bush, were booked separately as guests on Leno only one week before the vote on November 7. These historic bookings would become an important part of the story leading up to our nation's most controversial presidential election. Originally, only Bush was scheduled to appear. The Gore campaign had no plans to come to California, as polls indicated Mr. Gore was a shoo-in there. But on Friday, October 27, I got calls from both the *Chicago Tribune* and the Bush campaign saying they heard the vice president was doing the show on October 31, one day after Bush's scheduled appearance. When I checked with the Gore campaign, they denied the rumors at first but then confirmed them. Later that day, they again said they couldn't commit to the date.

By that point we had already begun recording our Friday show, during which we always promoted our scheduled guests for the coming week, and we made the decision to announce that Gore would be appearing on October 31. This upset the Gore campaign, but they changed their tune later that weekend and once again committed to the date. I learned later that the internal polls, conducted by the two campaigns, were showing Bush had moved significantly ahead of Gore. This may be the reason the vice president came in at the last minute.

While I was exchanging calls with Gore's people, I began getting calls from reliable Clinton insiders. They said President Clinton wanted to make a November 2 appearance with Jay on Gore's behalf. I tried to find out more from White House sources, but I got nowhere. When I checked with the vice president's aides, they abruptly said they hadn't heard about the idea and that Gore wouldn't like it.

In politics, ideas are always floated before being introduced. If that's what was going on, the chilly reaction from the Gore camp to Clinton's offer may have been the reason he never came on the show. I can't help but wonder: What if he had? Clinton is known as a legendary campaigner. Could he have changed the election's outcome? We'll never know.

It was now time to prepare for the two shows, starting with Bush's segment. Jay had final say about all questions, but we usually discussed them with the guests or their people. We weren't really a news show where guests are rarely informed about specific questions beforehand. While that never stopped

Jay from asking presidential candidates tough questions, he just didn't believe in playing the "gotcha" game.

My pre-interview with Bush's staff took very little time. I worked mostly with strategist Mark McKinnon, a low-key, former Nashville songwriter, who said any serious "news" questions Jay wanted to ask were fair game. So we focused on some lighter material about Halloween, which both Jay and Bush signed off on.

The Texas governor was willing to do a comedy sketch poking fun at his tendency to utter gaffes, so we opened the show (cold open) with a pre-recorded bit. It started with a shot of Jay lighting a candle in a jack-o'-lantern.

> Bush: You can't do that. It's flammablebablebable.
> Leno: I think the word you want, governor, is "flammable."
> Bush then pointed to a sign on the wall, which read: "Warning: Highly Flammablebablebable."

"You know, sometimes my mind gets ahead of my words. . . ." Bush said during the interview.

Later Jay pointed out Halloween was the next day, putting on a Bush mask. "That's scary, but this is more scary, Bush said, putting on a Gore mask.

Jay asked Bush about Gore's charges that he wasn't ready to be president. He replied that President Reagan received similar criticism and said, "The more time you spend in Washington, the less qualified you are."

The two also discussed the closeness of the race in Florida, where Bush's younger brother, Jeb, was the governor. Governor George W. Bush jokingly said: "[Jeb] recognizes that Thanksgiving might be a little chilly if things don't go well." Obviously, neither Jay nor Bush had any way of knowing just how tight and crucial the Florida vote would be.

Getting ready for Gore's segment was a little more challenging. I dealt primarily with his speechwriter Eli Attie, a future Emmy-winning writer for NBC's *The West Wing*. He made it clear that Gore wanted no serious questions, summarily rejecting my entire list of about thirty topics.

I understood what Attie was trying to do. Gore had a reputation for being stiff and humorless, and his people saw *The Tonight Show* as an opportunity to showcase him as a down-to-earth, funny guy to millions of potential voters.

We didn't have the luxury to ask Gore all puff-ball questions one week before the election. Some two hundred journalists would be at the taping, as they had for Bush's. They would eat us alive if the segment was all fun and games. Besides, Jay had definite questions in mind, including President Clinton's role in the Gore campaign in view of the candidate's strained relationship with the president and a recent *Rolling Stone* cover photo of the vice president in very tight, khaki pants. He also had some fun topics.

The Gore team eventually signed off on the questions. Of course, they didn't really have a choice. We opened his October 31 appearance with Halloween stories and pictures. The Gores were known for throwing elaborate Halloween parties in Washington, and we had some great pictures of them in costume. The best one featured Gore made up as Frankenstein while taking a call about national security. Buckley's *TV Guide* article described this picture as the "defining moment of the campaign."

Gore deftly handled Jay's serious questions about Clinton and the *Rolling Stone* cover. He said he decided not to appear with the president at rallies because he was running his own campaign. And he dodged Jay's reference to the "very sexy" photo with a clever one-liner: "I thought people read that magazine for the articles."

Interestingly, just before the show Gore cleared everyone out of his dressing room except for his twenty-three-year-old daughter Kristin, who was then a Hollywood writer, and myself. Together father and daughter went over the topics, and she gave him some jokes. In most cases he took her advice over his campaign staff, despite all their efforts. She also advised him to go with a casual look by wearing cowboy boots, which he did. And when he sat next to Jay, he crossed his legs several times to make sure they were noticed.

How much impact did Jay's Halloween interviews with the candidates have on the election? One can only speculate. Both were outstanding guests, and their appearances got extensive—and mostly positive—press, but I would give the edge to Bush. He seemed a little more relaxed and natural than Gore, who may have come across a bit contrived with his heavy reliance on written "funny lines."

Bush's internal poll numbers continued to improve after his Leno interview, and by Thursday, November 2, he was ahead by five points according to Joe Allbaugh, a Bush strategist. This was a definitive lead five days before the election. But then a story broke later that day that would change the course of the election.

It seems Bush had been convicted of a DUI infraction in 1976. While the Texas governor had been open about his past drinking problems, he had not publicly acknowledged the DUI because he didn't want his eighteen-year-old twin daughters to know. As a result, Bush's lead vanished almost overnight, and the campaign was once again a horse race.

I had witnessed both campaigns fashioning their battle plans based on the anticipated close outcome in Florida, but I was truly shocked, along with everyone else, at just how close the vote would be. When Bush was declared the winner, the Democrats responded with legal challenges until the US Supreme Court stepped in and decided in Bush's favor.

After the election, a political science professor offered to do a research project with me on the enormous impact Jay had on this historic election. I declined because I was too busy working on other *Tonight Show* projects, but I regret that decision.

In the next presidential election in 2004, President Bush faced off against Senator John Kerry. During the Democratic primary, Kerry reluctantly agreed to do our show after his campaign was in deep trouble. He was running a distant second to Howard Dean and was facing a growing image problem, as both the press and his political opponents were describing him as indecisive and elitist.

During our pre-interview, Senator Kerry frequently used four-letter words, which seemed odd. I wasn't aware he swore that much. Inconsistent behavior always raised a red flag for me. I couldn't help but think: *Was a major presidential candidate actually trying to impress me by being a potty mouth?*

Kerry said he wanted his segment to be really different, something that would result in a water-cooler moment for viewers the next morning. When I asked him what he had in mind, he told me he wasn't sure but welcomed my suggestions. While this may sound good, it was actually a bad sign.

Many guests said they wanted to reinvent Jay's show, but not once ever suggested how. They all said that was my job. These guests all shared a common trait: instead of looking within, they blamed *The Tonight Show* for being inadequate.

I recommended to Kerry, as I had to the actors, that the best thing he could do during his appearance was to be himself, and I would help him by suggesting topics. That would show people he was a person with three dimensions, not a black-and-white newspaper article or a sound bite on a newscast. But, like some actors, he rejected the idea.

One of our writers—a former Democratic strategist—suggested that Kerry make his entrance onto the stage riding a Harley-Davidson motorcycle. He loved the idea, which he thought addressed his wishy-washy image by showing he was a blue-collar guy. On the day of his appearance Senator Kerry put on a leather jacket, a denim shirt, jeans, and a helmet. Then he climbed aboard the Harley, dramatically rode it through the audience and up a ramp onto the stage, where he was greeted by Jay.

I'll admit it was a pretty good stunt that required some skill, and it would have been effective as a comedy bit had it ended there. But Kerry still had an interview to do, which included questions about health care, recent campaign staff resignations, and his strategy to beat Governor Dean. These were all serious topics, which he answered—while wearing his motorcycle jacket. For a guy so concerned about his image, he was certainly projecting a confusing one.

To make matters worse, he was preceded at the panel by Triumph the Insult Comic Dog, a puppet that was voiced and operated by a sarcastic comedian named Robert Smigel, who said, "The poop I made in the dressing room had more heat than John Kerry."

I believe Kerry's segment was the worst appearance ever made by a political guest. Jay was also unimpressed. Years after the Kerry guest spot, Jay told David Gregory on *Meet the Press* that Kerry was "pushing a little too hard. . . . He rode up a ramp on a bike, you know, and had the leather jacket—he's a regular guy, by golly."

Despite his *Tonight Show* fiasco, Kerry would go on to win the Democratic presidential nomination but would lose the general election to President Bush, largely because of a clever campaign ad inspired by a *Tonight Show* writer, Michael Jann. The ad featured video of Mr. Kerry windsurfing and compared it to his positions on Iraq, education, and health care, which shift "whichever way the wind blows."

He had come up with the original idea for Jay's monologue after seeing news footage of Kerry windsurfing, which struck him as the perfect metaphor for Kerry's tendency to change his positions. So he wrote this joke: "Can you believe John Kerry? Even his hobby depends on which way the wind blows."

Two days after the joke aired, the Bush campaign released the ad. Jann, a Bush supporter, never objected to his material being lifted. He had already been supplying jokes to the campaign, just as some of our other writers were sending jokes to the Kerry campaign. (I also have provided material to politicos.) This was routinely done in all the presidential campaigns during the Leno years. Jay himself sent jokes to selected candidates from both parties.

Hillary Clinton appeared as a presidential candidate on Leno in April 2008. She was in the middle of a hard-fought race against Barack Obama to be the standard bearer for the Democrats, which Mr. Obama would win a few months later. Unlike Mr. Gore, Mrs. Clinton rarely shied away from discussing touchy subjects during her visits with Jay, including a story that she falsely claimed she had been the target of sniper fire during a trip to Bosnia. When she came on the show, she told Jay: "I was so worried I wasn't going to make it. I was pinned down by sniper fire."

The only subject she refused to discuss with Jay was baseball. She had always claimed to be a Chicago Cubs fan and even threw out the first pitch at Wrigley Field in 1994. But in 1999 she professed her loyalty to the New York Yankees while planning a run for the US Senate in New York. This caused a huge backlash against her in both New York and Illinois.

She made her first on-air visit with Jay in 2000 during her Senate campaign. She brought along her own version of Jaywalking, in which she asked people on the street if she should go on Jay's show despite his "mean" remarks about her husband, then President Bill Clinton. "Hillary Walking" was a clever way of using humor to get around all those awkward Monica Lewinsky jokes Jay had been telling.

In a 2003 appearance, she dealt with her husband's dalliances by turning to comedy once again. A tabloid newspaper, *Weekly World News,* published a satirical article purportedly written by an alien named P'Lod that claimed he was having an affair with Mrs. Clinton. She brought the article to my attention, suggesting that Jay might want to bring it up. When he did, she played along, saying the press was blowing the story out of proportion. She insisted that P'Lod, an important official in the Intergalactic Council, had simply accompanied her to an official function at her request. Now he was being held up to undeserved ridicule, and she felt compelled to publicly defend his honor.

In the early years, most of our political guests were presidential candidates, but we made an exception for then GOP Speaker of the House Newt Gingrich, who had a reputation in the press as a firebrand. I began making him weekly offers in 1995, which he consistently declined. About a year later, I learned he was planning to visit the San Diego

Zoo's Wild Animal Park. Turns out he had always wanted to be a zoologist. Who would've thunk? So I invited him to come on the show with some animals. He quickly accepted.

We planned to have him on for two segments. The first would be a typical guest interview. The second would feature Newt as an animal expert along with a newt (naturally), a Sicilian donkey, and two Yorkshire piglets, one for Jay and one for Newt. Before he arrived, we did a rehearsal with the animals so the director could plan for the best camera angles. I stood in for Newt at the rehearsal, which went fairly smoothly except that Jay's piglet squealed whenever he picked it up. He told the animal handler to make sure Newt got that piglet. Then he winked, meaning, "Don't tell Newt about this."

When we did the show, Newt's piglet began squealing as if on cue while Jay's piglet remained calm. "It thinks you're going to eat him, Newt," Jay said. Then Jay exchanged piglets with Newt, just to show the audience that the pig was a squealer by nature and that the Speaker wasn't hurting it. But the little porker calmed down as soon as he got into Jay's arms. The pig wasn't coached to do that. It could have just been a coincidence, or maybe Jay just had a way with animals. Whatever it was, the audience loved it, and Newt appeared to take it in good stride. Besides his overall segment was excellent, and Jay invited him back.

About a year later, the Speaker returned to the show. Much news had happened in the interim and Newt was at the center of it, including an unprecedented balanced budget and an attempted Republican overthrow of Newt as the Speaker. Jay had a lot of questions for him and was very excited he was there. When I welcomed the Speaker back to the show, I had forgotten about the piglets. Unfortunately for me, Newt hadn't. He looked me straight in the eye and bluntly said, "You sabotaged me." I had no idea what he was talking about until he reminded me: "You deliberately gave me that squealing pig," he said.

I was stunned that he knew he had been set up—and that

he cared. So I came clean and admitted we swapped the pigs but insisted we had done it to protect him. I told him Jay's pig had relieved itself several times during the rehearsal and I didn't want Newt's suit to be soiled, so I made sure Newt didn't get that pig. I wasn't worried about Jay's suit because the wardrobe department had plenty of back-ups. I made up the story on the spot, and Newt called me out on it: "Do you think I don't have a back-up suit?" he asked, sarcastically.

I learned a valuable lesson that day: never try to beat one of the most politically astute men in the world at his own game. Much to my surprise, I noticed Newt wasn't really upset. He was just letting me know that no one puts one over on Newt Gingrich. After our exchange, he never brought up the pig incident again during subsequent appearances.

Newt's brusqueness often resulted in unflattering press, but he wasn't the most controversial political guest to come on *The Tonight Show*. That honor belongs exclusively to former vice president Dick Cheney, who was often compared to Darth Vader. When he left office, he wrote a major tome about his eight years in the Bush administration, serving as the country's "most powerful and controversial Vice President." All the major news shows were clamoring to book him, but he told his publisher his first choice was Jay Leno, who he watched every night.

But the show wasn't interested in Cheney at first. Some producers were hesitant to book "the most hated man in the world." But in the end they couldn't resist an exclusive late-night interview with the contentious former vice president who said he was willing to do or discuss anything with Jay. There were no conditions.

For his appearance, Cheney was in a comedy sketch dressed as Darth Vader. Later in his interview, he talked about his checkerboard background while growing up in Wyoming. He had been kicked out of Yale twice for low grades and bad behavior brought on by excessive drinking. He then went to work as an electrical transmission lineman, which he enjoyed. He also liked drinking with his work buddies every night and was arrested twice for driving while intoxicated. He only stopped drinking after his girlfriend and future wife Lynne threatened to leave him. Not exactly the Dick Cheney most people had come to know and despise.

Jay then moved on to more serious topics, such as waterboarding. But now he was no longer talking to the evil Dick Cheney but rather to a guy who had dealt with hardships in his life just like everyone else.

Sarah Palin is also one of the most embattled political figures in modern times. Unlike Cheney, she was never vice president, although she did seek the office as John McCain's running mate. I first learned about Palin while cruising the Inside Passage in Alaska in the summer of 2008.

I was watching the local news in Anchorage when I happened to see a story about "Governor Sarah." I was fascinated that the newscasters didn't even use the last name of this attractive governor. I did a little research and found that polls showed she was unbelievably popular, with approval ratings in the 90s. Some articles referred to her as "the most popular governor in America." *Who is this Governor Sarah, and why haven't I ever heard of her?* I thought.

I had a good working relationship with people at both presidential campaigns, and I called my contacts at the McCain camp to tell them about her. They had not yet picked a running mate, and I thought they might appreciate a report from the field. I'm sure my call didn't make any difference, but about a month later the campaign selected Palin.

I made numerous unsuccessful calls to the McCain campaign to secure Palin as a guest. I found out later that the campaign had been restricting press access to their candidate after her disastrous interview with Katie Couric on *CBS Evening News*, which I thought at the time was a foolish idea. Katie had been floundering as the anchor at *CBS Evening News* and needed a big opportunity, like a "gotcha" interview with Palin. This should have been obvious to any political professional. But it seems the McCain aide responsible for the booking, Nicole Wallace, was good friends with Katie. She denied it, but after the campaign Wallace was hired as a political consultant at *CBS News*.

Throughout the campaign, I never stopped trying to bring in Palin because I thought she had a magnetic appeal to many people. The Democrats also found her irresistible. They loved going after her verbal mistakes, which every politician makes on the campaign trail; but even they couldn't deny Palin held her own against her Democratic opponent Joe Biden in the vice-presidential debate. Biden graciously acknowledged that in an appearance on Leno: "You've got to admit, she has really captivated a large part of the American public. So, you know, I was just a bit player in that debate."

To his credit, Biden made fun of his own verbal gaffes on the campaign trail, including this one: "Jobs is a three-letter word." He told Jay, "Hopefully, you don't make a gaffe in policy. But look, I've made many a gaffe in my life, and I suspect I'll make a whole lot more." If Palin had made a similar appearance on Leno, she would have "killed." A Palin insider told me the McCain campaign's decision to keep her off Leno was just plain "stupid."

When Obama-Biden won in 2008, Palin went on to become a folk hero among conservative Republicans, and I continued pursuing her. After a year and a half she said she was interested, but only if we flew her and her family and friends from Anchorage to Burbank on a private jet. We agreed and leased a Learjet for $35,000 to do the job.

Despite the cost, she was a great get, and the timing was perfect for us, as we were launching Jay's reprised version of *The Tonight Show* after the failed *Jay Leno Show*. A lot was riding on this booking, and I knew we would be heavily promoting it. So just to add a little fun to the segment, I asked Palin to do a brief stand-up routine during her interview with Jay. She had already performed well in comedic sketches on *Saturday Night Live* during the campaign, which got heavy coverage in the media. I was hoping we might also generate a little interest.

I wanted Palin to do a few jokes, just to mix it up. I gave

her twelve jokes, courtesy of the writers, and told her to pick three. But when she read them, she insisted on doing all twelve. She really liked the jokes and was excited about doing something different. So we decided to go with it, promoting the idea that she would be doing a "full set" just like a comedian. The only other non-comedian guest who had done anything like this was—ironically—Katie Couric, who did a monologue.

Jay introduced Palin this way: "Tonight we have a young comedian from Wasilla, Alaska . . . making her first appearance on the show . . . please welcome, Sarah Palin.

She walked out to the mark where Jay did his monologue every night, and did a very respectable job with topical jokes about Alaska, Hollywood, the recent winter Olympics and, naturally, politics:

> It is so beautiful here. So warm. Back home it was freezing. It was five degrees below Congress's approval ratings.

> The truth is . . . I'm glad I'm not vice president. I'm glad because I would not know what to do with all that free time.

Bert Haas, owner of Zanies Comedy Club in Chicago, was so impressed that he gave her an "open invitation" to perform at his club, though she never took him up on it.

Laura Bush never performed stand up on the show, but she told one of the funniest jokes. In a 2004 interview, the charming First Lady mentioned she had been at a political rally in Las Vegas. Jay asked her if she played the slots or went to a Chippendales show. "Jay, what happens in Vegas stays in Vegas," she shot back.

The joke drew huge laughs because nobody saw it coming from the normally reserved First Lady, who got the line from her husband, President Bush. But she didn't stop there. When Jay asked her what the last argument she had with the president was, she deadpanned: "What happens in the White House stays in the White House." Mrs. Bush was one of Jay's most loyal guests. She never appeared on *Letterman*.

Mitt Romney, a Republican who made two unsuccessful runs for president in 2008 and 2012, also preferred Leno over Letterman. But getting him to come the first time in 2007 was no easy task. His senior adviser, Kevin Madden, was dead set against it.

After avoiding my calls for a month, he finally picked up only to tell me that Jay Leno ranked at the very bottom of his priority list: "I would much rather get my candidate on the local news in Hartford than on your show. Am I making myself clear to you?" he asked. He was, indeed. I tried not to take insults personally, but I was taken aback by Madden's rudeness, which served no useful purpose. He could have just politely declined. Besides, his behavior didn't reflect well on his boss, who was known as a decent person. But I'm grateful to Madden. If he had just said no, I might have dropped the matter. But whenever someone smugly tells me I can't do something, I like to prove them wrong. I'm sure Madden had no idea he could be so inspirational.

Actually, going around Madden wasn't too hard, although luck played a big role. Quite by chance, my wife, Mary, and I were good friends with a family (Dennis and Patti King) who knew the Romneys through the Mormon Church. Dennis and Mitt had taken their two-year Mormon mission trip together in France. They were also big fans of Jay and offered to contact the Romneys directly. Two days later, Mitt's son Matt called me to apologize for Madden's behavior and to assure me that his dad would come on the show soon. A few weeks later Mitt made the first of many appearances over a six-year period. His wife, Ann, also came on the show several times.

After Mitt lost the 2012 presidential election, he came on Leno, as well as a few other shows, a few months later to announce his retirement from politics. This was the first time a presidential candidate had chosen a late-night show to make such a momentous statement. After the show, Jay drove the Romneys to his warehouse in Burbank for a personal tour of his huge car and motorcycle collection, a privilege Jay offered to only a select number of guests.

Most of our biggest political gets took a lot of effort, but one just happened out of dumb luck. In January 2010, I booked Scott Brown within days of his stunning victory over his Democratic opponent for the Senate seat previously held by the late Democratic icon, Senator Ted Kennedy.

I thought I had landed the first Republican Senator elected in Massachusetts since 1979 because of my deft skills as a producer, but the booking had nothing to do with me. Minutes before Brown's satellite interview, he told Jay he was doing the interview for personal reasons. His dad, Bruce, had been a frequent guest in Jay's boyhood home after Jay's dad had hired him as a young insurance agent. The two men went on to form a close working relationship. Jay had not realized Brown was Bruce's son until that moment. He confirmed that his family was so close to Brown's dad that they named their dog Bruce. It was a great appearance, but Senator Brown never returned to the show. He lost his Senate seat in 2012 to Elizabeth Warren, a Democratic rising star.

A guest appearance by former senator John Glenn in 1999 also evoked strong childhood memories in Jay, who was in fifth grade in 1962 when Glenn became the first person to orbit the earth. Glenn was a national hero after carrying out his historic, dangerous mission in the midst of a heated space race between the United States and the Soviet Union, our enemy during the Cold War.

Jay's teacher, Mr. Simon, had assigned the class to write a paper about Glenn's historic feat. But Jay's paper came back with a grade of C-minus for substandard and incomplete work. When I booked Glenn, Jay got very excited and called his former teacher to tell him about his upcoming interview. After watching the show, Mr. Simon, who was still teaching in the same classroom, upped Jay's grade to an A, the only one he ever got.

Some of the most unforgettable appearances by political guests happened backstage. Senator Joe Biden came to the studio for an appearance in October 2008 as Barack Obama's running mate in his first presidential bid. I greeted him when he arrived. As I began escorting Biden to his dressing room, the late comedian Steve Bridges, who often parodied President Bush, came into view. He was there to appear in a comedy sketch as the president.

Fully made up, Steve looked strikingly similar to Mr. Bush. Trouble is, I hadn't yet told Biden about the bit, and he mistook the comedian for the president himself: "g—d—, is that you, George?" he yelled out. Steve reacted in character: "Well, why wouldn't it be me, Senator Biden?" he asked. Still in character, he did an exaggerated laugh, pumping his shoulders up and down, just the way President Bush does. Biden loved the performance and talked about it during his visit to the show.

One presidential candidate almost missed his interview with Jay even though he and his wife arrived at the studio on time. Like all guests, they went straight to the dressing room to prepare for his appearance, and everything seemed to be in order. But the door to his dressing room was closed and locked, and one of his aides told us not to bother him.

That was a little unusual, but it was nothing to be alarmed about. Politicians often needed privacy to make phone calls. Besides, we had fifteen minutes before the interview. But soon we were down to ten minutes, and the door was still closed and locked. With five minutes to go, the aide assured us the candidate would be out soon. Somehow, that didn't make us feel better. This was the kind of behavior we expected from a rock singer smoking pot or an actress primping, not a presidential candidate.

With two minutes to go, the director's booth was calling the stage manager demanding to know where the guest was. We had already been reminded several times of how late it was, and now we were being told in a no-nonsense voice: "*We have to go, and he needs to be out here now!*"

All of a sudden, the door opened and the candidate emerged, looking a little sheepish as he straightened his tie and said nothing. His wife, whose hair was mussed and whose lipstick was noticeably smeared, was smiling as she wished her husband good luck. We rushed to the backstage area, arriving just in the nick of time.

The candidate proceeded to do the best interview he had ever done with Jay, and after the show he and his wife left the studio acting as if nothing unusual had happened. And maybe nothing did. After all, no one knows what goes on behind closed doors.

Two guests used Jay's show to announce their political candidacies: Fred Thompson and Arnold Schwarzenegger. Both were actors and both were Republicans who began their campaigns late in the game. Thompson's announcement was highly anticipated, as he had dropped hints about it for months.

Thompson, a former senator from Tennessee, was best known for his role as Arthur Branch, the tough district attorney on *Law & Order*. He came on Leno in September 2007 to launch his bid for the GOP presidential nomination, which resulted in extensive press coverage. But a few months later, he dropped out of the race, giving his support to Senator John McCain, who would eventually become the Republican standard bearer in the 2008 election.

Schwarzenegger's candidacy had a different result. After hinting that he might run for the office of California governor, Schwarzenegger said he would announce his decision during an appearance on Leno in August 2003. This attracted worldwide attention, despite wide speculation he wouldn't run. Political experts and his closest aides believed the Hollywood action star wouldn't jump into the recall election. Arnold himself said he was having second thoughts.

Jay also assumed Arnold wouldn't enter the race and promoted the actor's upcoming appearance by saying he was curious which candidate Arnold would support. Fortunately, the mistake was caught, and Jay re-did the promo by telling viewers to tune in and see what Arnold's decision would be.

When the big moment arrived, Arnold pulled a fast one and announced he was running: "The politicians are fiddling, fumbling, and failing. The man that is failing the people more than anyone else is [California Governor] Gray Davis. He is failing them terribly, and this is why he needs to be recalled, and this is why I am going to run for governor."

Arnold's words caused panic in the studio, as Jay had prepared few questions about the election. He had assumed Arnold was primarily there to promote his new film, *Terminator 3: Rise of the Machines,* and was only using the gubernatorial race to draw attention to the film. During the commercial break, we quickly gave Jay some suggestions. He was up to speed about the election anyway, so the segment was seamless.

Two months later, Arnold won, and Jay introduced the governor-elect's victory speech, saying: "The critics said, 'Well, Arnold can't be an administrator. He is an actor. Oh, Arnold can't be an environmentalist, he is an actor. Oh, Arnold can't be governor, he's an actor.' And of course, Arnold was thrilled—for the first time in his career, the critics are calling him an actor, ladies and gentlemen! This is a historic night."

Jay's introduction drew heavy criticism from liberal pundits. One blogger labeled him a "Republican pawn." Nothing could be further from the truth. Jay participated in Arnold's victory celebration to support his long-time friend, who just happened to be a Republican. If he had run as a Democrat, Jay would have been just as supportive. Besides, Arnold was married to Maria Shriver, a Kennedy, America's most prominent Democratic family.

One question has always intrigued me about Arnold: when did he actually decide to run? He told *Vanity Fair* in 2011 that the idea came to him as he was en route to the show. "I just thought this will freak everyone out. . . ." he said. "It'll be so funny. I'll announce that I'm running."

He said he told Maria and everyone else that he wasn't going to do it. In fact, his announcement did shock his close aides in the studio that day. Their mouths collectively dropped. Maria had a different reaction. A year after the election, she said on Leno that she knew about Arnold's decision and that the two of them had many long and spirited discussions about it for a week.

Arnold's surprise announcement is certainly one of the

show's most memorable moments. But I believe the finest moment was inspired by the atrocities of September 11, 2001, when almost three thousand people died in the horrific terrorist attacks carried out by al-Qaeda.

NBC pre-empted Jay's show that day, which was the right decision. It was not a time for jokes. But when was the right time? A day later? A week? A month? We didn't know. How could we—a comedy and variety show—be relevant when people were in a state of shock and when the nation was essentially at war with an enemy we didn't understand?

Jay decided to call Johnny Carson, which he rarely did. He really needed his legendary predecessor's guidance. Johnny advised him to get back to work because the country was ready for some humor. He also had another recommendation: "When the country has just gone to war, you don't make fun of the king; you make fun of the enemy." Johnny was giving Jay permission to ease up on his jokes about President Bush and to turn up the heat on the terrorists, for the good of the country. He assured Jay that he would be doing jokes about the president again in a few short months and that he would know when the time was right. Jay took Johnny's advice.

Shortly after that, White House FEMA director Joe Allbaugh called me with a message from President Bush, urging Jay to help the country get back to normal by putting our show back on the air. Jay got a similar call from New York mayor Rudy Giuliani's office. We scheduled our first post-9/11 show for September 18, one week after the attacks.

Then we talked about possible guests. Mayor Giuliani was our first choice. As expected, he declined our invitation. Of course he had no time to come to Burbank, but we had to ask. We spent many hours discussing a long list of entertainers and political leaders before offering the spot to Senator John McCain, a long-time friend of the show and a national war hero. Jay himself called Mr. McCain to make the invitation, which he accepted.

The show began with no theme music. Instead, we opened with a somber introduction from announcer Edd Hall as Jay walked out to the monologue mark. But there was nothing funny about his monologue that night. It was still too soon for that. Jay said his prayers were with the families of the victims and those who had died trying to save them. He called the fallen firefighters, police officers, and the Americans who had fought with the terrorists on United Airlines Flight 93 "the greatest people of our generation."

Then he talked about being a Boy Scout at age twelve, admitting he wasn't a very good one. Jay's dyslexia made it difficult for him to do basic tasks like tying knots. His scoutmaster, a wise and compassionate man, designated him as the troop's "cheer master," telling Jay it was his job to tell jokes to keep the guys' spirits up. Jay realized even then that this wasn't the top job. But it was something he could do to contribute to the welfare of the troop. That's how he felt about going back on the air, he said. He knew he wasn't out there shoveling debris at Ground Zero, but at least he could bring a little cheer into the lives of people who needed it.

During his interview, Senator McCain spoke with a soft yet reassuring voice as he called America the greatest nation on earth, a "beacon of hope to everybody throughout the world," including Muslims. He described the terrorists as educated individuals in their forties, not young and impoverished as many commentators had wrongly led people to believe.

Most viewers were aware Osama bin Laden was the 9/11 mastermind. Beyond that, though, not much was known by the public. McCain explained bin Laden's background and motives, describing him as a wealthy Saudi Arabian who had fought against the Russians in the Afghan War. He had actually had a falling out with his own country and turned against America after our troops—who he considered infidels—had been stationed on Saudi soil during the Gulf War. McCain showed a firm resolve, assuring viewers that we would get bin Laden. "God may have mercy on terrorists, but we will not," he stated firmly. And almost ten years later in the dark of night, US Navy Seals would take out bin Laden in a daring raid on his compound in Abbottabad, Pakistan.

Chapter Eleven

News People

From the beginning of *The Tonight Show with Jay Leno*, we sought journalists—reporters and commentators—as guests. The show's original executive producer, Helen Kushnick, believed adding them to the guest mix would be one way to make the show different from *The Tonight Show Starring Johnny Carson*, which mostly featured entertainers. Jay himself was a news junkie, and she figured he would like interviewing journalists. They were also consistently good as guests. Most news people know how to tell a story well—better than most entertainers. Though they're pigeonholed as stuffy and dull, those stereotypes are rarely true. Inside almost every one of them is a comedian dying to get out.

In Jay's twenty-two-year run as host of *The Tonight Show*, only one person filled in for him as guest host, and it wasn't a comedian or an actor. It was a journalist: Katie Couric, the long-time popular co-host of NBC's *Today* show and one of Jay's best guests. Interestingly, we never asked her to be the guest host; it was Katie's idea. She pitched it as a fun opportunity for Jay and her to trade places. He would fill in for her on *Today,* and she would take over for him on *Tonight.* Jay, who had insisted that NBC never hire a permanent guest host for him, did not exactly embrace the job swap, but he didn't openly resist it, either. He told the press: "It's Katie's idea. It's a girl idea. Guys don't say, 'Let's trade places.'"

Katie described the swap as "a fun, goofy thing . . . it's just kind of a lark." In fact, she had carried out a three-year campaign at NBC to have her idea realized, starting with

Jeff Zucker, president of entertainment and her former executive producer at the *Today* show, who rejected the idea at first. But Katie was persistent and eventually prevailed. The job switch was finally approved and scheduled for May 12, 2003. Jay promoted it by attempting to lower viewer expectations: "Katie has the most difficult job. Her show's three hours a day instead of an hour. It's a combination of hard news and entertainment. And ours is just goofy. . . . My job is to make fun of the 11 o'clock news you just saw," he said. Katie, on the other hand, insisted Jay's job was tougher: "Jay has to carry *The Tonight Show* in a very palpable way. So much of the success of the show hangs on Jay's performance and sensibilities. . . . He has to be incredibly topical and funny. . . . I tell knock, knock jokes with my kids, but I'm not sure America is going to concur."

America did concur, and for good reason. "America's sweetheart" put on a respectable monologue and didn't try to pretend she was a professional: "Good evening, and welcome to *The Tonight Show,* or as I call it . . . Extreme Fear Factor." She showed that she could make the transition from news to late night when she drew attention to her "sexy" black cocktail dress. Motioning towards her chest with both hands, she said, "For all you people from LA who've never seen these before, these are actually real." Katie's interviews with guests Mike Myers and Simon Cowell were also excellent, as one would expect from an experienced *Today* show co-host.

At the *Today* show, Jay conducted a satellite interview with Secretary of State Colin Powell, who was in Jerusalem on a peace mission with the Israelis and the Palestinians. Jay's questions were pointed, relevant, and professional. He asked about concessions the Israelis would be willing to make and whether the new Palestinian prime minister could bring an end to suicide bombings. He also wanted to know if Powell would be golfing any time soon with Defense Secretary Donald Rumsfeld, a clever reference to the strained relations between the two men.

This was Jay's third interview with Powell. The first two

were on *The Tonight Show*. The two men were actually friends, sharing a common interest in cars. Powell's hobby was restoring old Volvos; Jay had given the former four-star general some rare Volvo repair manuals and had taken him on a tour of his collection of classic vehicles.

As a ratings stunt, the job swap was a big success. *The Tonight Show's* numbers climbed 40 percent, and *Today* show viewers increased by 9 percent. The switch is on every media list of the most memorable moments at *The Tonight Show with Jay Leno*. Why, then, did Katie push for the switcheroo? I don't think she was after Jay's job, although I do think she intended to show television executives she was capable of more than co-hosting *Today*. In 2012, she became the host of her own talk show called *Katie*. Coincidence? I think not.

Katie Couric wasn't the only talent we booked from the *Today* show. Matt Lauer, Meredith Vieira, Al Roker, Ann Curry, Natalie Morales, Savannah Guthrie, Kathie Lee Gifford, Hoda Kotb, Lester Holt, and Willie Geist were also our guests. We were particularly partial to Matt, who started appearing on Leno in 1994. A true professional who would go on to become one of NBC's biggest news stars, Matt knew what would play well on *The Tonight Show* and was willing to share self-deprecating stories about his well-know fear of germs. One of the most memorable was a tale about his attempt to conquer this fear by working as a garbage collector for a day. It was just one of his many sincere—but failed—efforts to overcome germophobia. He also shared a tip to determine the proper length of time required to wash your hands to make them adequately germ free: just sing "Happy Birthday" twice while scrubbing.

Matt took a hit when his *Today* show co-host Ann Curry was fired in June 2012. Stories surfaced that he disliked her and was behind the decision to get rid of her. In fact, Ann was released because *Today's* ratings took a hit following the departure of Meredith Vieira as co-host in 2011. I have no idea whether Matt Lauer liked Ann, but it didn't matter.

He didn't hire her. NBC executives did. According to press accounts, most of them knew she was a bad fit, but they were afraid she would jump ship to another network if she didn't get the job. So they settled on a co-host less than ideal for their number-one news celebrity and host of the most profitable show at NBC.

Matt's plight was something Jay and his staff could relate to. After all, NBC had fired Jay in 2009 as host of *Tonight* after notching number-one ratings in late-night for fourteen straight years. When his replacement, Conan O'Brien, failed miserably, Jay was demonized in the press and in social media for taking Conan's job. So in an act of solidarity, *The Tonight Show* booked Matt Lauer in May 2013. During the segment, Jay asked his friend and NBC colleague this heartfelt question: "You've been taking a lot of hits in the press lately. How have you been holding up?" Jay didn't frame his query in the context of his own experience. He didn't have to. Matt knew Jay was really saying, *I know what you're going through, and I support you.* At the end of the interview, Matt responded to Jay's words of encouragement: "Through good times and bad times you have been a terrific pal to me."

Brian Williams, known for his legendary sharp wit, was never funnier than in his 1996 appearance on *Tonight* with fellow guests Jane Fonda and Cher. Back then he was not the anchor of *NBC Nightly News,* and the two women didn't know who he was. Smitten by the handsome young newsman, they were giggling like school girls and speaking in hushed tones so he couldn't respond to them. He had lost control, a rare moment for Brian.

Finally, Jane spoke up: "Who is he? I think he's kind of cute." Cher agreed that he was good-looking, but "in a Republican kind of way." Without missing a beat, Brian shot back: "I guess I'm going to have to return my copy of *Half Breed* that I just bought."

Tim Russert, the legendary "blue collar" moderator of *Meet the Press*, was a regular guest for many years and a friend of the show. On June 13, 2008, he died suddenly of a heart attack while working on a *Meet the Press* segment. That night Jay paid tribute to his friend at the end of his monologue: "When you talked to Tim about politics, it was like talking to a guy on the bar stool next to you. He never talked down to you, even though he knew way more than you do." Jay brought up a historic moment in NBC's coverage of the 2000 presidential election when Tim held up a white board with the words "Florida, Florida, Florida" written on it. Long before other pundits figured it out, Tim had identified the election's pivotal state. Jay had done many monologue jokes about the white board, and during the Christmas season one year Tim came on with a gift: a white board with the words "Jay, Jay, Jay."

Whenever the NBC News Washington bureau chief was a guest, he and Jay had lengthy discussions about the latest news and gossip before the show, much to the chagrin of the stage manager who had the daunting task of keeping Jay on schedule. Tim's special relationship with Jay and the show was not only professional but also personal. Years ago, his beloved dad, "Big Russ," a salt-of-the-earth garbage truck driver, told Tim he'd know he made it when he got on *Johnny Carson*. And when we first booked Tim (September 8, 1992), he brought his dad to the show. Afterward, they went to dinner at the trendy Los Angeles restaurant Spago at the invitation of Maria Shriver, then an NBC news correspondent. Both men ordered pizza and beer, which baffled Maria. "I could have taken you guys to Shakey's," she said

In 2004, Tim wrote a best-selling book about Big Russ. He told Jay that working on the book made him closer with his own son, Luke, which led to a story about a tattoo Luke had secretly gotten on his side against his father's advice. Later, Luke accidentally disclosed the body art to his shocked parents. Tim angrily demanded that his son lift his arm and show him the full tattoo. When Luke reluctantly complied, Tim saw the letters TJR—Tim's initials, and also Big Russ's. Luke said he was inspired to order the tattoo after reading his dad's book. "I wanted you and Grandpa to always be on my side," Luke said. Tim said his son's story left him speechless, moving him to tears and laughter at the same time. Luke would decide to follow in his dad's footsteps, and today he is a reporter for *NBC News*.

Tim loved telling Jay fun anecdotes, such as his foray into booking music acts while in law school. He once took a huge risk by hiring an unknown singer named Bruce Springsteen to perform at a large venue. He filled every seat. Tim made both a great discovery and $4,000, enough to pay for a year of his law school education. He also went on to become friends with Bruce and often attended his concerts with Luke.

Tim tried for years to get Jay to ask him about his "favorite" story, but, sadly, he never did because of limited time. It was about Mary Matalin and James Carville, the married odd couple of politics. James is a Democrat, and Mary is a Republican. As regular guests on *Meet the Press*, they bickered frequently on the air, which was very funny. One of their verbal spats started in the MTP green room before the show and continued on the air and during the commercial breaks. When the program ended, they kept arguing while walking off the set. Tim looked out the window and noticed they were still at it in their car as they were driving away. Later, they were pulled over by a cop who became concerned after seeing them wildly waving their arms and yelling at each other.

Jay made one appearance (May 1994) on *Meet the Press*. I accompanied him to the show in Washington, DC, and I remember being struck by how convivial the mood was in the green room before the show. Tim was smiling as he introduced the guests to each other, and Jay was telling jokes. Then when the show started, Tim shifted into his MTP persona, putting all of his guests, except Jay, on the hot seat. Jay was asked what political stories his audience found funny: "Sex and money are always the best . . . they are the kind of jokes people understand. . . . Most people don't have nuclear weapons in the backyard, but they have, well, the guy next door," Jay said.

Meet the Press, the longest-running show on network television, was an American icon, but it was on life support when Tim took it over in 1992. In his seventeen years as host, Tim restored the venerable Sunday morning news program to its old glory as must-see TV for political junkies and an essential stop for the biggest names in politics. And as our show became known as an essential stop for presidential hopefuls, Tim was always available to help me with contact information for political guests, often making calls on our behalf. He was not only my good friend but also, I believe, the greatest American journalist of our time. When he died, he left a void that has never been replaced.

I knew columnist and commentator Tony Snow long before he was named President Bush's press secretary in 2006. He was a good person, and we soon became friends. A conservative, he was widely respected by people on the left and the right. When he got his own radio show in 2003, I sent him guest ideas and jokes on a regular basis, which he never forgot. When Tony was hired by the Bush administration, he invited my wife, Mary, and me to his new office in the West Wing of the White House. He was full of ideas on how to improve the administration's strained relationship with the press, which he shared with us. In the days that followed, he would become one of the most articulate and open press secretaries in modern times. About a year later he took a leave of absence to seek treatment for a recurrence of colon cancer, which was spreading to his liver. In September 2007, he decided to step down as the president's chief spokesman.

I booked Tony to do the show two weeks later. He updated Jay about his cancer, saying it was in remission after chemotherapy treatments and was treatable, but not curable. He said he would miss the small things about his job, like walking into the Oval Office to visit with the president or watching the Marine One helicopter lifting off from the South Lawn of the White House. Still, he believed cancer was the best thing that ever happened to him; it taught him to count his blessings, and he realized how much he loved and cared about people.

Tony then revealed that he was moving on from his position

not because of his illness but because he just wasn't making enough money in his government job. He was planning to give speeches and write books, which would be much more lucrative. It seemed like an odd statement to me. When Tony went to work for President Bush, he knowingly gave up a much higher-paying career as a journalist. I worried that the cancer was worse than he had led us to believe.

After the show that night, Mary and I had dinner with Tony to celebrate his successful appearance. That's when he confirmed what I had suspected. The cancer was fatal, and he was on limited time. The real reason he needed to boost his earnings was to ensure his young family's financial security when he was gone. There was no sadness in his voice, only cheerfulness, which I believe was rooted in a deep and abiding religious faith. Tony called me several times after that, mostly to cheer me up when the show was going through a rough patch. But I never saw him again. He died on July 12, 2008, at the age of fifty-three

After his first appearance on *The Tonight Show* in 2001, Chris Matthews quickly became our go-to news person. Steeped in Democratic politics before becoming a commentator on *Hardball,* his MSNBC show, he had been a speechwriter for the Carter administration and a top press aide to House Speaker Tip O'Neill. Chris had strong, edgy opinions and was a fast, enthusiastic talker. Fellow guest Chelsea Handler once teased him by asking if he could speak any faster. Without missing a beat, he replied, "My dear, you're beautiful, but if you concentrate, you can keep up."

Off the air, carrying on a phone conversation with Chris could be challenging. He would speak continuously in one long sentence, jumping from subject to subject. In one conversation with me, he rambled on for thirty minutes, cutting from President Obama to the Republicans to his upcoming airline reservations before I could even ask one question. There seemed to be no editing going on. Sometimes Chris engaged in stream of consciousness on MSNBC. While covering a 2008 speech by Barack Obama, then a presidential candidate, Chris said, "I have to tell you . . . it's part of reporting this case, this election, the feeling most people get when they hear Barack Obama's speech. My, I felt this thrill going up my leg. I mean, I don't have that too often." Chris never tried to distance himself from that remarkably honest remark, saying Mr. Obama represented to him the opportunity for the country to move beyond its racial divide. From that point, Chris appeared to take a turn to the left as a commentator. Then, in 2011, he started shifting to the right, calling the national media "a little liberal." And by 2013, the thrill in Chris's leg was a little less intense: "[President Obama] obviously likes giving speeches more than he does running the executive branch," he said on *Hardball*.

During his many visits with Jay, Chris discussed his struggle with liberal and conservative ideas, calling himself a liberal in his heart and a conservative in his mind. It was fascinating to watch. I believe he would have made an excellent moderator of *Meet the Press*. He had already been hosting a similar syndicated weekly program (*The Chris Matthews Show*) with much success. His interviews were tough but fair, in the great tradition of Tim Russert.

Unlike Chris, Rush Limbaugh never had any doubt about his political worldview. He was a conservative, through and through. From his earliest days on national radio, starting in 1988, Rush was a force to be reckoned with. He had tapped into a backlash against liberalism in the media like no one else before him, using sardonic humor and biting satire. He re-framed conservatism as an *us v. them* cause and re-defined mainstream media as posers who were actually "liberals" running America into the ground. His daily radio show rocketed to number one in the nation with twenty million weekly listeners, making him the most popular radio personality ever.

But at *The Tonight Show*, I couldn't sell Rush as a guest to save my soul. My colleagues thought he was too polarizing, too mean, and too bigoted. They were just citing what they had read in the media and heard from their friends in Hollywood. They didn't listen to Rush, as I did. Then one day Debbie Vickers, the executive producer, said she thought booking Rush was a good idea. She had heard from friends and family who were regular listeners and fans of the conservative talk show host. We ran the idea by Jay and he approved it. By this time, I had already been reaching out to Rush's chief of staff, Kit Carson. The popular radio pundit had his own doubts about Jay and his intentions. After all, Jay was in the mainstream media. Rush didn't get on board for months. Eventually, Roger Ailes, the executive producer of his television show, persuaded him that a spot on Leno could introduce him to a lot of potential new listeners.

In February 1994, Rush sat down next to Jay and talked about his early days as a disc jockey, when he got fired for playing "Under my Thumb" by the Rolling Stones too many times. Then he turned to politics, saying he would never run for office despite his strong political views. Why? To begin, "candidates have to spend too much time raising money," he stated. But if he ever did run, it would only be for one term. "That way no one would get any special favors," he said. This show, which did well in the ratings and got heavy press coverage, represented a sea change in our approach to bookings. My colleagues were now more willing to book controversial pundits they disagreed with. As for Rush, he was happy with his interview and even did a comedy bit with us shortly after that. Then a few years later Jay did a joke implying Rush was a racist and a Nazi. I got a call from Carson the next day saying the joke went too far and that Rush was deeply hurt by it. It would take years to mend that fence. Rush did not return until September 2009 for the new *Jay Leno Show* prime time program. This time my colleagues welcomed Rush with open arms. Our ill-fated 10 p.m. show was struggling from the beginning, and we needed all the help we could get.

Rush had agreed to be part of an ongoing feature called "The Green Car Challenge." In this bit, the guests drove an electric Ford Focus prototype around a track in the parking lot outside the studio, racing against the clock. The driver with the fastest time was the winner. The idea was to promote the "environment." A cutout of environmentalist Al Gore was placed on the track as an obstacle. If a driver hit "Al," they lost points. Rush, never a fan of the former vice president or electric cars, went out of his way to smash into "Al Gore." Then he backed up and hit the cutout again before completing the course with a record slow time, which was his intention. Rush turned the bit into a satirical farce, his stock-in-trade. It was a rare funny moment for a bit that was very unfunny and intolerably preachy.

Sometimes we just got off to a bad start with our guests. In 1994, liberal documentary filmmaker Michael Moore showed up for his scheduled guest spot with a short, "funny" videotape he was planning to show during his segment. He had our permission to do it, but we hadn't seen the tape until that day. When we watched the video, we killed it because we thought it was mean. The future Oscar-winning director wasn't happy with our decision, but he accepted it . . . until about forty-five minutes before the start of the show, when he walked into my office threatening that he would bolt if we didn't run his tape unedited. He knew as well as we did that he had us over a barrel, as there was no time to bring in another guest. So we gave in. I remember thinking during the confrontation that it felt like a stunt he would pull in one of his documentaries. We did not take kindly to Michael's demand, and we had a falling out with him that lasted ten years. By then he was an established documentarian and never made another unreasonable demand.

Like Rush Limbaugh, Michael made his final appearance on *The Jay Leno Show*. We gave him high-profile promotions, which surprised even him. He posted this message on his website: "Last night Jay Leno premiered his new prime time show on NBC. His in-studio guest was Jerry Seinfeld. Tonight (Tuesday), for his second show, his guest is . . . me! I know—that's crazy. My friends are taking bets on the exact hour today the executives at GE will call and pull the plug

on this insanity. Or not." During his segment he sang Bob
Dylan's "The Times, They Are a Changin'." He was not a
good singer, and his rendition was rough, even by Dylan's
standards. It was part of the format in the prime time show
called "Earn Your Plug," which required a guest to do a
"stunt" if they wanted to show a clip from their film or hold
up their book. Like most ideas on the show it was so bad,
it was embarrassing. But Michael was a good sport, and he
tried his best. This time, he didn't back us into a corner. We
did that ourselves.

Jay used to warn comedians who were political activists,
"You start out as a comedian, then you become a political
humorist. Then you become a political satirist. Then you
become a commentator. Then you're out of show business."
That's what happened to Al Franken, who made seven
appearances on *The Tonight Show* starting as a comedian
in 1992 and ending as a commentator in 2005. In 2009, he
was elected to the US Senate in Minnesota and out of show
business. By his last appearance, Al was hosting the premiere
show on the now-defunct liberal radio network *Air America*.
He made little pretense at being funny, and backstage his
behavior was very controlling. He wanted to see every single
page of the show notes in my hands, demanding that Jay not
ask any other questions than what we had agreed to. Jay
could ask anything he wanted, and he often did. I didn't tell
Al that. Confrontations just before show time were never a
good idea. I just said Jay would stick to the list. The interview
went on as planned, except Al wasn't funny.

Bill Maher, host of HBO's *Real Time*, followed a similar
path. Like Al, he was a comedian who became more and
more political, leaning to the left. But unlike Al, Bill never
forgot that his job was first and foremost to be entertaining.
He often blurred the line between being a comedian and a
pundit, and we sometimes didn't know if he was making a
joke or a serious point. Usually, it was both, and he did it
skillfully. He was a consummate professional.

Next to Terry Bradshaw, Bill made more appearances

than any other guest. He debuted as our first comedy correspondent in New York on New Year's Eve 1993. He and Jay were competitive but supportive of each other, eventually becoming friends. In 2002, ABC cancelled Bill's late-night show, *Politically Incorrect,* when he agreed with one of his guests that the 9/11 terrorists were not cowards: "Staying in the airplane when it hits the building. Say what you want about it. Not cowardly." It was a poor choice of words, but that can happen when you're doing an unscripted show called *Politically Incorrect.* Bill did not intend for his remarks to be anti-military, but that's how they were perceived. Jay backed him throughout the ordeal and booked him in 2003 to plug his return to the air as the host of *Real Time.*

At the height of the controversy with Conan O'Brien in 2010, when NBC offered *The Tonight Show* gig back to Jay, Bill came to Jay's defense on *Larry King Live:* "The one place I would criticize Conan and David Letterman was when they did these jokes along the lines of . . . 'You can have anything you want, unless Jay Leno wants it.' Okay, you're not a kid who had his ice cream knocked onto the sidewalk by Jay Leno. Jay Leno beat you for something because, for whatever reason, Jay Leno has his finger on the pulse of mainstream America better than anybody." I always enjoyed working with Bill and considered him a friend. Some of my colleagues thought he was testy, but I found him surprisingly friendly and supportive, although he was a bit idiosyncratic. He was a strict vegetarian and refused to appear on the show when animals were featured. He was also a night owl, so I could never reach him before 2 p.m. An avowed atheist, he despised organized religion. This was a subject Jay tried to avoid, but Bill slipped it into the conversation whenever he could. Atheism was his passion; in a way, it was his religion.

When I left *The Tonight Show* in 2010, Bill was the last guest I ever worked with. Although we were friends, I was at the opposite end of the political and religious spectrum from him, though I never let him (or any other guest) know my views. I decided on a whim to fess up to him that day. I told him I thought he was one of the funniest, most thought-provoking, and kindest people I ever worked with. Then I said: "I basically don't agree with anything you stand for. And besides, I teach Sunday school every week. I'm glad I got to work with you." He came over and hugged me, saying he hoped we could work together again someday. When I introduced him to my replacement he said, "You don't teach Sunday school, do you?"

Jay liked the ladies of *The View,* and so did I. Their daily "Hot Topics" segment, which featured their differing views about popular culture and politics, was entertaining. So I extended them a standing invitation to come on the show any time. But the women only made two appearances together, one in 2003 and the other in 2004. After that, Joy Behar said she wanted to be booked as a solo act. She considered herself a comedian and said she couldn't do her jokes while the others were out there with her. Trouble is, Joy's material was uneven, and she often forgot the first rule of comedy: you have to be funny. And being mean isn't being funny. In a 2010 appearance, she and Jay were talking about Glenn Beck, then a host on Fox News Channel. Joy claimed Glenn hated her. Jay said he often had people on his show whom he disagreed with and wanted to know if she would consider inviting Glenn to appear on her now-cancelled HLN cable show. She said she'd like to give Glenn a message: "Glenn Beck, from the bottom of my heart, I don't hate you. I don't give a flying f— about you."

Not everyone shared Joy's indifference toward Glenn. In September 2009, *TIME* did a cover story on the controversial host, featuring a picture of him sticking out his tongue with this headline: "Mad Man: Is Glenn Beck Bad for America?" When the story came out, I immediately showed it to my colleagues who, until then, had no interest in booking the hugely popular, wacky, firebrand conservative-libertarian radio and television host. They thought Glenn was a right-wing nut job. But now that *TIME* had "discovered" him, they were interested. Besides, I argued, we needed guests who could make a difference in the ratings with our failing prime time *Jay Leno Show,* and no other major talk shows were touching Glenn. We would be the first. Debbie Vickers and Jay agreed. I wasn't concerned about Glenn's political views, though I did worry that he might be a little crazy. I listened regularly to his radio show and knew he said some off-the-wall stuff, often embracing conspiracy theories that reflected his personality more than his politics. While other conservatives talked about the impact of the growing national debt, Glenn was predicting that economic collapse was imminent.

When I booked him in December 2009, some staffers complained that they were personally offended. I had no regrets as it was one of the most unique guest spots on *The Jay Leno Show,* as well as one of the best interviews Jay ever did. He called Glenn a polarizing figure as soon as he sat down. But Glenn insisted he was not divisive but rather a regular guy who "hated" both political parties. He said he was more Libertarian than Republican and admitted he would have preferred Hillary Clinton over John McCain in 2008. He quickly added, "That's like, gee, do I want to hang myself or shoot myself?" Then he made a case for cutbacks and sacrifices because "the debt is unsustainable," which he claimed the Obama administration didn't seem to understand.

To earn his plug, Glenn showed Jay how to make sugar cookies for Christmas using his grandma's "secret" recipe. It actually was fun watching the two men mix in excessive amounts of powdered sugar, flour, and other ingredients on a set that was festively decorated for Christmas. After the show, Glenn asked me to show him Studio 1, where Johnny Carson hosted *Tonight* for twenty years. An expert on the early days of broadcasting, he was very curious about everything. So I showed him the spot about forty feet back from the audience where Johnny did his monologue, along with the old seats—465 in all—built with a steep escalation right up against the back wall. He wanted to know all the shows that had been filmed there. I told him that list included *This Is Your Life, Truth or Consequences,* Bob Hope Specials,

Hollywood Squares, The Gong Show, and *The Tonight Show with Jay Leno* (for about a year and a half). A few months later, Glenn returned to Burbank with his wife, Tania, and his kids to see Jay's collection of more than two hundred cars and motorcycles. My wife, Mary, and I were invited to join in as Jay showed us his vintage Duesenbergs, Bugattis, Lamborghinis, Bentleys, McClarens, and Stanley Steamers.

Another controversial figure at Fox News Channel is Bill O'Reilly. A former reporter, Bill became a commentator when he launched his nightly *O'Reilly Report* in 1996 (renamed *The O'Reilly Factor* in 1998), which quickly became the most successful news show in cable. I thought he was the most compelling and unique commentator in television news. He is knowledgeable and capable of making the most complex topics understandable and interesting. He tends to be conservative on most, though not all issues, and he emphasizes his sharp, often acerbic opinions in his "Talking Points" segment at the top of his show every night. He is also confrontational with many of his guests, holding them accountable for their actions.

I began pitching Bill as a guest almost as soon as I started watching *The O'Reilly Factor* in 2000, but my colleagues thought he came across as too mean. It's true, he often has little patience for politicians and others who don't answer his straightforward questions, but he's also number one in the ratings. In time I wore my colleagues down, and we booked Bill for the first time in March 2001. He turned out to be charming and even amusing, as well as a ratings plus. We invited him back many times, and he went on to become one of our most popular news guests.

I continued to work with Bill each time he was on our show, and I have to give a shout out to him: the very idea of this book was his, and I thank him for it.

After I left *The Tonight Show* in 2010, Bill and his executive producer David Tabacoff met with me to see if I would be interested in booking Hollywood entertainers on *The O'Reilly Factor,* which had not featured many actors.

"You mean you want me to book the folks you call pinheads every night?" I asked. I just let that slip out without thinking, and I was worried about how Bill would take it. He thought it was funny, and that's when I knew I could work for him.

In January 2011, they hired me temporarily to help bring in Hollywood celebrities. When *The O'Reilly Factor* set up shop at the FOX studios on West Pico Boulevard in Los Angeles, I was curious to see how the number-one cable news program operated compared to the number-one late-night show. The two programs were similar in many ways, though they also had their differences. Both existed in a constant crisis environment, and both lived by one rule: the show must always go on, no matter what. Expectations were high at both shows. No excuses were tolerated for not producing the best program possible. At *The O'Reilly Factor* there was no such thing as a slow news day. Producers had to come up with good story ideas even if there didn't seem to be any. At *The Tonight Show*, writers had to come up with funny jokes, even in a news drought. And it was never acceptable for producers to say no good guests were available. We had to keep looking until we found them.

How were the shows different? Other than the personalities of the two hosts, there wasn't much difference. Both Bill and Jay were demanding of and loyal to their staffs, although Jay often relieved the constant stress with jokes. At *The O'Reilly Factor,* Bill worked closely with the producers, sitting in on their meetings and seeking their opinions, but he was clearly the final arbiter of every programming decision. Jay was more of a team player. He had control over the comedy, but he delegated decisions about booking guests to the producers. However, Jay could veto any guest idea he didn't like. Both shows were hugely successful on a level that may never be matched again in either news or entertainment.

Chapter Twelve

Sports Greats

Athletes appealed to viewers more than any other group of celebrities, including big-name actors. But Jay wasn't much of a sports fan, so we didn't book many athletes at first. However, nothing brought the studio audience to its feet faster than a sports superstar who had just led a team to victory in a championship game, such as the Super Bowl. I also think we're attracted to athletes because we sense they're basically freaks of nature, super humans able to accomplish feats we mortals can't even comprehend. Yet like us, they're vulnerable.

Most athletes liked Jay because he seemed like a regular guy, and they were impressed when he hung out with them in the dressing room before the show. I think it surprised Jay when he recognized he and athletes had common traits. Like him, they were competitive, had a strong work ethic, and believed in personal responsibility.

In September 1995, Major League Baseball's Cal Ripken Jr. broke Lou Gehrig's fifty-six-year record of 2,130 consecutive games. It was a huge story, and Cal would become our first big sports "get." This was a sports booking Jay could relate to.

After all, Cal was being honored for showing up to work every day and never calling in sick, no matter how he felt. In fact, he had a fever for the three days leading up to his record-breaking game and couldn't sleep. Still, there was no way he was going to miss it. By the time he retired in 1998, Cal had played in 2,632 consecutive games over a seventeen-year period. Like Cal, Jay would also work seventeen years without missing a day, notching 3,750 shows between 1992 and 2009. He called in sick for two days after checking into a nearby hospital, reportedly for dehydration, but he never missed a day of work after that.

In time, many of Jay's consistently best guests would come from the sports world, including the NBA Hall of Fame's Charles Barkley and Dennis Rodman and the NFL Hall of Fame's Terry Bradshaw. Terry, a four-time, Super Bowl-winning Pittsburgh Steelers quarterback, held the record for the most appearances on *Tonight* (almost sixty) and never made a bad one.

Audiences loved Terry's goofy, off-the-wall remarks, and so did Jay. Terry didn't hesitate to give Jay a hard time about embarrassing subjects like his ignorance of sports and, more recently, his impending retirement. In June 2013, he teased Jay: "You love cars, you love your wife, and soon you're gonna know how much you love her because you're not gonna have this gig anymore."

Athletes and their coaches were the most superstitious people I've ever met. Most were open about it, admitting their behavior was irrational. And it was understandable. They frequently had little control over the events in their lives, such as referees' bad calls, erratic weather, and injuries. Jay, who was also superstitious, never failed to cover their rituals and good luck charms. Here are some of my favorites.

Golfer Tiger Woods wore a red shirt each Sunday (usually the last day of PGA tournament play) because his mom, who read his astrological charts, said it was his strong color. The color was also a nod to his alma mater, Stanford University.

When Shaquille O'Neal played for the Los Angeles Lakers, he painted his toenails black for every game. It started when his big toenail came off during a game and he painted the nail-less area black. That night, he scored a career-high 61 points. He also wore a new pair of size-23 shoes in every game, which added up to about one hundred pairs a season. When Jay asked him if he did this for good luck, he said no, he just liked new shoes.

San Francisco 49ers quarterback Joe Montana, who owns

four Super Bowl rings, talked about a superstition his coach George Seifert believed in. Seifert always had to be the last one out of the locker room, but Joe, the team clown, would sometimes mess with his coach. They were usually the last ones in the clubhouse at the end of the day, and Joe would start to exit and then stop and turn around, saying he forgot something. Sometimes he did it several times, driving Seifert crazy.

Turk Wendell, who pitched for the Chicago Cubs in the 90s, shared with Jay his lengthy pitching ritual: he wore the number 13 for luck, chewed four pieces of black licorice, brushed his teeth between every inning, and never stepped on base lines. He also wore a necklace adorned with mountain lion claws and wild buffalo teeth. Turk would later be named the most superstitious athlete of all time by *Men's Fitness* magazine.

Turk was a perfect fit for the hard-luck Cubs, a team that has not won the World Series since 1908. Many people have attributed this dry spell to a long-standing superstition that began when a billy goat was refused admittance to Wrigley Field at the 1945 World Series. This upset the goat's owner, Billy Sianis, who declared the Cubs would never win another World Series. His declaration became known as the Billy Goat Curse. Some believe it has kept the Cubs from even getting into the World Series since that time.

In 1996, while *The Tonight Show* was taping in Chicago, Cubs star first baseman Mark Grace was booked to exorcise the curse. He introduced Sam Sianis, Billy's nephew, who came out with a billy goat and made this declaration: "I hereby remove the Curse of the Billy Goat. The Cubs are the World Series pick for 1996."

The Cubs did not make it into the World Series that year—or any other year since then. However, after being traded, Mark kicked off a Series win in 2001 with a single for his new team, the Arizona Diamondbacks. Sometimes, good luck has a mind of its own.

When the Anaheim Angels defeated the San Francisco

Giants in the 2002 World Series, five members of the team—
Tim Salmon, David Eckstein, Troy Percival, Scott Spiezio,
and John Lackey—came on *The Tonight Show* to give credit
to the "rally monkey" for their victory. The monkey first
showed up on the stadium's video board in 2000 during a
game when the Angels were trailing the Giants 5-4 in the
bottom of the ninth inning. The clip, taken from Jim Carrey's
1994 hit comedy *Ace Ventura: Pet Detective* showed a
monkey jumping up and down. Shortly after that, the Angels
scored two runs and won the game. Two years later, the
monkey would bring the team the luck they needed to win its
first championship in forty-two years.

In 2004, the Boston Red Sox swept the St. Louis Cardinals
in four games to reclaim the title World Series champions,
breaking an eighty-six-year losing streak, second only to the
Cubs. It was the biggest sports story to break during Jay's
run as host. And since Jay was from Boston, we pulled out
all the stops to get the team on the show. The Red Sox even
considered chartering a jet to fly the entire team to Burbank,
but the cost was prohibitive.

Instead, we booked five players: David "Papi" Ortiz,
Derek Lowe, Mike Timlin, Dave Roberts, and Alan Embree.
When star player Papi Ortiz balked, Jay, a Boston native,
got on the phone with his agent to make the case that Papi
should do the late-night show hosted by the hometown boy.
The agent quickly agreed to the booking. When the team
members made their entrance, they were showered with red,
white, and blue confetti, and later Jay literally ripped off his
shirt to reveal a "Who's Your Papi?" T-shirt.

He asked the players about a rumor that the team had
participated in a ritual: taking shots of Jack Daniel's whiskey
before each World Series game. They denied it (wink, wink).
But the real significance of the Red Sox triumph was that
they had finally overcome the so-called curse of the Bambino.
Like the Cubs, the Red Sox had been under the shadow of a
superstition, and they hadn't won a championship since 1918
when they beat—who else?—the Cubs.

The bad luck apparently began when the Red Sox traded Babe Ruth, known as the Bambino, to the New York Yankees. So it was only fitting that Boston would bounce back from a 0-3 deficit, winning four consecutive games to defeat the Yankees in the best-of-seven American League Championship Series, which led to the Red Sox's momentous championship.

Athletes told Jay inspiring stories of how they prevailed against all odds to achieve their goals. In 2000, Kurt Warner hurled a seventy-three-yard-touchdown pass to clinch the Super Bowl for the St. Louis Rams as they downed the Tennessee Titans 23-16. Five months earlier, he was the Rams' back-up quarterback, playing for a yearly salary of $250,000 (the minimum wage in the NFL). He was only moved up after starting quarterback Trent Green blew out his knee in a pre-season game, knocking him out for the season.

Then Kurt admitted to Jay that after he was let go by the Green Bay Packers five years earlier he was stocking shelves for $5.50 an hour at a grocery store in Cedar Falls, Iowa. He credits that job for helping him become a better player. He was working late hours when there were few customers, which allowed him to practice his passing by tossing Nerf balls, toilet paper rolls, and candy down aisle nine.

In 2010, hockey great Patrick Kane scored the winning goal in overtime against the Philadelphia Flyers, making the Chicago Blackhawks the Stanley Cup champions for the first time in forty-nine years. The team, once described by ESPN as the worst in all of professional sports, had undergone an unbelievable turnaround in three years, led by Patrick, Jonathan Toews, Duncan Keith, and Brent Seabrook.

Those four players showed up with the Stanley Cup at *The Tonight Show* five days later to celebrate their miraculous victory. The audience saw video highlights of Patrick's winning goal followed by footage of Duncan taking a puck to the face, which knocked out seven of his teeth. Still, he insisted on rejoining his team on the ice within minutes. He then presented Jay a necklace adorned with a prop tooth, which he wore for the rest of the show.

Some of the most outstanding coaches in sports made regular visits to the show. Phil Jackson holds a record eleven NBA titles as a coach and is arguably the greatest of modern times. He definitely gets my award as the most interesting coach to appear on *Tonight*. Known as the Zen Master, he had total control of his team and his emotions on the court and was soft-spoken off the court. Jay, not a fan of coaches in general, really liked Phil's understated style and genuinely enjoyed having him as a guest.

Phil's players included some of the greatest stars in the NBA, such as Michael Jordan, Kobe Bryant, Shaquille O'Neal, Scottie Pippen, and Dennis Rodman. Most of Phil's players loved and supported him, and he was a father figure to many. Some had huge egos, and Phil's challenge was to motivate them to become team players.

He regularly used his appearances on *Leno* and other shows to send messages to his players. He would criticize their play on the court, such as in this anecdote about Kobe Bryant: " . . . there was a game on Sunday night. He took the ball and went to the hoop immediately. That's not how I saw it. So we had to talk that out."

In May 2013, Phil, by then a former coach, opened up to Jay about his two biggest superstars: Kobe and Michael Jordan. He said they both had a "competitive zeal that was unmatched," but he gave the edge to Michael, who had "a little better shooting percentage" and who was "a little more consistent with the team system."

Something Phil never discussed with Jay was his practice of Native American exorcism rituals, which he performed annually and whenever the team was on a losing streak. He would light a bundle of sage and take it through the trainer's room, the locker room, onto the court, and into the weight room in an effort to cleanse the team of bad spirits. I have no idea how he pulled this off with some of the NBA's greatest stars.

Another great motivator was Pat Riley. In 2006, he coached the Miami Heat to its first NBA title, staging a dramatic four-game comeback against the Dallas Mavericks. Then he flew to Burbank to tell Jay how he did it. After the Heat lost its first two games, Pat told his players they would win the next four to claim the title. He wrote "6/20/06" on the board, which was the scheduled date of the fourth game.

Pat described "the pit" in the middle of the locker room floor, which was a large gold cutout shaped like a championship trophy. Only the team knew about this icon, which represented the NBA title. Pat said he and his players threw valuable items into the pit, including Pat's six NBA Championship rings, a map of the route of the Dallas Mavericks victory parade, and the rosary beads of Pat's mother, Mary, who had died during the season. This was done to honor her memory and that of family members the players had lost.

Then there was controversial firebrand Bobby Knight, who was the winningest college basketball coach when he stepped down in 2008 after forty-two years on the sidelines. The long-time head of Indiana University's hoops squad, best known for tossing a chair across the court and giving referees a hard time, was always on his best behavior at the show and was a good sport, to boot.

When he retired from his coaching job, he showed up on *Tonight* wearing a ref's black-and-white striped jersey. He told Jay he was looking for an easy job, like being a referee: "There are fat guys that referee, there are slow guys that referee. I mean, some of them don't see well, and a lot of them don't even know what the rules are. What better job could you have than being a referee?" "It's dangerous," Jay replied. "You could get hit with a chair."

Despite his bravado on the court, Bobby was known for emphasizing academics to his players off the court. A very high percentage of them graduated from college. When Jay asked the coach how he wanted to be remembered he replied, "I think the major responsibility that any college coach has that recruits kids is to see that those kids graduate. Why else are they there?" he said.

We developed relationships that lasted many years with star athletes and former players who became regular guests, including Michael Jordan, Magic Johnson, Joe Montana, Steve Young, Troy Aikman, Shaquille O'Neal, Tiger Woods and Kobe Bryant. But our ties with Tiger and Kobe went sour as experiences in their own lives became monologue material.

We first booked Tiger in 1996, long before he became the biggest name in golf. Still an amateur then, he was getting a lot of buzz on the sports pages. He soon became a pro and the number-one golfer in the world. By his next appearance in December 1997, he was named PGA Player of the Year, after winning the prestigious Masters Tournament at age twenty-one.

Tiger was a loyal guest, never appearing on Letterman. During his appearances he always got in a jab at his good friend and wannabe golfer Charles Barkley, calling the former NBA star the "worst golfer of all time" while showing video of his imperfect golf swing. When Charles came on the show, he got back at Tiger by calling him a cheapskate. It became a running gag.

In November 2002, Tiger brought his Swedish girlfriend— Elin Nordegren, a model—to the show with him. He was proud of her and wanted to introduce her to Jay. Tiger married Elin in 2004, and in 2006 he made a very touching appearance, telling Jay he wanted to have kids and that family would always come first. Then he paid tribute to his dad and "best friend," Earl, who had died earlier that year. Earl was Tiger's rock in life. I believe that loss led to some very unfortunate consequences.

On November 25, 2009, the *National Enquirer* ran a story that Tiger was having an extramarital affair. Two days later, another story surfaced: Tiger had left his home in Windermere, Florida, in his Cadillac Escalade SUV and collided with a fire hydrant, a tree, and several hedges on his street. He was treated for minor cuts to his face and received a ticket for careless driving. There were reports Elin had smashed the vehicle's back window with a golf club while attempting to get at her husband. The story ballooned into a major sex scandal, as more than a dozen women came forward claiming to have had affairs with Tiger.

Tiger's sordid affairs were perfect fodder for late-night humor. Jay cut loose with numerous jokes:

It's not looking good for Tiger Woods. According to a poll today, 88 percent of women have an unfavorable opinion of Tiger Woods. The other 12 percent are cocktail waitresses.

President Barack Obama accepted the Nobel Peace Prize from the Norwegians. This comes almost two weeks after Tiger Woods was crowned by a Swede.

Gatorade has officially ended their relationship with Tiger Woods. He was seeing at least five other sports drinks.

The jokes were funny, but I knew Tiger wouldn't like them. So I reached out to his long-time agent, Mark Steinberg, who was always gracious and polite. This time, though, he never called me back. Later, Tiger hired Ari Fleischer, President Bush's former press secretary and a friend, to handle the press.

Ari told me he missed the old days when life was easier. Back then he only had to represent a beleaguered president to the Washington press corps. Ari said he would get back to me if Tiger ever wanted to do the show. Of course, he never did. Tiger returned to the PGA Tour in April 2010 and divorced Elin shortly thereafter.

Kobe Bryant was only seventeen when he made his first appearance with Jay in July 1996. He had just been signed by the Los Angeles Lakers after deciding to go directly into the NBA from his high school in Philadelphia. Even then he had all the confidence of a superstar, predicting the Lakers would win ten NBA titles while he was on the team.

Kobe was close with his family, who often accompanied him to the show. In 1998, during his second guest spot, he talked about his dad, Joe "Jellybean" Bryant, who played with the Philadelphia 76ers for eight years. Joe taught his son how to play basketball, and by the time Kobe was fourteen, he could beat his dad in one-on-one play. At age nineteen, he was already being compared to the great Michael Jordan. Life was good, but it was all happening so fast.

At age twenty-one, Kobe met seventeen-year-old Vanessa Laine, and the two got engaged six months later. There were reports that his family did not approve of Vanessa. Then, in April 2001, he married her at St. Edward Roman Catholic Church in Dana Point, California. Neither his parents nor his teammates attended. Press reports later said that Joe was estranged from his son for about two years after that.

Two months after Kobe's marriage, the Lakers won their second NBA title under coach Phil Jackson. Kobe came on *Leno* to celebrate the victory and to talk about his new wife. He said it was love at first sight and that being married to her made him a better player. Then he showed off his wedding ring, which Vanessa helped design. Kobe's family members did not show up for the taping that day. I had heard there was a falling out, and I wondered how it would affect Kobe's life, as his family had served as an important buffer to his crazy, topsy-turvy world.

In July 2003, Kobe, then twenty-four, was charged with sexual assault of a nineteen-year-old woman who worked in a Colorado hotel where he was staying. With Vanessa at his side, Kobe said at a Los Angeles press conference that he was guilty of adultery but not rape. In September 2004, the case was dropped after the woman refused to testify in court. She later filed a civil lawsuit against him, which was settled out of court.

Jay's monologue had some jokes about the incident:

Kobe Bryant and the Lakers are playing the Nuggets in Denver tonight. Kobe's wife is excited because any time Kobe goes to Colorado she gets jewelry.

Kobe Bryant got a technical foul last night. But he says he didn't foul the guy. He says it was consensual.

My contacts with the Lakers told me Kobe was not happy with the jokes, which I understood. Even so, I extended him a standing invitation through his agent, but he never came back.

Former vice president Dick Cheney appeared in a comedy sketch as Darth Vader in 2011. (Photo by Paul Drinkwater/ NBC/NBCU Photo Bank via Getty Images)

Jay Leno with the Kings, the Romneys, and the Bergs. (l-r) Dennis King, Patti King, Mitt Romney, Ann Romney, Jay, Mary Berg, me. The Kings were responsible for persuading Mr. Romney to appear on Tonight *after an aide had nixed the idea.* (Courtesy NBCUniversal Media, LLC)

Senator John McCain with his wife, Cindy, and me in the dressing room during Mr. McCain's 2008 presidential bid. (Courtesy NBCUniversal Media, LLC)

Jay with Arnold Schwarzenegger as he announces his intention to run for governor of California in 2004. (Photo by Paul Drinkwater/NBC/NBCU Photo Bank via Getty Images)

Jay with the late Tim Russert, then moderator of Meet the Press, *holding up a white board, his trademark prop during presidential elections.* (Photo by Paul Drinkwater/NBC/NBCU Photo Bank via Getty Images)

The late Tony Snow, former press secretary to President George W. Bush, and me. Tony made one appearance on Jay's show. (Courtesy NBCUniversal Media, LLC)

Fox News Channel anchor Bill O'Reilly and me. I booked Bill's appearances on The Tonight Show *and later worked as a producer for* The O'Reilly Factor.

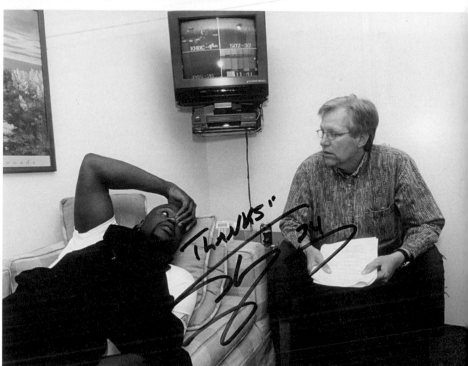

Shaquille O'Neal, former Los Angeles Laker, with me in his dressing room while resting. One of the NBA's greatest players, Shaq was also very entertaining. (Courtesy NBCUniversal Media, LLC)

Chicago Blackhawks on stage with Jay. I'm in a black jersey just to Jay's left. The entire team came to the show and appeared in a comedy sketch with Jay in March 2010. Shortly after that, the Blackhawks won the Stanley Cup championship for the first time in forty-nine years, and four members of the team returned with the Cup to make another visit. (Courtesy Chicago Blackhawks)

Phil Jackson, former coach of the Los Angeles Lakers, with me on stage. Phil was Jay's favorite coach. (Courtesy NBCUniversal Media, LLC)

Jay drove a different vehicle to NBC in Burbank every day, but on February 7, 2014, the day after the finale of The Tonight Show with Jay Leno, *his parking space was sadly empty.*

Comedian Larry the Cable Guy talks with Jay Leno during a commercial break on January 1 *2014. Larry was a "friend of the show" who made twenty-five appearances. This was his las* (Photo by Paul Drinkwater/NBC/NBCU Photo Bank via Getty Images)

The Berg family with Jay on stage. (l-r) Melissa, David, Jay, Mary, me. (Courtesy NBCUniversal Media, LLC)

Executive producer Debbie Vickers and me in front of the booking board in the conference room where the producers planned the show.

During his final appearance on Tonight, *NBA great Charles Barkley presented Jay with this framed denim jersey, signifying his twenty-two years as host. Borrowing from a sports tradition, Charles said he was "retiring" Jay's famous article of clothing. The shirt was mounted to the wall in* The Tonight Show *studio.*

Some sports heroes achieved victories and record-setting feats that were so extraordinary, they bordered on the unbelievable. That's because they were. I wonder if we need to put an asterisk next to their appearances with Jay.

Of all the sports titans, cyclist Lance Armstrong appeared to be the greatest. It seemed that no other athlete—including Michael Jordan, Tiger Woods, and Wayne Gretzky—had prevailed so triumphantly over such impossible odds. On the set, the cyclist told his amazing story of being diagnosed with an advanced stage of testicular cancer from which he was not expected to survive, but did. And after enduring three operations and aggressive chemotherapy treatments, he was declared cancer free in 1997. By January 1998, he returned to serious training. And between 1999 and 2005, he won the Tour de France, the world's most grueling sporting event, seven consecutive times.

He would always share little tidbits about the three-week Tour, which spanned 2,300 miles. He said he rode five to eight hours a day, going 70-80 mph downhill and 30 mph on the flats. He never stopped to take bathroom breaks, instead relieving himself while riding. He also told heart-warming stories about his single mom, Linda, who struggled just to make ends meet, even as she encouraged him to accomplish great things.

Lance went so far as to say his cancer was a blessing in disguise because it humbled him. After he was stricken with the disease, he became a better person, surrounding himself with the right team and setting goals that changed the world of cycling.

Still, there were persistent doping allegations in the news, which actually made Lance look like the persecuted hero. In his last interview with Jay, he staunchly defended himself, citing the countless drug tests he had passed. Then he said such allegations would never go away because "anyone who runs fast or jumps far will be suspect."

But in 2012, Lance publicly admitted that he was doping.

He was stripped of his titles and banned from cycling for life. I look back and wonder how we all got taken in by him. He did show signs that something was amiss. Backstage, he always seemed distracted, though never rude. He once brought along Sheryl Crow, then his girlfriend, but didn't introduce her to anyone, including Jay. It was an awkward moment because Jay didn't recognize her at first.

When San Francisco Giant Barry Bonds sat down next to Jay in 2002 to talk about his record seventy-three homeruns the previous season, he was considered the best player in baseball. He expressed his disappointment with former baseball players who claimed that steroid usage in the sport was widespread, because it put false notions in the minds of kids. He said he didn't take steroids and supported drug testing in Major League Baseball. Although I invited him back many times after that interview, Barry never returned.

The following year, MLB would begin drug testing. And in 2011, Barry was convicted of obstruction of justice for lying to a grand jury about using steroids and human growth hormones. In 2013, he was denied entry into the National Baseball Hall of Fame in his first year of eligibility.

Barry's baseball career was controversial long before the steroid era. He was known in the press as an arrogant, volatile guy who wouldn't even autograph baseballs for children. An off-camera incident backstage at *The Tonight Show* seemed to support that theory. In 1996, we invited him to do a comedy sketch poking fun at his "reputation" for being mean to kids. He agreed to do it.

In the pre-taped bit, Barry was in the dressing room autographing a baseball for three young, admiring kids (who included my children, Melissa and David, along with a friend). They were all excited to be there to do a sketch with a famous baseball player. The plan was to have Jay introduce Barry during the monologue by saying he thought Barry was getting a bum rap and was actually a nice guy. In the next shot, the audience would see a smiling Barry Bonds interacting with the kids.

The bit went very smoothly during the show, but while we were rehearsing, the director called for a re-take right after Barry had autographed the ball and handed it to one of the kids. As soon as the cameras stopped rolling, he grabbed it back from her. "Gimme that ball. That's worth fifty bucks," he said. The kids were taken aback, but Barry was dead serious.

In 2007, baseball great Pete Rose told ESPN radio that he bet on the Cincinnati Reds "every night" while he was the manager of the team. His statement caused quite a brouhaha in the press. Following a permanent ban from baseball in 1989 for wagering on games, he insisted for years that the ban was unfounded. Then in 2004 he admitted to Jay and others that he had been gambling. I booked Pete on Leno to find out what this new development was about.

During his appearance, Pete dismissed the ESPN story as old news, but then he tried to justify his betting. He said he always bet for the Reds, which he believed showed he had faith in his players: "It was like my sons playing for me . . . I bet on them every night. . . . It was wrong, but it's kind of human when you think about it." Pete denied he was addicted to gambling, but he would not reveal the size of his wagers.

After the show, an incredulous Jay Leno told me he didn't think Pete showed the slightest hint of contrition throughout the interview. Noted clinical psychologist Stanley Teitelbaum, who watched the interview, had the same impression and wrote about it in his book *Athletes Who Indulge Their Dark Side*: "[Pete Rose] conveyed an attitude that suggested he did not feel like he did anything wrong, with the rationalization that his betting did not hurt his team."

Jay had a joke in 2002 that I think best sums up Pete's moral confusion:

> Baseball commissioner Bud Selig was with Pete Rose this week to discuss reinstating him to baseball. I guess the talks were going pretty good until Rose said to Selig, "So, what are the odds?"

The biggest names in racing also stopped by to chat

with Jay, including NASCAR legends Jeff Gordon, Jimmie Johnson, the late Dale Earnhardt, and Dale Earnhardt Jr. But the most memorable appearance by a professional driver was that of the late Paul Newman, who in 1995 accepted Jay's challenge to race in Go-Karts through the corridors of NBC.

Just before the competition, Jay joked that he would kick the eighty-year-old Oscar winner's "ass"—and then proceeded to get his own backside handed to him. Jay absolutely loved the experience. When he complimented Paul on how smoothly he took the curves, he replied, "I wish I was seventy-nine again."

Paul, known later in life as much for his racing as his acting, told Jay that he didn't get into the motorsport until age forty-seven. He had tried skiing, tennis, and other sports but was never able to "find grace" until he got behind the wheel. Jay invited the veteran actor back for a rematch a year later and lost again. However, that wasn't Jay's last race.

In 1995, Jay competed against the elder Earnhardt in a tractor race that began in Studio 3, snaked around some hay bales on the tarmac in the "Midway" driveway outside, and ended up back in the studio. The legendary NASCAR driver, known to this day as the greatest ever, quickly pulled ahead of Jay, who then gunned it and was tire-to-tire with the "great intimidator" at the halfway mark. The race came right down to the finish line, when Jay managed to pull ahead of "number 3" by a nose.

Tonight Show prop man and NASCAR enthusiast Greg Elliott said only a professional driver of Dale's ability could have pulled off such a "close loss" in the dramatic fashion that he did. In his interview with Jay, Dale said he didn't consider racing dangerous unless there was a crash. He even considered freeways so risky that he refused to drive on them. NASCAR's "bad boy" died on the track on February 18, 2001, after crashing his car into the wall on the last turn of the last lap of the Daytona 500.

Many people assume Jay, who boasts a huge collection of cars, is a racing enthusiast. He actually isn't, although he has driven the pace car at major racing events. However, one sport he did take an interest in was boxing.

Jay's father, Angelo, was an amateur boxer, and Jay was fascinated by the brutality of the sport and by the fact that there can only be one winner. He talked knowledgably about "the gentleman's sport" with boxing greats such as Lennox Lewis, Evander Holyfield, Bernard Hopkins, Sugar Shane Mosley, and Wladimir Klitschko. Of all the boxers, it was lightweight Oscar De La Hoya who made the most stops at the show.

We first booked Oscar at age nineteen after his dramatic victory at the 1992 Barcelona Olympic Games. He captured America's heart with a story about his late mother, Cecilia, who raised him in the barrio. Just before she died of breast cancer in 1990, he promised her he would win a gold medal for her. Then he told Jay about his recent visit to the White House, where he and other Olympic champions were invited for a special ceremony. At one point during this auspicious occasion, he had to go to the bathroom. He said of being in a presidential restroom, "I thought, wow, to sit here where George Bush sits is a real honor."

Oscar, known as the "Golden Boy," would become boxing's biggest attraction, winning ten world titles in six divisions over a sixteen-year career. In that time he had some great anecdotes about the life of a pugilist. Like most boxers, Oscar abstained from sex before every fight because he believed it was physically draining and, therefore, detrimental to a peak performance in the ring.

Jay loved teasing him about the challenges of being celibate while lying next to his beautiful wife, Millie Corretjer, sometimes resisting her charms for up to five months. Dr. Phil was once a fellow *Tonight Show* guest during one of these discussions. When Oscar asked him about the legitimacy of this boxing custom, Dr. Phil just laughed.

In 2007, I attended one of Oscar's last big bouts, which he lost in a close, split decision to Floyd Mayweather. Naturally, I was rooting for Oscar, who I thought was the clear-cut winner. But after the fight I booked Floyd Mayweather to appear on Leno. After all, there's only room for one champion in boxing.

One of Jay's most beloved guests was the two-time heavyweight champion George Foreman. George was also one of our funniest sports guests. I'll never forget his best line: "I got ten kids. All the boys [five] are named George. When you're a boxer, you gotta make preparations for memory loss."

By the time he started showing up on *Leno* in 1992, most people were more familiar with him as the spokesman for the George Foreman Grill than as a boxer. The champ told Jay that when a business partner and friend suggested the idea of putting his name on a small, slanted grill, he wasn't interested and quickly forgot about it. Then his wife, Mary, tried the grill and liked it because the grease rolled right off. She fixed him a burger and he loved it, but he never expected to make any money on the deal. George said he was just hoping to get sixteen free grills for family and friends. As it turned out, he made tens of millions of dollars by endorsing the product. Some estimates put the total amount at more than $200 million, far more than he ever made in the ring.

In 1997, George did a cooking segment—one of the show's funniest—to display the wonders of The George Foreman Lean Mean Fat-Reducing Grilling Machine. He was also promoting a cookbook he had written, and that night he was planning to prepare mustard lemon chicken, one of the recipes in the book. Halfway through the demonstration, George forgot the ingredients, so he just started saying the machine would "knock out the fat." Jay "helped" by mixing in huge quantities of spices and seasonings willy-nilly. No matter: at the end of the segment, Jay pulled out a sample of the entrée that had been pre-cooked to perfection by a food stylist.

George frequently discussed his mixed feelings about retiring from boxing. At age forty-five, he had been the oldest man ever to hold the title heavyweight champion. At age fifty-five, he was planning to make yet another go of it, but Mary was adamantly opposed. George reasoned that when you're more afraid of your wife outside the ring than the guys inside the ring, it's time to quit.

Dallas Cowboys quarterback Troy Aikman made his debut appearance on *The Tonight Show* in February 1993 following his team's Super Bowl victory. He admitted he was overwhelmed by the experience, considering his record in his rookie season four years earlier was 0-11. He led his team to two more championships in his twelve-year career for the Cowboys, making many more *Tonight Show* stops along the way. Never one to get emotional, Troy let down his guard when he appeared with Jay in 2001 to talk about his decision to step down from the game he had been playing since he was seven years old. He said he would miss the camaraderie in the locker room after a big game and would never be able to duplicate the highs and lows he felt while playing football. In an attempt to lighten the mood, Jay asked Troy to name the first football team he played for. The question caused Troy to pause and smile for the first and only time during his interview. "It was the Henrietta Fighting Hens," he said.

Standing at seven foot one and weighing 325 pounds, Shaquille O'Neal was the largest, most imposing player in the NBA during his career. He was also a daredevil and would regale Jay with tales about skydiving, bungee jumping, and riding motorcycles. Shaq wasn't completely fearless, though. One day he made an appearance with an animal act that came on right after him. When the animal ambassador showed up with a large, scary-looking snake, Shaq's eyes got as big as saucers and he stood up and bolted from the stage. It wasn't an act.

To me, our all-time dopiest sports moment involved an all-American swimmer, who was an Olympic contender. But that's not why we booked Matt Zelen in 1998. We brought him on because he had recently lost his swimsuit while competing in a meet—and had gotten a lot of exposure in the press.

The meet was a major invitational hosted by his school, St. John's University in Minnesota. Nine schools participated and six hundred people attended. The crowd made the twenty-one-year-old competitor nervous about the race, and he forgot to tie his suit. The moment he hit the water, he felt it slip to his knees, then to his ankles, where it was causing drag. So he kicked it off, which meant he was buck naked for most of the 100-meter butterfly swim.

Now Matt had a dilemma: It was a big meet. His parents and his grandmother were there, and he was off to a good start. Should he stop or continue? He decided to go for it. He could hear the crowd cheering louder and louder as he passed his suit floating in the water three times, once with every lap. When the heat was over, he had won by over two seconds but was disqualified for violating the uniform code.

Matt later checked with his grandmother, who said she was okay with his decision to keep going. "I promised her if I had been swimming the backstroke, I would have quit right away," he told Jay.

Chapter Thirteen

The Audience

Jay wanted to keep his studio audience happy, and it wasn't just because he was a nice guy. He believed they and the viewers at home were as essential to the program's success as the guests, the band, and even Jay himself.

To David Letterman, the audience doesn't seem as important because he sees himself as a comedic artist. Letterman's show pages go out of their way to make sure the audience is packed with fans who will laugh on cue. However, David isn't playing to them because he believes he is producing art. Or at least, that's his public persona.

Audience members had an important role at both shows, but the audience experience was as different as the hosts themselves. People who attended both told me that *The Tonight Show* treated them like guests while *Late Show* regarded them as groupies and even encouraged them to act that way. People had to stand in line outside for several hours at both shows, which was never any fun. At *Tonight's* Studio 11 in Burbank, all were made to feel welcome. By contrast, at Letterman's Ed Sullivan Theatre in New York, prospective audience members can only be there if they've passed a test. According to *The Late Show's* website, "a ticket will only be issued to those individuals who correctly answer a random trivia question about the show."

Those who get into Letterman's studio are told they are welcome, but they are not an essential part of the show, as audience sounds could easily be dubbed in. Nevertheless, they are expected to laugh loudly and often because they will be witnessing a rare comedic talent, Or as the Letterman website puts it, "there is no off position on the genius switch."

Just before Letterman's show begins, a staffer conducts a briefing on how the show works and what is expected of the audience—which is to laugh, or else. Pages closely monitor the audience throughout the recording, issuing frequent reminders to jump up and clap often. One person told me a page warned him to applaud with more energy. When he didn't, he was moved to another seat out of camera range, presumably where Letterman couldn't see him. David is reported to be cold and distant during the commercial breaks, leaving his guests alone at the panel while he retreats to a corner at the back of the stage, where he stands with his arms crossed.

At Studio 11 in Burbank, a comedian warmed up the crowd before the show with some amazing physical antics and bits. Most recently this was the job of the talented Don Reed. I watched his routine many times, and his approach cut a stark contrast to Letterman's somber pre-show directives. Don put Jay's audience in the right frame of mind, but his act was also stand-alone funny. He described it this way to the *San Francisco Chronicle*: "I really try to make them laugh and feel uplifted. I feel if you don't make the audience genuinely laugh, you're not starting the engine correctly."

Don was joined every night by Jay, who came out in his denim shirt and jeans. It was a much more informal time than the show, and people were able to see how quick-witted Jay could be without scripts or cue cards. Many told me the pre-show was the best part of their experience, and I could understand why. Jay would tell a few jokes, answer questions, and even invite a few lucky audience members on stage for a photo op. He would start with the perfunctory, "What's your name? Where are you from?" He then always had a joke ready tailored to the person who came up.

To a group of young, attractive women:

Jay: So did they tell you how these photos work?
Women: No.
Jay: Okay, well, there might be some partial nudity required.

To a young man:
  Jay: So what do you do?
  Man: I'm an actor.
  Jay: Ah, so you live with your parents.

When the show started, Don would continue to be a strong, positive presence from the sidelines, encouraging the audience to be enthusiastic, throwing out show merchandise to the studio fans. During commercial breaks, Jay would banter with his guests onstage or prepare for his next segment. Occasionally, he would wander into the audience to greet fans.

Jay thought of the studio audience as customers, and customers were always right. If they weren't laughing at the comedy, then it wasn't funny—literally. Jay could tell the greatest jokes in the world—by his standards. But if people didn't react, it didn't matter. The material bombed, as far as Jay was concerned.

If a joke fell flat and Jay couldn't save it with a comeback, it was often edited out before the show was aired. If a prerecorded comedy sketch was dying in the studio, it was shortened or even taken out altogether. Guests who droned on with boring stories were probably not blathering as long during the actual broadcast.

Jay never assumed his audience wasn't bright or hip enough to understand his material. He knew people were busy leading their own lives and not always aware of the latest news, the source of his topical humor. Jay described it this way to the *New York Times Magazine*: "You really have to put yourself in the place of the people in the audience. . . . If I see someone who's not laughing, my instinct isn't to get annoyed—it's to figure out why they don't understand."

His emphasis on the audience paid off handsomely. Not only did he bring in the numbers, but for many years his show was also the most profitable one on television, taking in 15 percent of NBC profits.

But according to Rob Burnett, David Letterman's onetime executive producer and former head writer, Jay was no David. Burnett dismissed Jay as a mere "wrestler" (Jay once participated in a World Wrestling Federation match as a stunt) and told the *New York Times'* Bill Carter: "There are two parts to the so-called late-night war. One is: Who's the best? That part of the war is over. Dave won."

As for the other part, Burnett long contended that Leno beat Letterman in the ratings only because he had more viewers leading into his show than Letterman did. In the 90s, NBC had stronger network programs from 10 p.m. to 11 p.m., especially on Thursdays when *E.R.* aired.

Of course, NBC's ratings dynasty came to an inglorious end years ago. Meanwhile, CBS prime time has climbed to the number-one spot, giving Letterman those lucky lead-ins. Still, Burnett insisted that, despite CBS's ratings dominance, NBC affiliates drew more viewers to their 11 p.m. newscasts than CBS affiliates, giving Jay the edge. And when NBC started airing Sunday Night Football in 2006, it attracted a larger male audience than CBS on that one night during the football season. According to Burnett, that somehow gave Jay the upper hand in lead-ins over Letterman for the rest of the week.

If you ask me, when you insist that your guy is an artist, as Burnett did, you have to let the art speak for itself and let the chips fall where they may. You can't obsess over viewership when your own host acts as if he's above it.

I think David's too-cool-for-the-room attitude comes through to viewers. Dave Hinckley of New York's *Daily News* put it this way: "Not everybody likes Dave. Not even close. Not only does the CBS *Late Show with David Letterman* draw fewer viewers than Jay Leno's *The Tonight Show* over on NBC, but in any random group of 100 TV viewers, several dozen will say they just don't like Dave."

Jay believed pleasing his audience was part of his job. He would advise young actors to be accommodating to their adoring fans even if they weren't in the mood. "People don't realize you're just having a bad day," he'd say. "Once they hate you, they will hate you forever."

Being nice to fans comes naturally to Jay, though it also

makes good sense. To him, show business is as much about the business as the show, and his primary job was to deliver more demographically correct viewers to the advertisers than Letterman did. Art had nothing to do with it.

Still, ratings were often *The Tonight Show's* only validation. Neither critics nor Emmy judges ever liked it. *Tonight* received one non-technical Emmy in 1995 for Best Variety Show, while Letterman's *Late Show* has garnered nine wins from countless nominations. Nielsen doesn't consult with the Emmys, the press, or the critics when it tabulates ratings, and that's why I believe Nielsen, with its pulse on the people, is the only judge that counts.

The media has always seen Letterman as the rightful heir to Johnny Carson because they think David's humor is sophisticated, urbane, edgy, and unpredictable—and, therefore, inherently better. But critics speak from their points of view, not from that of the audience. They love the idea that you never know what David will do next, even though it's often contrived for the sole purpose of self-promotion. For example, the media couldn't wait to see what David would have to say about his emergency quintuple heart bypass surgery, his bout with shingles, or his wedding and the birth of his son. When David admitted to having sex with female staffers and being blackmailed, the media went into a tizzy.

David has dealt with these personal experiences by turning them into promotable events on his show, which has resulted in ratings gold. His revelation about his affairs boosted his viewership 38 percent in a week. Letterman does best when his show is about him rather than his written material and his guests. I have no problem with that, but I do take issue with critics and even industry executives who think his antics are comedic genius.

It's ironic that David's heavy reliance on contrived events represents the very antithesis of what his hero, Johnny Carson, was about. He became an icon because people genuinely liked him, not his stunts. That's also why people preferred Jay. To me, the most memorable *Late Show* episodes come off like reality TV because they've been staged. I think that's an insult to viewers, but the press tends to love those episodes.

The media bought into a sixteen-year "feud" between David and Oprah, despite the fact that it was obviously phony. It started when Oprah told *TIME* magazine in 2003 that she felt uncomfortable during two appearances on Letterman. That part was true, but David exaggerated what she said, and he openly taunted her on his show by saying she didn't like him, which was just shtick. He was badgering her for no other reason than to create an issue, which he has also done to many other celebrities.

In February 2009, actor Joaquin Phoenix appeared on Letterman sporting a long, bushy, and unkempt beard. He appeared to be almost catatonic as he grunted a few monosyllabic responses to David's questions. People thought Joaquin was serious, and the press bought into it, too. They thought it was a genuine train wreck. Except it wasn't! To me, Joaquin's performance wasn't even believable. He appeared to be struggling to keep from laughing, as David looked more bemused than angry while giving quick, clever responses. Too clever.

And here's the real giveaway: Joaquin had filmed a so-called documentary called *I'm Still Here* that supposedly examined his descent into madness. Wouldn't it be logical to assume that Joaquin's odd behavior was only done to promote his film? He was having an apparent meltdown on Letterman, and his film was about being mad. How hard is it to connect the dots? Turns out, the film was eventually revealed to be a fake—a "mockumentary"—by its director, Casey Affleck. And Joaquin made another guest appearance on *The Late Show* admitting his previous appearance was just an act. At David's urging, Joaquin revealed that Letterman's staffers were aware of it, though David was not. But Bill Scheft, a Letterman writer, had already told nuevo.net that it was a performance and that David had been in on it: "Dave loved it because he could play along. He could do whatever he wanted with it. And he did, and it was great television."

Great television? Not if it's an act. Cynically playing the audience for a sucker is condescending and insulting. Jay never treated his viewers that way because he respected them.

Some time ago, publicists for the publishing industry invited me to New York to take part in a panel discussion on late-night television. I jumped at the chance to go. *The Tonight Show* had been consistently losing key bookings of celebrity authors to Letterman, and I thought the panel would give me an opportunity to make a strong pitch on Jay's behalf.

The Tonight Show was clearly the late-night ratings winner, even in New York, so it made no sense for the publishers to favor Letterman. Why did they? I suspected three reasons:
1. David was the home-town guy.
2. The publishing industry was based in New York and always kicked off media tours there.
3. Because of numbers one and two, they probably concluded that Letterman was the top-rated late-night show. Perception always trumps reality—and often logic.

I was the only late-night producer to accept the invitation until a Letterman producer learned I was coming and decided to join the panel. Soon after, producers from three other shows decided to take part. I figured I needed to educate the room about the ratings when the moderator asked us the big question: *What can your show do for us?*

Letterman's producer immediately answered with absolute confidence and conviction that ratings didn't matter because David was simply the best and everyone in the room knew it. I thought that was presumptuous, but then I realized she actually believed what she was saying and was simply mimicking the accepted mantra she had heard at CBS and had read in critics' columns. And she was certain everyone would agree with her because she viewed New York publishers as hip, smart Letterman aficionados who "got" Dave.

Uh-oh! My gut was telling me a serious discussion about ratings wouldn't work because many of the people in that room probably agreed with her. So I decided to talk business from the publishers' point of view. I acknowledged that many people, including myself, considered David to be an artist. "But what we do at *The Tonight Show* ain't art," I said. "We wouldn't be caught dead doing art. There's no money in it."

Then I said: "Funny thing about our viewers. They read and buy more books than Letterman's viewers. I learned this from a recent internal survey I read, conducted by a major publisher here in New York . . . so if you want to book your authors on a show hosted by an artist, that's great. Or you could book them on Jay Leno, who has an audience that will read their books. Your choice."

A good friend in the publishing industry—and a Jay Leno fan—had shared this inside information with me in confidence. Of course, I made sure not to give away his identity. And the tip paid off. Going forward, I got considerably more celebrity author bookings. One of them was John Kennedy Jr., Jay's all-time favorite guest. More importantly, he was an audience favorite, as well.

Chapter Fourteen

Jay Leno's Garage

It just makes sense that a behind-the-scenes look at Jay Leno and his *Tonight Show* would also include a behind-the-scenes look into his garage. In many ways, Jay's legendary collection of more than two hundred cars and motorcycles is as much a part of him as his late-night television program. Representing more than one hundred years of automotive history, it is valued at $50 million. Some would consider this a pretty expensive hobby, but to Jay, it's a bargain: "It's cheaper than hookers and cocaine. Most guys in Hollywood have twenty girlfriends and one car, and I have twenty cars and one girlfriend."

He keeps his vehicles, classic automotive posters, and other artifacts at Big Dog Garage near the Burbank airport. It includes five attached solar- and wind-powered warehouses totaling seventeen thousand square feet. I've toured this amazing facility, which is comparable to the world's finest automobile museums. Then again, it technically isn't a museum because Jay's vehicles aren't just for show. He drives them all and would take a different one to the NBC studio every day.

Truth is, Jay doesn't even think of his vehicular possessions as a collection. He just buys the cars and bikes he wants and never sells anything. As a result, his "non-collection" is wide-ranging: "I like anything that rolls, explodes, and makes noise. Motorcycles, cars, steam engines, trucks; I love 'em all," he said during my tour.

Jay particularly loves fast cars—and has plenty of them—but he's not the racing enthusiast many people think he is. Even so, he has the distinction of being the first person to have driven the official pace car at all the major NASCAR races. And he's one of only a few people to have held that honor for both the Daytona 500 and the Indianapolis 500.

He once set a speed record . . . well, sort of. He was clocked for going 76 in a 55 mph speed zone while driving his 1906 Stanley Steamer, making it the oldest car ever pulled over by the California Highway Patrol. It's also the oldest vehicle he owns, one of many vintage cars in his garage filled with Duesenbergs, Bugattis, Lamborghinis, Bentleys, McClarens, and more Stanley Steamers. Jay's collection of contemporary vehicles features a jet-powered motorcycle with a 320-horsepower engine that can go up to 260 mph. It literally sounds like a Boeing 737.

The Leno fleet is overseen by a staff of three mechanical wizards, including the head mechanic, an engineer who designs and makes parts, and an automotive body man.

Jay is also an excellent mechanic in his own right. He once did new-car preparation and light maintenance for Foreign Motors, a Rolls Royce and Mercedes Benz dealer in Boston. Part of his job involved driving new Rolls Royces to customers in New York, where he would also do his stand-up routine at comedy clubs such as The Improv or Catch a Rising Star—all while he was still a student at Emerson College in Boston.

Like most of Jay's cars, the parts he needs to keep them running are no longer manufactured, so he also has a state-of-the-art shop in the garage to fabricate them. It includes a computer-controlled mill, a water jet cutter, sheet metal equipment, a lathe, and welding equipment. The shop even has an industrial, refrigerator-sized 3-D printer, which literally produces computer-designed parts by a process known as plastic extrusion. It's ironic that such a futuristic device makes old car parts.

The garage itself has a huge gourmet kitchen where Jay often prepares meals for his crew as well as the many celebrities and others who stop by for a tour. And yes, it really is gourmet in an automotive way. Jay once did a cooking segment in his kitchen for Martha Stewart's show, preparing his Uncle Louie's Chicken Wings Marinara for twenty guys. He used a sixty-ton press, applying four thousand pounds of pressure, to crush a clove of elephant garlic. He also proudly showed off his unique salt-and-pepper shaker, made out of a carburetor.

Jay is truly an expert in all things automotive, including restoration, mechanical repairs, and the history of the industry worldwide. He writes a car advice column for *Popular Mechanics* and has an Emmy-winning web series called *Jay Leno's Garage,* which features his and others' vehicles as well as commentary from automotive experts.

The anecdotes he tells when he's giving a tour make his vehicles fun to learn about, even if you're not interested in cars. And, of course, he always has lots of funny stories. That's why the best part of Jay's garage is Jay himself.

No tour led by Jay would be complete without a reference to the first car he ever bought—his beloved 1955 black-and-white Buick Roadmaster. He paid $350 for it in 1972 after reading about it in a PennySaver ad. He literally lived—and often slept—in that car during his early days as a struggling comedian. He and Mavis took it out on their first date, and in 1977, he drove it to Studio 1 at NBC, where he made his first appearance on Johnny Carson's *Tonight Show.*

Jay eventually moved on to another car, but he never sold the Roadmaster. Instead, it sat in his mother-in-law's driveway for almost sixteen years. In 2002, he decided to restore it and soup it up with a 620-horsepower engine, a Corvette suspension system, shiny chrome, new interiors, and custom hubcaps.

During our tour, Jay talked about the classic film *Chitty Chitty Bang Bang,* which was based on a famous children's novel about a magic car. The story by Ian Fleming, creator of James Bond, was inspired by an actual series of racing cars named Chitty Bang Bang that was designed in the 1920s by racing enthusiast Count Louis Zborowski. No one knows for sure the origin of the cars' odd name. It's thought to have come from the sound of their Maybach aero-engines.

According to Jay, though, there's another explanation: the name is a British slang expression dating back to World War I that means having sex in the back seat of a car. Jay was bemused that the Brits have probably had quite a laugh about this at the expense of the Yanks, who associate *Chitty Chitty Bang Bang* with Dick Van Dyke and a cute, flying car.

In a world of electric and hybrid vehicles, Jay proudly claims ownership of three alternative-energy cars. His, though, aren't hot out of the factory. His newest was built in 1925. The oldest is a 1909 Baker Electric car that can go eighty miles on one charge.

Unlike other cars of its day, the Baker didn't smell of gasoline, and it didn't need any cranking, which greatly appealed to women. As a result, the Baker became the first car ever marketed to women. Jay described the interior of his model, which even featured a makeup kit, as "froufrou." The women who bought Bakers tended to be well off, including Henry Ford's wife, Clara, who wouldn't drive a Ford Model T.

Baker was ahead of its time with both its product and its marketing techniques. In fact, they were too far ahead for the company's own good. Baker Motor Vehicle Company went out of business because, at that time, men bought the cars, not women. And no man was going to buy a car that had cut-glass flower vases in it.

People often ask Jay which of his cars is his favorite, a question he usually deflects with one of his own: "Which of your children is your favorite?" Nevertheless, he does have his favorites.

He once wrote in his *Popular Mechanics* column that he prefers old cars, ones that need him: "To me, cars are like screen doors. I know that if I jiggle the latch and move it this way, it will open for me and no one else. And that's the kind of cars I like."

He's partial to Duesenbergs, Packards, and Bugattis. His 1932 Duesenberg Model SJ is at the top of his list because of its sturdiness and strength: "You can drive it like a modern car even though it's sixty-five years old or more. You can comfortably go 70 to 80 mph on the freeway."

My favorite is a classic fire truck, which looks like a big toy, similar to the one pictured on the cover of the children's book *Number 9: The Little Fire Engine* by Wallace Wadsworth. It turns out this truck—a V-12 American LaFrance—featured state-of-the-art technology when it was built in 1941. Its 256-horsepower engine was the most powerful one made in its day, and its aerodynamic design was tested in a wind tunnel, a first for a fire truck.

Warner Brothers Studios in Burbank was the truck's original owner. After twenty years of service, it was passed on to the Burbank airport, where it served for decades as a wind shield for a runway. By the time the airport offered the truck to Jay, it had seen its better days. The price was right: he could have it for nothing if he towed it away. This was a vehicle that definitely needed Jay's touch, and he predictably agreed to the deal.

Jay's crew did a basic cleanup on it, using ten-ton jacks to hoist it, and had the engine running in no time. The body, however, was another story. It was in horrible condition after baking in the California sun for years, but the crew was able to restore it to mint condition in only ten days by using sand paper. They also pulled out the water tank in the back and put in a tailgate lift, making the truck the most useful vehicle in the garage. Now it's used to pick up broken-down motorcycles on the road.

But practicality is not what makes this fire truck endearing to me. You can't help but smile at the site of Jay driving around Burbank in a big, old fire truck, waving at everyone. He once took Tom Cruise for a ride in it.

Jay even drove it to a movie screening at Warner Brothers that my wife and I attended. Afterward, Jay, Mavis, and a few of their friends took it for a spin around the parking lot, sounding the siren and the bell several times. I still regret that we didn't join the ride in Number 9 that day. All I had to do was ask.

Jay and his team also restored another classic fire engine called a Christie, named after the engineer who built it. This one is a 1914 steamer that had been refurbished by the Burbank Fire Department and put on display. The truck didn't run, so the firefighters took it to Jay's shop for help. He and the boys got to work, and soon Jay was driving the steam-powered Christie on the streets of Burbank at speeds up to 25 mph.

This amazing machine, one of only six in the country, was originally an adapted version of a horse-drawn cart (the horse bit was replaced by the engine). Horses had been a fixture in the fire department for about seventy-five years, and the firemen actually didn't like the new technology at first. They thought it detracted from the romance and adventure of their job.

In 1928, "Christie" was acquired by Warner Brothers Studios in Burbank, making appearances in films with the likes of Charlie Chaplin and the Three Stooges. In the 1940s, the vehicle was given to the Burbank Fire Department. When Jay completed the job of fixing up and restoring the Christie (at his expense), he made a video of it for *Jay Leno's Garage* and then returned it to the firefighters.

Jay is rarely mentioned in the tabloids and gossip websites because he doesn't engage in behavior they would consider newsworthy. On the rare occasions when the rags do uncover something about him, it almost always has to do with one of his cars.

The *London Daily Mail* published some pictures of Jay riding around North Hollywood in one of his Stanley Steamers while talking on a cell phone, which is illegal in California. The online headline said in large, bold print: "Time to put the brakes on the chat! Talk show host Jay Leno appears to use his phone while out in his vintage wheels." And the caption under a close-up picture of Jay said: "Surely that's not allowed. Jay Leno was spotted chatting on his mobile phone in California. . . ."

Ironically, the article cast Jay in a positive light, calling him the "world's greatest car collector." It even had a touch of classic, wry British humor, saying, "His other love: In his spare time Leno hosts NBC's *The Tonight Show with Jay Leno*."

The tabloids have printed a number of stories about Jay as the Good Samaritan on the freeways, which he is. The *National Enquirer* reported that he came to the aid of a "damsel in distress" by the side of the road whose car had a flat tire. Turns out she was a production assistant for Conan O'Brien's TBS show and was worried about being late for the show, which Jay said he would watch.

A man who routinely and happily helped staffers and stars get the best deal on any car, he also diagnosed their cars' mechanical problems and was hardly ever wrong. I once owned a beat-up old van. One day during my morning commute to the studio, the van started stalling. By the time I got there, it died. Of course, I was grateful I wasn't stranded on the freeway, but I was upset because I had just replaced the van's defective starter.

What is it now? I thought. I would never have imposed on Jay by asking him for help, but he overheard me telling my colleagues about my car problems and immediately identified the starter as the problem. When I told him I had just put a new one in, he said it was probably a rebuilt starter, and they're sometimes faulty.

I dismissed his diagnosis because I was certain the mechanic had put in a new starter. Then he offered to take a look at my van. His assistant, Helga Pollock, reminded him he had a phone interview with the *New York Times* in ten minutes, but he didn't seem to care. He told Helga to have the reporter wait.

Jay immediately took off for the parking lot at his usual pace, which is twice as fast as a speed walker. I ran to keep up with him so I could answer the technical questions he was asking me on the way. As we approached the van, I wondered what Jay was thinking. Unlike him, I wasn't a car guy. To me, a car served only one purpose: getting me from point A to point B with as few hassles as possible.

There it was: my old, banged up van sitting next to a Mercedes, a BMW, and a late-model SUV, all owned by my colleagues. Jay took one look at the van and paused. I knew a joke was coming: "Where did you get this piece of sh—? Don't I pay you enough?"

First, he tried to start the van—to no avail. Then he looked under the hood. Next, he got down on his knees and began poking around the floorboard area on the driver's side. By now I was a little nervous about the *New York Times* interview he was blowing off so he could work on my "piece of sh—." I told him not to waste his time, but he ignored me.

The next thing I noticed was his feet sticking straight up from behind the steering wheel. I couldn't believe what I was seeing. I wish I had thought to take a picture, even though I have an indelible imprint of that moment in my memory. Jay then got out of the car, wiped off his hands on a rag, and said: "Yea, it's a bad starter." Then he rushed off to his phone interview.

I paid to have my car towed to the shop, and the next day my mechanic told me he would cover the cost of the tow and the new starter he was installing to replace the defective rebuilt starter he had originally put in. He also asked me if Jay wanted a job at his garage.

Chapter Fifteen

Trying Times

I would never trade my eighteen years at *The Tonight Show* for anything. I met and worked with people who were making a difference in the world, and it was exciting. But from my first day on the job to my last, I could never relax. Not one single day. The work environment was constantly unsettling and frenetic for my colleagues and for me.

We never even felt comfortable going out to lunch, though we could order in any meal from any fine restaurant in town at the show's expense. I usually just had soup and salad. In that environment, I was too distracted to taste my food.

Were we paranoid? No. Worst case scenarios such as last-minute guest cancellations frequently happened while producing a daily comedy program. But throughout the show's twenty-two-year lifespan, we were also dealing with constant threats to our survival. Most of them came from within, starting with Helen Kushnick, the original executive producer.

Helen established a bunker mentality from the day she took over, wreaking extensive havoc during her short reign of terror. Her aggressive, often underhanded approach resulted in short-term gains but would soon do her in and tarnish Jay's nice-guy image.

In February 1991, a story appeared on the front page of the *New York Post* that said NBC was pressuring Johnny Carson to leave so it could replace him with Jay Leno, who was attracting younger audiences as the show's guest host. There was just one problem: Kushnick, then Jay's manager, had made up the story and planted it in an attempt to strong-arm NBC into signing Jay as Johnny's successor. When Jay heard rumors that Kushnick was responsible for the story, he confronted her, but she denied having anything to do with it.

In the spring of 1991, CBS offered Jay an 11:30 p.m. show to compete with Johnny. Kushnick used this as leverage to secure a deal with NBC, guaranteeing that Jay would get Johnny's job when he retired. Soon after, Johnny announced that he would be stepping down in May 1992, which, of course, meant Jay would be the new host of *The Tonight Show*.

Lost in the mix was David Letterman, then the host of a late, late show that followed Johnny on NBC. David had not actively pursued the position, assuming NBC would give it to him. In reality, he hurt his cause by bashing NBC executives on the air. Jay had spent years lobbying for the job, and as Johnny's guest host he visited each and every one of the more than two hundred NBC stations around the country. Affiliates are an important part of every network, and keeping them happy is important. Jay spent time with general managers and news departments, shooting promotional videos and schmoozing. While the reclusive Letterman would never have considered pressing the flesh with the locals, Jay, who had always thought he would be a salesman, was happy to make the rounds. His efforts didn't go unnoticed by the NBC brass, who were impressed.

I had a good feeling about Jay, as well. I was thrilled when I learned he and the staff for his new show had moved into an office right down the hallway from mine at NBC in Burbank. I had just been laid off after working seven years as a producer for NBC News and three years as West Coast bureau chief for CNBC. The business cable network allowed me to use my old office to look for a job, but so far there didn't seem to be many.

I called my wife, Mary, to tell her about my new neighbor. She asked me when I would be stopping by Jay's new office to fill out an application. In response, I told her that *The Tonight Show* would never hire me, a journalist with no experience in entertainment. "What do you have to lose?" she asked. She was right, but I had heard horror stories about Kushnick.

Later, Mary called again to find out if I had been down to

Jay's office. I told her I was too busy but planned to drop by first thing the next morning. Besides, it was already 4:45 p.m., and I didn't want to be late for dinner. She told me dinner could wait. I grabbed my resume, headed for the offices of *The Tonight Show with Jay Leno,* and tried to put Kushnick out of my mind.

When I got there at 4:50 p.m., the receptionist said I was the last person applying for a job there. All applications had to be in by 5 p.m. The next day would have been too late. I started mumbling nervously. "I'm with NBC News. You're an entertainment show. Could you use somebody like me? It doesn't hurt to ask, right?" I often tell people it's a lesson in how *not* to get a job.

It wasn't exactly the best sales pitch, but I was hoping to find out if there were any openings I was even remotely qualified for. Then I heard a voice—loud and shrill—coming from a nearby office: "Get in here now. I want to talk with you!" *That's Helen Kushnick*, I thought. She didn't look scary, just frenzied. She quickly greeted me without any pleasantries, grabbing the resume from my hand as if she had been expecting me and I was late. She scanned my resume, nodding her head in approval while saying "good." Then she looked me straight in the eye, and said, "I think you're the person I've been looking for."

"Really?" I said incredulously.

But she didn't hear me. She just kept talking: "I want someone with your background. Jay likes the kinds of people you're around every day: journalists, economists, people in the news. Guests like this would make Jay look smart, and you don't see them on Johnny. But I'm going to change that. I'll be changing a lot of things."

Then she abruptly ended the conversation and said she'd be calling me soon. I walked out of the office, stunned. A few minutes earlier I had absolutely no job prospects. Now I was certain I had a good chance of becoming a producer for Jay Leno. When I told Mary this she, ironically, tried to tamp down my enthusiasm: "It's *The Tonight Show.* Don't get your hopes up. I know I told you to talk with them, but it's a long shot!"

But it wasn't a long shot. The very next day, Kushnick called and asked me to come down to meet Jay. When I saw him, I was overwhelmed. *What am I doing here?* I thought. I admitted my self-doubts to him, which he quickly dismissed. He told me he was glad Kushnick found someone with my background. Kushnick again emphasized she would be making changes and that I would have a big part in it. Then she hired me. It was the easiest job I ever got and the hardest job I ever had.

Kushnick threw a barbeque for the new staff of about one hundred fifty and their families at her beautiful ranch-style home in Hidden Hills. She owned several acres and kept horses on her property for her twelve-year-old daughter, Sara, who liked to ride. I arrived with my wife; my seven-year-old daughter, Melissa; and my three-year-old son, David. We were all dressed in new summery outfits Mary had purchased just for the party. When Jay saw us, he quipped, "You guys look like you're right out of the Sears catalog!"

That's exactly what we looked like, but I was embarrassed because I thought he somehow didn't approve. This was our first Hollywood party, and I wasn't sure how people were supposed to dress. But I would soon learn that Jay often joked about what people were wearing—and anything else that came to mind. We all came to love those jokes, which helped ease a lot of tense moments over the years.

Kushnick was a gracious host that day, smiling as she introduced her new hires to each other and making sure we got enough to eat. But just below the surface lurked a deeply troubled person we would all soon get to know better. At forty-six, she had experienced numerous personal tragedies, including the loss of her husband, Jerry, to cancer and her three-year-old son, Sam, to AIDS from a tainted blood transfusion. She herself was battling breast cancer and had undergone a mastectomy.

Helen's dark side began to emerge at the office as she bullied and embarrassed staffers, often in front of others. She was even insulting to Jay, often telling him to go away and work on his "little monologue" so she could get some work done. She was fond of saying that Jay liked steak and that she was the one who butchered the cow. But he didn't need to know how it got done.

Her contempt for Johnny Carson never faded. She regarded him and his inner circle as members of the "old boys' club" who would never willingly let her or Jay in. She believed the Carson crowd dismissed her as a woman who was too pushy, and Jay as a comedian who was too ethnic and not from the Midwest.

Johnny was a god at NBC, and I always winced when she spoke ill of him. Still, she was drawing on a grain of truth. An appearance on his show could make or break entertainers, and his producers knew it. They could be arbitrary and arrogant; comedians resented it, but they had no choice. There was nowhere else to go. Jay himself turned in a substandard performance in his fourth appearance on Johnny and was not invited back for eight years.

When Jay's show debuted on May 25, 1992, it drew a whopping sixteen-million viewers. We were off to a great start, except for one thing: Jay never mentioned Johnny's name. It wasn't an oversight; Kushnick was adamant that Jay should not acknowledge Johnny in any way since Johnny had not mentioned Jay on his final *Tonight Show* broadcast. Critics picked up on Jay's faux pas, which would haunt him for years.

Kushnick never realized how incredibly petty and foolish it was to disrespect Johnny Carson. Like him or not, he was a living legend. And she insisted Jay had made major changes to the way Johnny had been doing the show. In truth, our format was almost identical to Johnny's.

The changes we did make were cosmetic: There was no sidekick, like Ed McMahon. Our announcer, Edd Hall, was off-camera. And our music director, Branford Marsalis, played more contemporary jazz than his predecessor, Doc

Severinsen. Gone was the multi-colored curtain from which Johnny emerged at the top of the show. In its place were pre-taped multiple curtains. And there was a new backdrop featuring an illustration of the Pacific Ocean.

In time, Jay would put his own unique imprint on the franchise with a longer, more politically relevant monologue and the addition of newsmakers to the guest mix. Kushnick laid the groundwork for these achievements, as she understood and encouraged Jay's passion for politics and news. But none of it would happen on her very short, chaotic watch.

A speech by Ronald Reagan on the opening night of the Republican National Convention in August 1992 marked the beginning of the end for her career as executive producer. The former president was delivering the closing speech, and running long. Kushnick insisted that NBC News pull out so *The Tonight Show* could begin on schedule. The news division refused, and rightly so. They had no problem putting *Tonight* on a little later. You don't pull the plug on a beloved former president. But there was no reasoning with her. She cancelled *The Tonight Show* that evening and sent the studio audience home, prompting NBC executives to decide then and there she had to go.

Soon after that, *Entertainment Weekly* came out with a cover story about Jay's late-night competitor Arsenio Hall, featuring his face under the headline: "I'm Going to Kick Jay Leno's Ass." Arsenio's nasty remarks about Jay were largely a reaction to Kushnick's underhanded tactics with publicists who had booked their clients on Arsenio's show. She was demanding that the bookings be cancelled if the clients ever wanted to come on Leno again. She had already carried out her threats against NBC News talent Maria Shriver, singer Rodney Crowell, and her own personal friend Elizabeth Taylor. Kushnick called the Oscar-winning, legendary actress herself. My colleagues and I could hear her yelling from behind her closed office door. When the door opened, Kushnick came out swearing like a sailor about the audacity of Taylor to appear on *Arsenio*.

She also put the screws to lesser-known performers, such as Travis Tritt, an accomplished country guitar picker and singer but not a big star, even among country artists. His manager, Kenny Kragen, was shocked when Kushnick called him and threatened to permanently bar Tritt from Leno if he didn't cancel Arsenio: "You and I will be in this town for a long time and we'll see each other, and we're never going to talk again. It's your loss and the record company's," she said, according to Kragen. Then she hung up.

After that, a *Tonight Show* producer told Kragen that Kushnick would be cancelling a booking he had made for another client, country singer Trisha Yearwood. Kragen, a respected, experienced manager, didn't like to play games, so he took the story to the *Los Angeles Times.* The article quickly resonated with publicists, managers, and agents who were also victimized by Kushnick's high-pressure tactics. They went public, as well. Warren Littlefield, the president of NBC Entertainment, supported Jay and saw this as the perfect opportunity to fire Kushnick. She had gone too far, and she wasn't showing any signs of letting up.

Helen made a bizarre appearance on the Howard Stern radio show, denying Kragen's allegations and accusing NBC executives, Arsenio Hall, and others of a sexist conspiracy against her. When she came into work the following Monday, she received a letter of dismissal. But she told me and several others that everything was fine and that she and Jay would be staying. Later, she said Jay would walk out with her if she was fired.

Throughout the day we heard noises coming from behind the closed door to her office, as she was presumably throwing things against the walls. Jay went in to talk with her and closed the door, but we could still hear her screaming at him.

Meanwhile, we had a show to do with guests Scott Bakula, Paul Reiser, Kristoff St. John, and Blue Man Group. Somehow Jay put on his game face and got through the monologue and interviews as if it were any other day. After the taping, Helen left the lot, never to return. At every entrance, guards posted a black-and-white head shot of her with a message that she was banned from the lot. The photo looked like an FBI poster of a wanted criminal. It was surreal.

The next day, Jay spoke to the staff at our noon production meeting. He acknowledged that something was wrong with Kushnick and apologized for the "insanity" she had caused. Then he took responsibility, saying he didn't know about the problems, but should have.

In the midst of the frenzy, Kushnick admitted to Jay that she had planted the phony Carson story, insisting she had done it for Jay's own good. Upon hearing this, Jay knew he could no longer support her. When she was fired, his first order of business was to apologize to Johnny, who accepted graciously. Jay also made many other calls to try to mend the fences Kushnick had broken, but much of the damage would never be undone. Jay continued to be portrayed in press accounts as a guy who would stop at nothing to get what he wanted.

The two people in Kushnick's life who meant everything to her were her daughter, Sara, and Jay, whom she discovered in 1975 at the Comedy Store in Los Angeles. An intensely loyal person, Jay made a promise to her husband, Jerry, on his deathbed to take care of his wife and daughter. When she left *The Tonight Show*, Kushnick was beyond Jay's help. Nevertheless, he reached out to her and Sara, going to their house for a dinner of chicken wings, a meal she had often served him. Sara told *Entertainment Weekly* the evening was like old times when Jay would hang out at the house. A few years later, on August 28, 1996, Helen died after a nine-year struggle with breast cancer.

In February 1996, HBO made a film about Helen's beleaguered stint as Jay's executive producer. Called *The Late Shift*, it was based on Bill Carter's book of the same name. Actress Kathy Bates captured Helen's troubled personality perfectly, winning a Golden Globe for Best Supporting Actress. Her performance was so eerily accurate that to this day I wince when I look at her.

For all of her faults, Helen always believed in Jay, unlike NBC's East Coast executives. In December 1992, CBS signed a late-night deal with David Letterman for $16 million a year. This led to a panic among NBC's suits, who were beginning to have second thoughts about Jay despite his respectable ratings. NBC had thirty days to make a counteroffer to David, which they seriously considered.

On December 21, NBC president Bob Wright met in New York with David to find out what it would take to keep him. His answer: *The Tonight Show*. No surprise there. Wright would make no commitments, but he reportedly came away from the meeting with positive feelings about David. News of their meeting quickly got back to Jay in Burbank. That night, the staff was gathering in Studio 9 on the NBC lot for the first *Tonight Show* Christmas party.

Some saw Jay talking angrily with West Coast executives, and word quickly spread that he was reacting to news that Mr. Wright had decided to pick Letterman. No such decision had been made, but it didn't matter. We thought it had happened. The festive celebration of our first successful year, in spite of the Helen Kushnick debacle, quickly turned somber.

At one point, the late Fred de Cordova, then a consultant for our show, attempted to cheer us up. Johnny's long-time executive producer said Jay was proud of us and assured us that our show would go on for many years. But Freddie's words fell flat. No one could have inspired the room that night. Like many of my colleagues, I was certain I would soon be out of a job. The memory of the evening was so distasteful that the staff would never have another Christmas party.

The next day Jay went directly to the press, citing growing ratings, happy advertisers, and satisfied affiliates. He didn't understand NBC's wishy-washy support: "I feel like a guy who has bought a car from somebody, painted it, fixed it up, and made it look nice, and then the guy comes back and says he promised to sell the car to his brother-in-law." Nobody was better at automotive analogies than Jay.

He also said that he would go to CBS if they offered him

a late-night show and NBC gave the 11:30 slot to David. Jay even used his monologue to mock NBC's indecision, saying NBC stands for "Never believe your contract." He would reuse this joke years later when NBC executives again displayed a lack of confidence in him.

On January 6, 1993, Jay slipped into a small, out-of-sight guest office in Burbank to listen in on a bi-coastal conference call among NBC executives set up to discuss who should host *The Tonight Show*. He later told *Playboy*, "My career was at stake. I had to know where I stood. Am I dead meat? Who's on my side and who isn't? I had my supporters . . . but it was also fascinating to hear my own eulogy."

Jay's eavesdropping incident was obviously wrong, and it was also a tactical error. He was taking a huge risk that had no practical payoff. The call simply confirmed what he already knew: The East Coast executives favored David, and the West Coast guys wanted Jay. To make matters worse, Jay brought up the event to *Playboy* without any prompting. This bizarre story has played into the hands of Jay's many detractors and critics, who continue to use it to portray him as a ruthless schemer.

Not long after the call, NBC made an offer to Letterman that his team rejected. The deal would have required that they wait until Jay's contract was up a year and a half later, which they weren't willing to do. They reasoned that was too much time and would have allowed Jay to establish a solid audience, putting David at a disadvantage.

Then there was their attitude. According to Warren Littlefield, David's team talked themselves out of a contract by taking the intractable, arrogant position that their guy was Johnny's rightful heir. They were "so aggressive and so difficult in their negotiation assuming they had Johnny the King, and they didn't," Littlefield wrote in his book *Top of the Rock*, published in 2012.

Jay had dodged another bullet, bringing great relief to all of us. But it wasn't long before the next crisis came up. On August 30, 1993, *The Late Show with David Letterman* debuted on CBS with huge numbers. The news got massive press, as Leno vs. Letterman had become the media story of the year.

David's ratings triumph had legs, continuing night after night, week after week. After ten weeks it was clear: David was number one. Executives from NBC and GE, its parent company, called a meeting to discuss their late-night problem. They decided to stay the course after GE's then CEO, Jack Welch, strongly supported Jay. Warren Littlefield, one of Jay's biggest supporters from the beginning, agreed.

Welch, a tough, no-nonsense guy who transformed GE into an international powerhouse, was considered by many to be one of the world's greatest CEOs. He was ultimately responsible for hiring Jay in 1991 and had stood by him through thick and thin. I was always curious why Welch picked Jay over David. Trained as an engineer, he had no background in comedy. I got my chance to ask him when he was a guest on the show to plug his book *Jack: Straight From the Gut*. He told me he didn't pretend to know whether David or Jay was funnier. He made his choice based on gut instinct alone. He had met both men and liked what he saw in Jay. "Your boss was comfortable in his own skin," he told me, "and the other guy [David] wasn't."

In 1994, when Letterman was at the zenith of his late-night run, Bill Carter's influential book *The Late Shift* boldly announced that the late-night war was over, and Letterman was the winner. He declared that Littlefield's decision to support Jay over David was his biggest mistake, one which cost NBC millions. Carter then offered words of consolation to Littlefield, saying his strong family and sense of perspective would help him accept his blunder. Carter then concluded his well-researched but misguided book with a touch of melodrama about Letterman: "And so the successor to Johnny Carson packed up his office, his talent, and his vision and walked out of NBC forever, taking with him the last great franchise in the network television business: late night."

It sounded so definitive, but there was just one problem:

the self-appointed television prophet was dead wrong. The war wasn't over. It was just beginning for Jay. Carter wasn't the only scribe to jump to premature conclusions; he was just the most prominent one. There was Richard Zoglin of *TIME:* "Now that the dust has settled, it all seems too obvious. Of course, David Letterman was the logical person to take over *The Tonight Show* when Johnny Carson retired." *People* magazine concurred: "For all its hype, the Great Late-Night War of 1993 turned out to be something of a nonevent. . . . An astonishingly revitalized David Letterman, 46, strode authoritatively to the head of the pack, without even breaking a sweat."

But Jay had no intention of giving up the fight. His general in this battle was Littlefield, who came up with a plan to modernize the show, which was still using Johnny's old format. Littlefield's ideas included a new comedy segment after the monologue featuring recorded sketches by "comedy correspondents" covering actual events.

The number of guests on the show was reduced from four to three: two talking guests followed by a music performance. Most music acts had only niche appeal, so they were placed in the last segment where major tune-out would have the least effect on the ratings. Jay agreed with Littlefield's new approach, telling *Playboy:* "I was trying to do *The Tonight Show* exactly the way Johnny had done it, and it didn't work."

Jay also decided it was time to move to a new studio. We had been using Studio 1, where Johnny taped his show. Jay had never felt comfortable there, and, to be honest, neither did the rest of us. It was as if we were trespassing on hallowed ground. Of course, Johnny was still alive, but it felt as if he was always there, watching. Johnny's cavernous studio, designed in the 1950s for black-and-white shows, had a huge audience capacity of 465 seats, and the monologue mark was set way back (about fifteen yards) from the audience. Studio 1 was cool and distant like Johnny, not warm and friendly like Jay.

So we moved to nearby Studio 3, which was actually a mirror image of Studio 1. Still, it was Jay's, and he had plans to give it a major makeover. Per his specifications, we built a new $2 million set based on the design of Studio 8H in New York, home of *Saturday Night Live*. With a sweeping stage built close to the audience, it was designed to look like a comedy club with fewer audience seats (360), more color, and wackier designs. The new stage had an extension, called a tongue, allowing Jay to do his monologue right next to the audience, just as he had done in clubs for twenty years. An overhead boom camera provided dynamic moving shots, while a handheld floor camera captured dramatic close-ups. We also got rid of the curtains as well as the pre-taped "video curtains" in our show open. Jay now made his entrance at the beginning of the show through a doorway in the set, which looked more contemporary.

Guitarist Kevin Eubanks also took over as music director, replacing jazz great Branford Marsalis, who never really worked out as Jay's sidekick. Branford's sophisticated jazz selections lacked the driving rhythms necessary to bring out guests and to go to commercial breaks. Kevin's rock-and-roll was just what was called for, and he himself became a perfect foil for Jay's monologue jokes, filling the void left by Ed McMahon.

Jay also brought a new edginess to his monologue. He decided early on the OJ Simpson trial was a circus and treated it that way with his jokes. Then he came up with the Dancing Itos, a group of professional dancers dressed to look like the trial's judge, Lance Ito. The Dancing Itos quickly became a hit with viewers, including Judge Ito himself. They made numerous appearances, once with a dancer performing as prosecuting attorney Marcia Clark. Later, he added the Monkee Itos, the Dancing Lenos, the Dancing Unibombers, the Dancing Rodmans, the Dancing Belgium Waffles, and the Dancing Jerry Springers. By May 1995, *The Tonight Show with Jay Leno* had reinvented itself, and the changes were making a difference. Nearly two years after the premiere of Letterman, Jay pulled within .1 of a ratings point of his competitor on CBS.

The *Los Angeles Times* took notice, running a piece with this headline: "The Nice Guy Gets an Edge . . . and He's Gaining on Letterman." The article described Jay as a guy who had finally hit his stride: "More than anything, Leno feels he has finally proven himself—to network executives, critics, celebrities—which frees him up to be himself."

And then the talk-show gods blessed us. On July 10, 1995, British actor and heartthrob Hugh Grant made an appearance on Leno after his highly publicized arrest with a Hollywood prostitute. It attracted a huge number of viewers (almost eleven million), which launched Jay to the number-one spot and ended Letterman's highly-touted late-night reign. *The Tonight Show* maintained its ratings superiority from that day forward, except during the seven-month period in 2009-2010 when Conan O'Brien hosted.

New challenges soon replaced old ones, and holding the ratings was never easy. The Writer's Guild of America staged a strike in November 2007, forcing all the late-night shows to go into reruns. Two months into the strike, the WGA struck a deal with Letterman's production company, allowing *The Late Show with David Letterman* to return to the air with its writers in January of 2008. No such deal was made with *The Tonight Show*. Jay knew that he would soon lose his ratings edge if Letterman was producing new shows every night while *Tonight* was in reruns as the strike lingered on. So he made the difficult decision to cross the picket line to save his show. Putting the show back on the air was messy; the WGA decided to get tough, accusing Jay of strike violations for writing his own jokes. But this was the least of our problems.

Even as Letterman was featuring a bevy of stars—including Robin Williams, Tom Hanks, Denzel Washington, Katie Holmes, Diane Keaton, and Vince Vaughn—we were not able to book any big-name celebrities, as they refused to cross the picket line. The stars we contacted said they were getting calls threatening that they would never work in Hollywood again if they crossed the line. We wondered how the union found out who we were making offers to, but we soon learned we had a mole on the inside who was taking advantage of our open environment.

Our conference room, where we booked guests, had a big glass window. Anyone could look in, or even come in, to see the 3x5 offer cards on the big cork boards that had the names of potential guests. It didn't take long to discover the culprit, a production assistant, who wasn't very good at covering his tracks. He soon became an ex-production assistant.

After that incident, booking the show became a covert operation. We covered the window with black paper and locked the conference room door at the end of the day. Nevertheless, big-name celebrities continued to stay away in droves. At least they weren't being intimidated.

Our guest list, once primarily made up of stars, now consisted of animal acts, comedian Larry the Cable Guy, and just about every reporter and commentator at NBC News. Then there were the plate spinners, two guys on flame-throwing pogo sticks, and a pigeon lady who may have been a man. Our biggest celebrities were Republican presidential candidates Mitt Romney, Mike Huckabee, John McCain, Rudy Giuliani, and Ron Paul. Democratic presidential candidates would not cross the picket line. John Edwards even joined the striking writers on the line, but only while the news crews were there.

The producers also took over some of the writing duties. I came up with a bit called Priest, Rabbi, and Minister jokes, told by actual clergy. It was a big hit and led to lawyers telling lawyer jokes, doctors telling doctor jokes, and sales people telling sales jokes.

I also helped with Headlines. In this bit, Jay showed actual headlines, stories, and ads, submitted by viewers, that were unintentionally funny. Every weekend I brought home five bushel baskets of clippings to go through. That's a lot of news! Fortunately, I had some help in this task from my adult Sunday school class, who willingly agreed to skip our Bible lesson. Maybe too willingly. And they were especially talented at spotting double entendres. Maybe too talented.

After one hundred days, the strike ended. During that time Jay continued to be the number-one late-night host, beating Letterman without any writers or Hollywood stars. Well, except for Larry the Cable Guy. Jay's gutsy decision to put the show back on the air in defiance of the WGA probably saved the franchise. Of course, when our writers returned, we welcomed them with open arms. They were the best in the business, and we missed their immense talent.

We had been beset with so many crises threatening the existence of the show that we came to accept them as part of the job. As always, Jay turned to humor to help us get through such times: "Keep your enemies close and your friends closer," he would say. I thought this twist on an old adage was great advice on the importance of eternal vigilance. But none of us, including Jay, was prepared for our next mishap.

Jeff Zucker, president of NBCUniversal, had always been a friend of the show—or so we thought. We had known him for many years, going back to his days as executive producer of the *Today* show when Katie Couric was the co-host. Whenever he traveled to Burbank from his office in New York, he would stop by to visit with Jay and the producers, spending at least ten or fifteen minutes with us. No company president had ever done this.

Then one day in March 2004, Zucker popped into the producers' meeting, said "Hi," and quickly left, heading toward Jay's office. Normally an upbeat guy, Zucker seemed somber this time. We all sensed something was amiss. But we weren't in suspense long, as Jay soon came into the room. He told us Zucker had just fired him. There was no hint of emotion in his almost-inaudible voice and his expressionless face as he explained that he would be keeping his job for another five years, at which point Conan O'Brien would be taking over.

We were angry, and we let Jay know it. How could Zucker be doing this to his most loyal employee, a man who also just happened to be the number-one late night guy for many years? We urged Jay to fight back, but he seemed resigned to his fate and said there was nothing he could do. "Once the girl says no, you just have to accept it and move on. She'll never change her mind." It was a very strange response for Jay, who wasn't a quitter.

Over the next few days Jay was more forthcoming, telling us his meeting with Zucker was merely a formality. He had already made the deal with Conan because he was concerned the younger host would bolt from NBC without a succession plan that guaranteed him Jay's job. Jay felt pressured to accept the deal. He had grown tired of being routinely portrayed by the press and Letterman as the underhanded sneak who had stolen a job that was David's birthright, and he didn't want to be subjected to further scorn when it came to Conan.

Jay said he would go along with the plan if NBC announced his five-year extension prior to and separate from Conan's deal. That way it wouldn't look like Jay was being pushed out the door. Zucker agreed. Shortly after that, NBC put out the announcement, which made no mention of Conan.

Six months later, on the 50th anniversary episode of *The Tonight Show,* Oprah made a "surprise" visit with a birthday cake, and Jay made a "surprise" announcement that Conan would succeed him in 2009: "This show is like a dynasty. . . . You hold it and then you hand it off to the next person . . . Conan, it's yours. See you in five years, buddy." It was important to Jay that he not only make the announcement but also give it the appearance of a personal blessing. But his words would come back to haunt him years later when the transition began unraveling.

As 2009 approached, Jay continued to be the champion of late-night ratings, and he was having second thoughts about retiring. He told *USA Today* he was looking elsewhere: "I'm not a beach guy, and the last time I was in my pool was to fix a light. Don't worry. I'll find a job somewhere." These weren't empty words. He had options.

Early in 2008, Hollywood trade publications reported that ABC, FOX, Sony Pictures Television, and others wanted to talk with Jay about late-night possibilities. But according to the terms of Jay's contract with NBC, they couldn't reach out to him until November 2009. ABC's deal appealed to Jay the most because it was exactly what he wanted—the 11:30 p.m. slot on a broadcast network—which would allow him to go head-to-head with David and Conan. The alphabet network was willing to cancel its half-hour *Nightline* news program weeknights at 11:30 p.m. and move Jimmy Kimmel's late-night show from midnight to 12:30 a.m., which Jimmy agreed to do.

One day Jay called me into his office and asked me if I would be interested in working with him if something came up but said he couldn't be specific. I said yes and thanked him. I was fairly certain he was talking about ABC. A well-connected friend who worked there had been keeping me in the loop about ABC's plans to make a deal with Jay. My friend even gave me a tour of the studio and sets ABC was already designing for the show.

At a Beverly Hills press conference for television critics in July 2008, ABC's entertainment president Steve McPherson openly welcomed Jay to his network if NBC did not find a new job for him. He took a question from Jimmy Kimmel, who was posing as a reporter. Kimmel asked about media reports that ABC was courting Leno. "I can't believe they are going to let this guy go at the top of his game," McPherson responded. "If that happens, I guess we'll look at it and we will talk. And Jimmy will be involved in those discussions, and that will be that." By using Jimmy to ask the set-up question, McPherson was signaling to Jay that Jimmy was aware of ABC's interest in him and had embraced it.

Taking a cue from Jimmy, Jay showed up as a "reporter" the following week at an NBC news conference. Wearing a bald cap, fake goatee and glasses to disguise his identity, he asked, "When is Leno's last show?" Ben Silverman and Marc Graboff, the NBC executives conducting the session, were in on the "joke" and answered his question as if he were a real reporter: Jay's last night would be May 29, 2009, and Conan's first would be June 1, 2009.

Then "reporter Jay" brought up a topic that had not been pre-arranged, referring to Brett Favre, the retired quarterback who wanted his job back with the Green Bay Packers. "Well, everyone's entitled to change their mind, but I would imagine that puts management in an impossible situation," Graboff said. Then he threw out an olive branch: "He's [Leno] the hardest-working man in show business. He knew he was going to continue working. Our goal is to try to work with him to come up with an alternative to [*The Tonight Show*]."

Jeff Zucker offered these alternatives to Jay: a few Bob Hope-style specials a year, a nightly half-hour comedy show at 8 p.m., a nightly late-night show on the NBC-owned USA Network, and a Sunday late-night version of *Saturday Night Live*. Jay rejected all the ideas. He was only interested in a daily late-night, network entertainment show. In other words, *The Tonight Show*. Of course, that choice wasn't available.

So Zucker went back to the drawing board and came up with something that got Jay's attention: a nightly prime-time show at 10 that would have the look and feel of late-night but with more comedy. Jay resisted the idea at first, but he eventually agreed to do it. Zucker was thrilled he had figured out how to keep Jay. Sources at NBC reported executives there feared Conan would not have fared well going against Jay on ABC.

Putting Jay on at 10 p.m. five nights a week also helped Zucker solve another problem. NBC was not performing well at that hour with scripted, highly-produced, expensive programs. Zucker didn't expect Jay to bring in higher numbers, but he was hoping Jay's show, which was going to cost much less to produce, would attract enough viewers to satisfy advertisers. This would actually improve NBC's bottom line, which was more important to Zucker than the ratings.

A highly produced hour-long drama like *ER* costs $3.5 million per episode while five Leno shows would run only about $1.5 to $2 million. NBC's financial experts estimated Jay would need a 1.5 rating point in the coveted eighteen to forty-nine age demographic (almost two-million viewers) to attract our target advertising revenue of $300 million. Since Jay was getting a 1.3 to 1.5 rating at 11:30, it seemed like a reasonable goal.

The new program, called *The Jay Leno Show,* was unveiled to the press in December 2008. Jay did some interviews, attempting to lower expectations. He told the *New York Times* he did not expect to beat ABC's *Private Practice* or CBS's *CSI* franchise: "I just want to do well enough to get established. I'm a realist. I know it's going to be different." He said he would be producing forty-six weeks of original programming while the competing dramas would be doing twenty to twenty-two originals. That was the essence of his competitive strategy: "Those are well-produced, slick shows," he acknowledged. "But in the re-runs and other times, that's when we catch up. The tortoise and the hare: that's the key." It seemed like a daring and bold idea at the time.

On the eve of the show's September 2009 debut, the media was calling it a potential game-changer. *TIME* ran a cover story with this headline: "Jay Leno Is the Future of TV. Seriously." It described the low-budget, prime-time experiment as the new way of doing business in network television, which was struggling to reach a big, homogeneous audience of tens of millions. Former NBC president Fred Silverman was also impressed: "If *The Jay Leno Show* works, it will be the most significant thing to happen in broadcast television in the last decade."

Unfortunately, it didn't work. Despite all the fanfare, the show was cancelled after four months of tepid ratings. This time there was no cover story from *TIME* offering profound insights into NBC's noble but failed grand experiment. Instead, there was a story in *Entertainment Weekly* describing *The Jay Leno Show* as the biggest bomb in the history of television. On the cover, it featured a picture of Jay in tattered clothes, as if he had just survived a real bomb.

Some critics faulted the new show for being essentially the same as Jay's old *Tonight Show,* but there were actually numerous changes, imposed mostly by NBC executives. They pushed us to de-emphasize guests and to add more and different comedy in the second act following the monologue. We took on a whole stable of "young and hip" comedy correspondents who no one had ever heard of. They had a lot of attitude but few funny ideas. Most of the comedy was simply bad, and it would never have passed muster on the old show.

The funniest material continued to be Jay's old standbys: Headlines and Jaywalking. At the request of the affiliate stations, we had to hold those bits for the last act so they led into the local stations' newscasts. If we had been able to position our best comedy right after the monologue, we could have boosted our ratings. Contrary to what the critics said, I believe the show did badly because we didn't continue with our old format.

Ironically, the show was actually hitting the target viewership numbers set for it by NBC management. We were only expected to match the ratings and demographics of the old show, and we did. But while NBC was satisfied with our performance, the affiliate stations were not. Jay's weak lead-ins for local NBC newscasts were taking down their ratings. Some major markets were losing up to 50 percent of their audience, which begs the question: did anyone at NBC consult with the affiliates about this possibility before putting the show on the air?

The whole experience was demoralizing for Jay. I think he mentally checked out two months into the show as the ratings were plummeting and critics were relentlessly pummeling the program. He summed up his feelings in this monologue joke:

> NBC said the show performed exactly as they expected it would, and then cancelled us. Don't confuse this with when we were on at late night and performed better than expected and they cancelled us. That was totally different.

A guarded person by nature, Jay could be surprisingly candid on the air. During one of the last episodes of *The Jay Leno Show*, he calmly revealed his pent-up frustrations, referring to his fateful meeting with Jeff Zucker in 2004, though he didn't mention Zucker by name:

> I'm sitting in my office, an NBC executive comes in and says to me, "Listen, Conan O'Brien has gotten offers from other networks. We don't want him to go, so we're going to give him *The Tonight Show*." I said, "Well, I've been number one for twelve years." They said, "We know that, but we don't think you can sustain that." I said, "Okay, how about until I fall to number two, then you fire me?" "No, we made this decision." I said, "I'll retire just to avoid what happened the last time."

He said he never wanted to do *The Jay Leno Show*, but NBC wouldn't let him out of his contract, which meant he couldn't go anywhere else for a year to eighteen months. Yet Jay wasn't entirely helpless. He could have gone to ABC, even if it had taken longer than he preferred. If he had, there's a good chance he would have continued as the ratings leader on network television, going head-to-head against David. And the fiasco known as *The Jay Leno Show* would never have happened.

As for Zucker, I believe he made a valiant effort to keep both Conan and Jay at NBC. The 10 p.m. prime-time show was a gutsy, new idea that didn't work. I think he, like many other NBC executives before him, never had enough faith in Jay, despite his consistent ratings victories. Instead, Zucker chose to back Conan.

This misguided decision led to a debacle described by former NBC executive Don Ohlmeyer as "the dumbest thing in the history of television." He was right. And if Jack Welch had still been at GE during the Zucker era, I firmly believe Jay never would have been fired and Conan never would have been hired to replace him.

Conan—who had a background as a writer, not on-air talent—struggled from the beginning as a late-night host at NBC, relying on quirky, juvenile jokes and bits. He ignored suggestions from NBC executives to appeal to a wider, mainstream audience on *The Tonight Show*, as Letterman had successfully done when he moved to 11:30 at CBS.

Jay was coming off a fifteen-year run as the late-night leader when he handed off *The Tonight Show* franchise to Conan on June 1, 2009. In nine days, Letterman surpassed him in the overnight ratings. By the end of Conan's run seven months later, he had hemorrhaged 50 percent of the viewers Jay had built up. While it's true that Jay's 10 p.m. show was providing Conan weak lead-ins, Jay had always kept his ratings crown in place throughout long stretches of feeble NBC lead-ins.

When NBC Entertainment chairman Jeff Gaspin announced the network was pulling the plug on *The Jay Leno Show,* an old dilemma re-emerged: who should host *The Tonight Show,* Jay or Conan? According to the Hollywood trades, Gaspin came up with a compromise, proposing that Jay do a half-hour comedy program at 11:30 and that Conan do an hour-long *Tonight Show* at midnight. Jay accepted the idea, but Conan strongly rejected it, saying he would not participate in a plan that would destroy *The Tonight Show.*

I believe NBC's offer to Conan was more than reasonable. He had already shown he was incapable of connecting with a mainstream audience. Legendary NBC executive Dick Ebersol put it more succinctly: "What this is really about is an astounding failure by Conan." In the end, NBC bought out Conan's contract, and he walked out the door with $45 million.

This led to a huge, worldwide story pitting Jay against Conan. The media and Jay's late-night rivals once again painted him as a schemer, this time pushing poor Conan out the door after Jay had announced he was retiring and handing off the late-night crown to Conan. In reality, Jay didn't have the power to manipulate anyone. He was literally fired, and he wasn't given a choice in the matter other than to accept or reject an offer to work five more years. Zucker allowed Jay to announce his "retirement" so he could save face.

Conan ended up signing with cable outlet TBS to do a late-night show after FOX turned him down. His new show debuted in the fall of 2010, and within a year it lost 60 percent of its viewers. These days, Conan lives in talk show oblivion, averaging fewer than a million viewers a night.

Jay came back to *The Tonight Show* on March 1, 2010. In his first month, *Tonight's* Nielsen ratings shot back to number-one in all demographics. Jay averaged 4.9 million viewers, while Letterman garnered 3.7 million. *TV Guide* called Jay's comeback "miraculous." Still, there was lingering fallout from the disastrous *Jay Leno Show* experience. The ratings tapered off in time, but Jay maintained his ratings dominance.

In 2011, Comcast acquired NBCUniversal from GE, and in August 2012 it made cutbacks totaling $25 million at *The Tonight Show with Jay Leno*. Twenty staffers lost their jobs, and Jay took a 50 percent pay cut to avert even more layoffs, according to NBCUniversal. Comcast insisted it was only trying to make back its investment, yet the company extended no public or private show of confidence to Jay following the cutbacks.

Why would the new owners gut the budget of its one and only consistently number-one franchise and leave their other shows untouched? The cutbacks weren't strictly about budget. Comcast was sending Jay a message that he would not be their chosen one in late night. Jay shot back with thinly-veiled jokes in his monologue: "Welcome to *The Tonight Show,* or, as Comcast calls us, "The Expendables."

By February 2013, Comcast, which had already been making great strides at dismantling the once-proud peacock network, reached record-low Nielsen numbers. Jay responded with jokes such as this one: "For the first time in history, NBC is going to finish fifth in the ratings period. We are behind the Spanish-language network Univision—or as we call it here in Los Angeles: Cinco de Ratings."

NBC's Entertainment chairman Robert Greenblatt reacted sharply to the jokes, complaining about them in an angry email to Jay. Jay was shocked and replied that all late-night hosts make fun of their bosses, going back to the days of Johnny Carson. But Greenblatt already knew that. His real purpose was to intimidate the late-night host.

Back in January, Greenblatt told the press that NBC was extending Jay's contract through September 2014, avoiding questions about rumors that NBC's thirty-eight-year-old late-night star Jimmy Fallon would be taking Jay's job. But according to the *Hollywood Reporter,* by March NBC had already devised a plan to make Jimmy the host of *The Tonight Show* when Jay's contract expired.

Jay was reportedly upset when he heard about the story, but not because he would be losing his job. He knew he had no future with the Comcast executives, who didn't show Jay the respect he deserved. They never once bothered to come to the studio to watch his show. Jay was not happy because he believed NBC leaked the story to the *Hollywood Reporter,* and he didn't want to go through yet another public late-night war in which he was portrayed as the bad guy.

On St. Patrick's Day, Jay responded to the story with this joke: "You know the whole legend of St. Patrick, right? St. Patrick drove all the snakes out of Ireland, and they came into the United States and became NBC executives."

Shortly thereafter, NBCUniversal CEO Steve Burke entered the fray in an attempt to fix the damage inflicted by Greenblatt. The *Hollywood Reporter* announced that Burke met with Jay to smooth things over. Later, Greenblatt had dinner with Jay, and the two apparently came to terms about the succession. Jay's show finale would be February 6, 2014, and Jay would be paid through September, according to his contract. As always, he put his staff first and insisted that they also receive wages through that same time period. Greenblatt agreed. Jimmy would take over the show on February 17.

As his show entered the home stretch, Jay put on some of his finest performances. He had some great monologue jokes about President Obama, including this zinger delivered during his final broadcast: "The worst part about losing this job, I'm no longer covered by NBC. I have to sign up for Obamacare." Jay, who had always been considered the milquetoast comedian by critics, was getting into edgy territory, as the other late-night comedians, particularly

Letterman, had been staying away from Obama jokes. After a while, they had no choice but to follow Jay's lead.

Viewers appreciated that he was carrying on the great late-night tradition started by Johnny Carson of lampooning whoever was president, regardless of party. I believe this was a big reason Jay increased his ratings dominance over all the other shows in the late-night ratings to the highest level in three years. In his final season, Jay's nightly viewership averaged more than four million, which was 25 percent greater than Letterman's and included 35 percent more eighteen- to forty-nine-year-old viewers. This capped Jay's unbelievable run as the number-one late-night host for almost two decades.

Comcast had a right to replace Jay with Jimmy Fallon, who is young and talented. Jay himself has been very supportive of Jimmy, and he has said on numerous occasions that it was the right time for him to step down. Nevertheless, I have no doubt Jay would have continued to be number-one in late night for several more years if his contract had been renewed.

On March 10, 2014, the Television Academy recognized Jay's unique contributions to the medium by inducting him into its Hall of Fame. Bill Maher, a frequent guest on Jay's show, introduced his long-time friend at the ceremony. He took the occasion to attack critics and others for perpetuating the myth that Jay was mediocre as a host, while his predecessor, Johnny Carson, was "rebellious" and "edgy" by comparison. "[Jay was] suited to his time, just as Carson was when he hosted *Tonight*," Bill said.

The *Real Time* host also berated the media for buying into the idea that "Jay Leno stole Conan O'Brien's dream" when NBC rehired Jay to host *Tonight* after the show's ratings plummeted in 2009 during Conan's watch.

Bill's strong defensive posture may have seemed out of place at an awards ceremony, but I believe he did the right thing by setting the record straight about Jay's amazing legacy to late-night television, a legacy that has too often been misunderstood, not only by media critics but by NBCUniversal executives, as well.

Chapter Sixteen

The Future

Jay Leno hosted 4,610 episodes of *The Tonight Show*, seventy-nine more than Johnny Carson, who held the job for thirty years. In twenty-two years as host, Jay delivered approximately 160,000 monologue jokes and interviewed more than 14,000 guests. In his final episode, he described the experience as "the greatest twenty-two years of [his] life." He got teary-eyed as he summed up what it all meant to him: "The first year of this show I lost my mom; the second year I lost my dad. Then my brother died. After that I was pretty much out of family. The folks here became my family." So now what? Will Jay just quietly walk away from what he called "the best job in show business"? There's been much speculation about his future.

Jay has been very open about the fact that it wasn't his idea to leave *The Tonight Show* in February 2014. He was fired at age sixty-three for the second time. He said if it were up to him, he would have stayed for another year or two. I personally suspect Jay would have continued doing the job for another five years, assuming he continued his lead in the late-night ratings. He once told me that hosting a late-night show is like golf: "You can play the game pretty well into your 70s."

Of course, Jay wasn't offered the opportunity to keep his job—one he was performing better than anyone else at the time. His departure from *The Tonight Show* has left a huge void for his viewers. Who will they spend time with now just before they go to bed?

The so-called "late-night wars," which have always been

associated with Jay (Leno vs. Letterman, Leno vs. Conan, Leno vs. Kimmel, etc.) will not fade away just because Jay is no longer a player. He actually brought stability to the increasingly fractured late-night competition because everyone knew he was the top dog.

The only certainty is that the wars will intensify, as the growing number of late-night shows battle for a limited supply of A-list celebrities, advertising revenue, and viewers. It will soon become apparent, if it hasn't already, that Jay Leno was not responsible for cut-throat competition in the late-night environment. He just played the game better than anyone else.

NBCUniversal has entrusted its storied *Tonight Show* franchise to Jimmy Fallon, an enormously talented performer who excels at comedy sketches and musical numbers with his guests. He has brought many new, young viewers to the table and has enjoyed an initial ratings success, as well as critical acclaim. But late-night is a long-distance race. David Letterman learned this lesson the hard way. He reigned as the late-night ratings king for two years but lost his crown to Leno in 1995 and never got it back.

For all of his talent as a performer, Jimmy needs to work on his interviewing skills. Successful late-night hosts need to know how to talk with their guests about a variety of topical subjects, including serious ones. Jimmy loves playing games (charades, Catch Phrase, Pictionary) with his guests, and it's entertaining to watch. But one gets the feeling he's doing it because he doesn't know how to have a serious conversation with them. His monologue was also a little weak at first, but it has improved.

Fallon faces fierce competition from his late-night rivals, who include Jimmy Kimmel, David Letterman, Jon Stewart, Stephan Colbert, Chelsea Handler, Arsenio Hall, and Conan O'Brien. But of these, Kimmel represents the biggest threat. Like Fallon, Kimmel specializes in quirky comedy sketches, which appeal to young viewers. Kimmel is also a stronger interviewer than Fallon. That may be why Kimmel seems to be taking a page out of Leno's book and making a strong push to land interviews with political figures. Such interviews often resulted in strong ratings and great press for Leno.

In April 2014, David Letterman, always a strong presence in late night, made a surprise announcement on his show that he would be stepping down as the long-time host of *The Late Show* some time in 2015. His decision came less than two months after Fallon replaced Leno at *The Tonight Show*.

In 2013, CBS extended Letterman's contract from the fall of 2014 through the end of 2015 amid widespread speculation that he had been planning to call it quits. I suspect Letterman, who perennially trailed Leno in the ratings, wanted to stay in the game a little longer in hopes of finally achieving the ratings crown once Leno was out of the picture in February 2014. But Fallon's strong ratings may have proved to be too much for Letterman, who will be replaced by *Comedy Central's* Stephen Colbert.

There's another possibility here that must be examined. In the not-too-distant future, there may not be any late-night television as we know it today. Many viewers, especially younger ones, are no longer watching television shows, including late night. Instead, they are viewing video clips from these programs on the Internet. If this trend continues, Jimmy Kimmel, Jimmy Fallon, and their colleagues would essentially become performers in self-contained, five-minute comedy routines.

So where does this leave Jay? Would he want to get back into the fray? He has said that he has come to terms with the idea of moving on from late night. Some of my former *Tonight Show* colleagues believe he is happy with the idea of going out at the top of his game as the long-time, undisputed champion among viewers, if not among the critics. The staffers say Jay is ready to devote all of his time to doing standup comedy and working on his classic cars and motorcycles. I don't believe it.

There's no question Jay is booking more stand-up appearances. He has always first and foremost considered himself a comedian. Even with his *Tonight Show* duties, he did about

150 gigs a year at corporate events, casinos, comedy clubs, and fundraisers for police, firefighters, and others.

Jay will also devote more time to cars, but he won't just be working on them. He will, no doubt, write more articles and columns for automotive publications and the general press. He may even create documentaries about cars and conduct more interviews with automotive experts for his Emmy-winning internet show, *Jay Leno's Garage.*

But will life after *The Tonight Show* be limited to cars and stand-up comedy for Jay? Not a chance. I worked with him for eighteen years, and I know he has the mentality of a champion fighter. No boxer would ever walk out of the ring in the middle of a fight in which he was pulverizing his opponent. I have no inside information here, but I just don't see Jay hanging up his gloves in daily television.

So where will Jay go? NBC Entertainment chairman Bob Greenblatt has said he would love to keep Jay in the fold: "Nothing would make us happier than to have him à la Bob Hope—stay on the network." Hope had a long and fruitful relationship with the "Peacock Network," hosting many variety specials, but he never did a daily comedy program.

Jay lives, eats and breathes monologue jokes that feature topical and observational humor. I don't think he has any interest in doing an occasional, or even a regular, variety program. When Jay was fired the first time, he was offered a similar gig and turned it down flat.

Other media companies and individuals have been courting Jay, including the Tribune Company, *American Idol* producer CORE Media Group, and former NBC chief Jeff Gaspin. The most intriguing possibility is FOX, the only major broadcast network without a late-night entertainment show. FOX would provide Jay the opportunity to return to a daily late-night show, allowing him to go head-to-head with his competitors. Several prominent people have publicly backed this idea.

One of Jay's most vocal supporters is Fox News Channel host Greta Van Susteren. In a blog post, she urged her employer to hire Jay: ". . . I think Fox broadcast should sign him up and compete against his old network." Steve Pruett, the chairman of the Fox affiliate board, floated the idea of having Jay host a late-show on FOX in the *New York Post,* saying the board would be interested with the right business plan.

However, according to one former FOX executive, a late-night show for Jay on FOX isn't very likely. He told me he would be surprised if the FOX affiliates, who turned down a deal with Conan because it didn't appear profitable, offered a five-year contract to Jay, who would be in his mid-sixties. I certainly wouldn't discount a FOX show, but it's by no means a done deal.

That leaves the most bizarre possibility: CNN. *Variety's* TV columnist Brian Lowry was the first person to suggest the cable news network would make an ideal home for Jay. Media commentators quickly picked up on this quirky, crazy notion. After all, CNN Worldwide president, Jeff Zucker, is the former NBC executive responsible for firing Jay the first time. Lowry admitted he was pushing the Leno-CNN matchup because he loved coming up with an ironic solution that could actually work.

CNN's ratings have been sagging in recent years, so the network could potentially benefit from a show hosted by Jay—and the publicity it would generate. Why would Jay want to have anything to do with the guy who canned him in the prime of his career? First of all, Zucker probably didn't act on his own. Decisions of this magnitude are never made in a vacuum at global corporations like GE, then the owner of NBCUniversal. Others at the highest levels were surely involved, but they never owned up to it. Jay, one of the savviest entertainers about the business of show business, is surely aware of this.

Jay went through fourteen NBC presidents. Of all the executives, he got along best with Zucker, a likable and charismatic man. He and Jay shared a competitive spirit and a tenacious desire to vanquish David Letterman in the ratings.

Zucker also served as an unofficial producer of *The Tonight Show,* frequently suggesting guest ideas and personally calling celebrities to invite them on the show.

I have no way of knowing what Jay's future will look like, but he has said he doesn't want to do another version of *The Tonight Show.* Still, I believe he would love to continue doing a daily, scaled-down show that includes monologue jokes and guest interviews. The format could include a panel of commentators, which Jay would moderate. It could work. CNN, or another cable news network, could afford him that opportunity.

Whatever Jay does, one thing is certain: He won't be quietly fading into the woodwork, as Johnny Carson famously did when he retired from *The Tonight Show.* Jay was fond of saying that hosting *Tonight* was like being the most popular kid in high school. It wasn't just a joke. He liked that job more than anything else in the world.

Acknowledgments

This book has my name on the cover, but it was a team effort. I am grateful to the other name on the cover, Jay Leno. Without him, there would be no book. I only hope *Behind the Curtain* does justice to the great legacy he leaves to *The Tonight Show*.

I am truly thankful to all my former colleagues at *The Tonight Show*. I think of them as family, especially executive producer Debbie Vickers, whose support was unwavering. Thanks also to my fellow co-producers Stephanie Ross, Bob Read, Ross Mark, Tracie Fiss, Mike Alexander, and Barbera Libis. Others at the show provided helpful ideas, including John Melendez, Michael Jann, Greg Elliot, Joe Drago, Rene Mooshy, Denise Walker, Denise Soulam-Banks, and Mark Zawacki.

I have to credit Bill O'Reilly for planting the seed to do this book. I politely rejected his advice at first, insisting no one would be interested in what I had to say about Jay or *The Tonight Show*. Bill persisted for three years, offering specific suggestions and help, and I thank him for doing it.

I am deeply indebted to Gene Del Vecchio for his tireless help and encouragement in pitching the manuscript. I also want to thank Kathy Cannon and John Tenorio for enlightening me with their marketing savvy. A heartfelt thank you to Jessica Quinn for selflessly sharing her media-relations knowledge, and to Kristin Maynard for her insights about social media.

I truly appreciate Geoff Verhoff for always being there to answer endless questions about every subject under the sun and for pushing me to make difficult choices I didn't want to make. Thanks also for helping me land some of Jay's biggest political gets. I also want to reach out to Joe Allbaugh, Matt Romney, and other politicos who provided me with essential details for many of the stories.

A special thank you to Diane Prettyman, Robin de la Llata Aime, and Linda Vanek for their editing expertise. It's a thankless but essential task. I am thankful to my sister Michelle Berg, Amanda Gibbon, and Dana Gibbon for their enthusiastic efforts in setting up the website. And a shout-out to Cory Gilbride for sharing his photographic and technical knowledge, and to Nancy Baughman for her invaluable practical suggestions.

I wish to thank D.J. Snell and Crosland Stuart at Legacy Management for believing in this book and tirelessly working on my behalf, and I greatly appreciate Pelican Publishing for its support, especially my editor, Erin Classen.

I am most grateful to my family for providing me stability during the many highs and lows we experienced during my tenure at *Tonight*. My daughter, Melissa, and son, David, grew up hanging around the studio and covering the walls of my office with their artwork from school. David's wife, Anne, joined our family at the studio for my last day on the job. My wife, Mary, is the reason I got the job, encouraging me to apply for it despite my objections. She is also the uncredited co-writer and co-editor of this book.

Finally, I have to say Amen to God for showering me with blessings beyond belief. May any good that comes from this book be to His glory.

Index